Love in a Torn Land

Other books by Jean Sasson

The Rape of Kuwait: The True Story of Iraqi Atrocities against a Civilian Population

Princess: A True Story of Life behind the Veil in Saudi Arabia

Princess Sultana's Daughters

Princess Sultana's Circle

Ester's Child

Mayada, Daughter of Iraq

Love in a Torn Land

Joanna of Kurdistan:
The True Story of a
Freedom Fighter's
Escape from
Iraqi Vengeance

JEAN SASSON

John Wiley & Sons, Inc.

This book is printed on acid-free paper. ∞

Copyright © 2007 by Global Women Group LLC. All rights reserved

Published by John Wiley & Sons, Inc., Hoboken, New Jersey
Published simultaneously in Canada

Design and composition by Navta Associates, Inc.

All photographs courtesy of Joanna al-Askari Hussain, Ra'ad al-Askari, Sa'ad al-Askari, Alia al-Askari, and Hady Sarraj, from their personal collections.

Map on page xv © Red Lion maps c/o Transworld Publishers

Wiley Bicentennial Logo: Richard J. Pacifico

For general information about our other products and services, please contact our Customer Care Department within the United States at (800) 762-2974, outside the United States at (317) 572-3993 or fax (317) 572-4002.

Wiley also publishes its books in a variety of electronic formats. Some content that appears in print may not be available in electronic books. For more information about Wiley products, visit our web site at www.wiley.com.

Library of Congress Cataloging-in-Publication Data:

Sasson, Jean P.
   Love in a torn land : Joanna of Kurdistan, the true story of a freedom fighter's escape from Iraqi vengeance / Jean Sasson.
      p. cm.
   Includes index.
   ISBN 978-0-470-06729-1 (cloth : alk. paper)
   1. Hussain, Joanna Al-Askari. 2. Women, Kurdish—Iraq—Biography. 3. Kurds—Iraq—Biography. 4. Anfal Campaign, Iraq, 1986–1989. 5. Iran-Iraq War, 1980–1988—Personal narratives, Kurdish. 6. Iraq—Ethnic relations. I. Title.
   DS79.66.H86S27 2007
   956.7044'1—dc22
   [B]

2006029950

Printed in the United States of America

10 9 8 7 6 5 4 3 2 1

To Roxanne

—Jean Sasson

To my own courageous Peshmerga, Sarbast,
and our two sons, Kosha and Dylan

To Auntie Aisha

To the brave wives of the Peshmerga

—Joanna Hussain

When I was a child, I built a wall of hatred around me.
When I was asked, "From what did you build this wall?"
I replied, "From the stones of insults."

—PROVERB

CONTENTS

PREFACE

On my life's journey I have traveled to many corners of the world. During my travels, I have been privileged to meet and come to know many fascinating women, some of whom I've shared with the world through the pages of best-selling books. During the writing of *Love in a Torn Land*, the true story of a Kurdish woman, once again I found myself in a unique position to explore an exotic culture while coming to know a true-life heroine.

Joanna al-Askari grew up in Baghdad, but her heart belonged to Kurdistan. She steeped herself in the magic of Kurdistan at her mother's knee, absorbing from her a deep devotion to Kurdish traditions and the pull of the Kurdish homeland. Her childhood holidays were spent in her mother's hometown of Sulaimaniya in Kurdistan. Playing there with her Kurdish cousins, Joanna was unaware of the frightful fate awaiting her and many other Kurds. The brutality festering in the heart of a man named Saddam Hussein had not yet been unleashed.

No one was surprised when as a young woman Joanna fell in love with a handsome Kurdish freedom fighter. When the man she loved retreated from the cities of Iraq to live in the mountains of Kurdistan, Joanna joined him. As a young bride in Bergalou, Joanna barely survived the early chemical attacks ordered by Saddam on the Kurds. Forced to flee to seek safety in neighboring Iran, it seemed that Joanna's dreams were shattered—but that was not the case. Joanna and her husband forged a new life even as the dreams of freedom for Kurds were renewed with the ouster of Saddam Hussein.

I consider my journey with Joanna a great gift that I now pass to my readers through the pages of this book.

Please visit my Web site, www.jeansasson.com, for additional information.

Jean Sasson

I have described to the author Jean Sasson the details of my life, including what I saw and felt during the terrifying days and nights my husband and I were fleeing for our lives. We survived extreme physical danger, including chemical attacks and bombings. We made our way through the mountains and villages of Kurdistan to seek safety in neighboring Iran. While everything in this book happened to me, it is important for the reader to remember that during the chaos of war I was occupied with surviving. I was not keeping a diary. In the event that the confusion of war and the fog of time obscured my memory, there may be a possibility that I have erred as to the exact timing of certain events. But the reader can be confident that I lived through every incident described by the author.

Joanna al-Askari Hussain

ACKNOWLEDGMENTS

I'd like to thank Ra'ad, Hady, Ranj, and Eric for their help with so many things during the writing of this book. Ranj, you made enormous efforts to help your aunt Joanna and me.

I'd also like to also thank my nephew, Greg, for always being there and listening to me during so many telephone calls during the difficult time of writing. The same goes for my dear friend Danny. And Jack is always there for me.

I would like to thank my aunt Margaret, Alece, and Anita for their enthusiasm for everything I write. You'll never know how much your comments spur me on.

This book really would have been impossible without the valuable input from my literary agent, Liza Dawson.

I was so exhausted by the end of this process that I really could not have carried on to the finish line without my British editor, Marianne Velmans, and my American editor, Hana Lane. You are both greatly appreciated.

I thank you all.

MODERN-DAY IRAQ AND IRAN

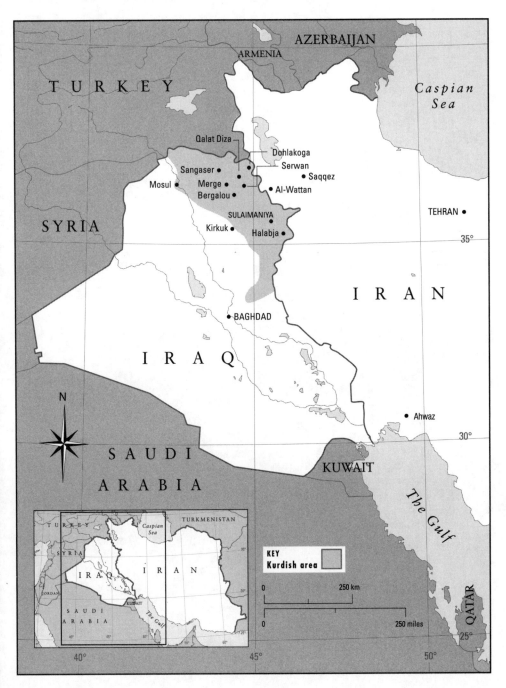

Prologue

Suddenly, I was startled by the roar of an unexpected artillery bombardment. While we were always subject to attacks, our enemy was off their usual schedule. Generally, we could set our watches by the afternoon and evening bombardments.

I felt a rush of confusion. I was too far from our house to make a run for safety, so I darted off the trail, crouching and waiting for an opportunity to dash home to take cover in a corner room.

Just then I noticed something strange. These artillery shells were different. Once airborne, they fell silently, puffing up dirty white clouds. I continued watching the strange spectacle, my mouth dry with anxiety, not letting my imagination go to the worst scenario. Perhaps the silent canisters were harmless?

Then another strange thing occurred: birds began falling out of the sky! I instinctively cried out, "It's raining birds!"

The combination of silent bombs and plunging birds stirred my disbelief. I whipped my head from side to side, searching all around me. The edge of the afternoon sky was dotted with flashes of color, gaudy specks plummeting to earth. Those colorful specks were more birds. The poor creatures were fluttering helplessly, falling as heavily as stones, down, down, down to the ground.

I winced as I heard dreadful thumps all around me.

I had always loved birds. I couldn't bear to see the pitiful disaster. If birds were dropping from the sky, I knew that I should move, and move fast, to run to the shelter. But I was literally frozen in place.

I searched the trail for sight of my husband. If he knew that I was in danger, he would come to me. But perhaps he would think I was already in the shelter. Because of the suddenness of the danger, perhaps he would be forced to seek cover in the communal shelter in the village center.

I bit on my lower lip as I continued to search the path for my husband's brawny frame, feeling a rush of panic for his safety.

No doubt, Bergalou was in the middle of what was quickly unfolding as a dire emergency.

Just then a bird fell directly at my feet, the dull thud of its impact causing me to gasp. The creature was in great distress. Its tiny black beak scissored vigorously, then more slowly, pitifully sucking at the air.

I stayed put, for the silent canisters were still dropping from the sky. I could hear my heart thumping loudly, noticing that those strange canisters were still billowing smoky puffs that turned into a dirty brown-colored cloud that hugged the ground.

Another bird fell nearby.

I was smart enough to know that animals provide the first indication of a chemical attack. Was this the poison gas attack promised by Ali al-Majid?

With that chilling thought I threw caution to the wind, leaping to my feet and sprinting down the path home in fear for my life.

Everything was a blur, but I did catch sight of an untethered mule as it snapped and bucked into a frenzy. That mule hustled past me on the path, trotting so fast he seemed to dance. Never had I seen a mule move that rapidly.

I kept running, trying to avoid the splayed birds strewn in my path. Finally, I dashed into the house, gasping for breath. Safe!

Seconds later, my husband burst in through the open door. I stared at him, mouth open, panting, without speaking.

He yelled out, "Joanna, upon my honor, this is a chemical attack!"

Yes! I knew it! I now recognized the unpleasant odor I had heard about from survivors of previous chemical attacks: rotten apples, onions, and garlic. We *were* under chemical attack!

My husband moved quickly, reaching high above to a shelf above the side door. He was getting our masks, I thought with relief, as he shouted, "Joanna! Put this on!" He handed me a gas mask as he pulled a second mask onto his own face, tightening the small bands that fastened it around his head.

I held my breath while I fumbled with the strap. In all the excitement, the simple task felt cumbersome. While we had discussed those masks several times, with my husband urging me to familiarize myself with the apparatus, I had stupidly failed to do so.

Finally, my husband grabbed the mask from my hands and slipped it into place over my head and face. Hand in hand, we ran together to our earthen shelter, crawled down and as far back into the hole as possible.

Once we were settled, I realized that I had been holding my breath the whole way. I hungrily drew in a much-needed mouthful of air, but all I accomplished was to strain my throat muscles. I could not capture a single breath!

My husband had no idea of my problem. Desperate, I yanked at the mask until it slid from my face, shouting, "I can't breathe in this thing!" Finally, I had his full attention, and he wiggled toward me. He grabbed my mask from my hands and examined it.

Feeling that I was about to explode, I was forced to breathe in the foul gases. My eyes were beginning to feel the effect of the gas as well. I felt as if my eyes had been set on fire. The pain was so intense that hot needles probing my eyeballs could not have hurt any worse. I could not stand it another moment. I started rubbing my eyes with my hands, not caring that I had been warned never to rub my eyes during a chemical attack.

"The gas is in my eyes!" I screamed, as I began to choke on the poisoned air that was fogging the shelter.

The gases were settling low over the ground, filling the shallow dugout. My husband moved quickly, crawling out of the shelter, then pulling me out behind him. With my mask in one hand, he grabbed my other, pulling me back into the house.

I thought we should run up the mountains, for I distinctly remembered instructions telling me that one should seek low shelter during a conventional bomb attack, and to climb as high as possible during a chemical attack.

But first I must have a working mask.

My throat was aching; my eyes were stinging. I crumpled to the floor and my husband knelt beside me. A clammy fog was clotting my senses and muddling my thinking.

Well, hello, death, I thought to myself.

PART ONE

Childhood

1

Little Peshmerga Girl

BAGHDAD
Saturday, July 8, 1972

In a country where Kurds are hated, I am a Kurd.

Although I was born and grew up in Baghdad, my heart belonged to Sulaimaniya. Baghdad was the city of my Arab father, and Sulaimaniya was the city of my Kurdish mother. Sulaimaniya is 331 kilometers north of Baghdad and is in Kurdistan. For ten long months of every year, from September through June, I plodded along in dusty Baghdad, dreaming of July and August, which I called the "happy months," when I would leave behind the drab-brown plains of Mesopotamia to journey with my mother and siblings to the color-splashed mountains and valleys of Kurdistan.

I well remember one particular travel day in 1972 when I was ten. I was so excited about our trip that I was called a pest by my mother and siblings, who were getting ready for our departure. I felt ignored. But when my dear uncle Aziz, who had lived with us for several years, noticed me standing listlessly in the kitchen, he led me to stroll into the back garden where a flowering bougainvillea climbed our garden wall.

To help the time pass faster, he encouraged me to pick lemons and naranjas. We had a wide variety of fruit trees and berry bushes in our back garden, including oranges, apricots, plums, naranjas, and dates. How fortunate I was to live in a land where luscious fruits grew like colorful jewels all around me. Of all the fruits, the naranja, an orangelike citrus fruit, was my favorite. When it was ripe, it was squeezed into juice and poured into ice trays to freeze. My mother would serve frozen cubes of naranjas in glasses filled with icy water and sugar while family and visitors lounged on the veranda.

I loved such occasions, acting as if I was all grown up as I crossed my legs like a lady and sipped the delicious drink, loudly interjecting my opinions into adult conversations. Because at ten I was the youngest child, and greatly loved, they pretended to take me seriously.

To my excitement, my older brother Ra'ad, who was eighteen years old and set to begin college in the fall, appeared at the back door and called out, "Joanna, go! Keep watch for the taxi."

Uncle Aziz nodded, holding out his hands for the fruit I had picked. Then I dashed through the kitchen where Mother and Muna, my fourteen-year-old sister, were preparing a picnic of chicken sandwiches and date cookies to eat while on the road. I skipped through the house to the front porch, standing first on one foot and then the other, impatient, willing the taxicab to arrive so we could leave for the bus station.

I kept a watchful gaze on the boulevard, wishing that we owned a car so that we could travel to the north in fine style.

The families of our al-Askari cousins all owned expensive automobiles. That was because they were rich. Unfortunately, we were poor. But even if we had been wealthy, my father would not have been permitted a license to drive a motorized vehicle because he was unable to hear the warning roars of automobiles, buses, and donkey carts that raced through the streets of Baghdad. My father had been deaf since childhood. His only means of transportation was an old blue bicycle.

I stared at his bicycle parked against the garden fence. How I longed to jump on that bicycle and ride away! But I was not allowed on it although my brothers were, with Ra'ad balanced on the back and Sa'ad perched on the front. I was envious of my brothers, but regardless of my pleas, such a thing was not considered proper for a girl in Baghdad.

To take my mind off the injustices of my life, I forced myself to concentrate on the city street in case the taxicab accidentally passed by our house.

It was fun to watch all the activity. The kaleidoscope of a Baghdad morning was in full swing. Human figures shimmered like a mirage, with men hurrying to reach the neighborhood café while harried housewives rushed to the market. Older boys were amusing themselves with marbles, calling out their negligible bets, while small boys shouted as they played hopscotch. There were few girls in public view because in those days respectable girls were expected to remain inside once the school year had finished.

I was thankful that Mother didn't oblige me to help with the housework, because I hated chores. Although she maintained the cleanest house in all of Baghdad, and my older siblings had specific duties, I was excused because I was the youngest.

"Salt! Salt!" The cry of the nomad camel driver drew my attention as he made his weekly pass through the neighborhood. Many were the mornings I had heard his hoarse cries while I curled up under the warm covers of my bed, so I stared at him with interest.

He kept up a steady bellow. "Salt! Salt!"

Dressed in a frayed gray shirt and worn brown trousers, he was a dark-skinned, craggy-faced man with arched eyebrows. A knotted rope of red and blue wool was looped from his arm around the long neck of a small camel. I instantly loved that camel, with her blond wavy coat and bowed lips curled into a smile, shuffling and rocking as if she were moving to the beat of a song. Her precious cargo was packed in rough cloth bags that swayed on either side. But when her master tapped her on the rump with his stick, she belched a rumbling complaint, and frothing saliva gathered at the corners of her open mouth.

"Salt! Salt" the hawker yelled as he puffed on a cigarette that hung from the side of his mouth. He raised his eyes to meet mine, plucking the cigarette out of his mouth as a hopeful smile crossed his face. His eyes widened and his head bobbed with anticipation.

I shook my head no and waved him off, aware that Mother still had an unopened bag of his salt in the kitchen. He shrugged good-naturedly and turned away, shouting, "Salt! Salt!"

My eyes were lured to a young peasant woman dressed in a billowy blouse, a colorful skirt, and a carefully twisted turban with a large round tray balanced on top. White cloths were wrapped around her feet and ankles for protection from the heat.

I knew enough to see that she had come from the south, from an area of Iraq called the Marshes. Women from that region were known to be as beautiful as the landscape.

She was peddling buffalo cream stored in round wooden containers on the tray on her head.

I watched as she ambled out of a side street, a trail of mangy neighborhood cats at her shuffling feet. The cats darted from side to side, meowing expectantly at the scent of the fragrant cream. Despite her youth and beauty, she appeared weighed down with resigned despair.

I felt sorry for her, and if I had had money in my pocket, I would have purchased all the cream her buffalo could produce. I was pleased to see a customer approach, his outstretched palms indicating the quantity of cream he wanted to purchase. The unsmiling girl unhooked a thin steel needle hanging from her waist, reached over her head, and grasped one of the wooden containers. Then she used the needle as a tool to slice through the congealed buffalo cream.

The cats looked on hopefully, on the ready for any spills, but the girl was too skilled for such carelessness.

After dropping a few coins into the girl's waiting hand, the customer left with his precious purchase.

The cats around her feet increased in number, but the cream peddler didn't seem to notice them, or me, as she slunk past our front gate. I thought that her life must be very hard to be so permanently gloomy. Her petulant lips made that clear.

As she strolled away, I tried to imagine that young woman's life, so unlike my own, for I knew even then at my young age that Iraq was populated by a huge variety of people with vastly differing lifestyles and beliefs.

After World War I and the defeat of the Ottoman Empire, the British and the French resolved that three main geographic regions would be joined together to make up modern Iraq. The central part of Iraq was the largely limestone plateau where Baghdad was located. Although modern Baghdad was not considered a beautiful city, it did claim a unique and glorious past, boasting palaces, mosques, markets, and gardens.

Iraq's second region was the wet lowland plain of the south known as the Marshes, home to the sad-faced buffalo cream seller. A marvelous variety of fish, birds, and plant life was abundant there. An old Arabic text says that the distinctive landscape resulted from the aftermath of a devastating flood so powerful that mud houses melted back into mud while the land itself split into thousands of tiny islands. The survivors of the great flood lived in huts on boats called *mash-houfs*, pieced together with reeds and bitumen.

Iraq's third region, the north, famed for its many snow-clad mountains and lush forests, was a place of beauty with waterfalls and orchards. Because of its cool temperatures, many vacation resorts had sprung up in that area. While Arab Iraqis had simply referred to the region as northern Iraq, Kurds called the area by its true name: Kurdistan.

I searched the street once more for the taxicab and caught sight of a group of young neighborhood bullies, a gang of four boys near to my own age who always took great pleasure ridiculing me for being a Kurd. When our eyes locked, they began to leap about on their bare feet, jeering laughter interspersed with hateful chants, "House of the Kurds! Kurd Girl!" One particularly spiteful boy laughed the loudest, shouting, "*La! La!* Girl of the deaf and dumb!"

My eyes met his. For a moment his words drove all the power and feeling out of me, but my passiveness lasted only as long as it took me to sail off the porch. I shouted, "Hey!" barely pausing long enough to gather several loose stones from under Mother's sweet-smelling *yass* bush, which I tossed as hard as I could. I had never reacted in such an aggressive manner before, but recently I had resolved to be more like Father, a bold man who always defended himself, even if it meant a physical fight.

Unaccustomed to a girl who would defend herself, the boys were so startled by the turn of events that they instinctively turned and ran.

I hit one of the boys on his arm. When he shrieked, the others fell over their feet to avoid the same fate. How stupid they looked!

I laughed aloud, feeling enormous satisfaction as I watched those cowards run down the street. And they were running from a girl, which made it all the more sweet.

I had never felt so powerful. Never would they frighten me again. Never!

I was smart enough to know that I must hide my deed, for my family would be horrified for a daughter to behave in such a rough manner. I quickly rubbed the dirt off my palms. When I glanced up to make certain my tormentors had not returned, I saw that the taxicab had finally arrived.

"He's here!" I cried out, running toward the house. I opened the door and shouted as loudly as I could, "The taxi driver is here! Come on!"

It was a mad dash with everyone rushing and grabbing suitcases from the front porch to pack in the taxi trunk.

The skinny taxi driver jumped from his taxicab. He shouted loudly as he directed the loading of our cargo.

Although Mother had taught me not to stare at people, I gawked at his brown face, so wrinkled and worn. His hands were gnarled, and he nervously rubbed them on his ragged, threadbare trousers. He was a poor man, I realized.

Truthfully, most people in Baghdad were poor. I glanced at Father, Uncle Aziz, and my brothers. Despite the fact that we were poor too, they were all attired in neat, clean clothes, free of tears or holes.

I glanced down at my bright pink dress. For the most part, Arabs in Baghdad wore dull colors, generally black or dark blue, but not we Kurds. We relished vivid colors. My pretty pink dress was freshly washed and ironed and smelled new, even though it was not.

Mother knew how to keep everything perfect. Mother kept her home and family so clean and tidy that it was possible that our enemies didn't know we were poor; we certainly didn't *look* poor. Perhaps our tidiness intensified their hatred.

The men were having difficulty closing the trunk. I helpfully pointed out, "This automobile is leaning to one side."

The taxi driver saw what I saw and began yelling directions as he inspected the weight on the tires. Those tires looked thin, even to my untrained eye, but I decided to keep that information to myself. Mother might insist on canceling that taxi and calling another. I did not want our trip delayed another moment, as I had been eagerly anticipating the trip since we last left Sulaimaniya, a year ago in August.

When the taxi driver felt everything was secure, he slid into the driver's seat shouting "*Yella, yella!*" Let's go.

Mother and Muna joined me in the backseat. Uncle Aziz came around to my side and gently pushed me to the center. Although he would accompany us to the station, it had been decided that he would not go with us to Kurdistan.

In 1962, the year I was born, my uncle was a student in Sulaimaniya when he was arrested simply for the crime of being a Kurdish. The torture he endured changed his life forever. Since that time, he had been unable to cope with life in the north, where his imprisonment and persecution had occurred. That is why he had moved to Baghdad to live with his older sister, my mother.

Even years after his torture, there were occasions when something would trigger bizarre behavior, when my uncle might refuse to speak or to come out of his room. For years he was incapable of attending college or holding down a job. But he was a greatly loved uncle, always willing to join in silly games with me.

So he would remain behind in Baghdad without us, while we visited my grandmother Ameena, my aunties, and all my cousins in Sulaimaniya.

The taxi driver shouted loudly that he was in a hurry, that we must go. Ra'ad and Sa'ad quickly shoved into the front seat with the driver.

As the taxi pulled away from the curb, I remembered that I had forgotten to say good-bye to my father. My father rarely traveled to Kurdistan with us. He was not Kurdish himself, but even had he been, he would have stayed behind in Baghdad to work, never having enough money to join his family on vacation. Poor Father.

As we drove away, I twisted around until I could see his face through the window of the taxi, his brown eyes crinkling, his lips stretching into a smile. I stared back at his kindly face until he reached down to pick something from the ground. His scalp was exposed, his hair plastered down in some places and sticking out in others. He had obviously worked up a sweat during the loading of the taxicab.

Suddenly, I had a queasy feeling in my stomach, a flutter of unexplained apprehension over my father's well-being. But I quickly pushed that bad feeling aside as we made our way into the thick of midday Baghdad traffic.

Unlike most cities, Baghdad did not grow from a small village but instead was designed according to a master plan. The year was

A.D. 762 when Caliph Abu Ja'far al-Mansur was struck with the idea
of creating a city of circled enclosures. His dream was for a circu-
lar city with three distinct enclosures on the west bank of the Tigris.

Caliph al-Mansur ruled from the innermost enclosure, the army
was housed within the second enclosure, and the citizens lived in
the outermost enclosure. But modern Baghdad had spread well
beyond its carefully laid out circles, losing what charm it might have
had.

With only a few main roads, Baghdad was chaotic as well.

Our driver nosed his taxi onto the thoroughfare, competing with
hordes of people, donkey carts, cars, and minibuses to bully his way
onto the main road.

Colorful billboards advertised Western products. Others touted
the advantages Iraqis were supposedly enjoying under the current
government of the Baath Party, the latest political party that had
come to power during yet another government coup four years
before, in 1968. I had overheard my brother Ra'ad jokingly call the
Baathists the "comeback kids," because they had been in power
once before, in 1963, but had been quickly deposed due to the dis-
order and malice demonstrated during their first attempt at govern-
ing. But everyone said the Baathists were now firmly entrenched.

Although I was too young to understand politics, I was aware of
the destructive effects of the 1958 revolution that had caused
deaths in my family and my father to lose his business. I was more
attentive than most children my age, and I was aware of optimistic
whispers regarding Iraq's new government. I knew that the adults
wanted only one thing: an end to the confusion and upheaval that
occurred each time there was a change of government in Iraq.

But on that sun-drenched July day so long ago, who could have
guessed the heartbreak and terror that the Baathist government and
Saddam Hussein would ultimately bring to all Iraqis? It was good
that none of us were aware of the dreadful days coming.

In years past, our family had traveled by train from Baghdad to
Kirkuk and from there to Sulaimaniya by car. But that particular
summer of 1972 Mother said we must save money; thus, we were
traveling by bus. Soon, we arrived at the Nahdha bus station in
downtown Baghdad. More travel bedlam erupted as we piled out of
the taxi and waited while Ra'ad, Sa'ad, and Uncle Aziz reversed all
the work just accomplished, unloading and stacking our bags.

A porter appeared and for a small tip eagerly helped transport the luggage. We walked hurriedly to the designated area of the station where the minibuses to Sulaimaniya were parked haphazardly, awaiting passengers. Suddenly, we were confronted by one of the bus drivers, an older balding man with a thick mustache that was so long it drooped down on either side to his chin. He was extremely friendly, encouraging us to board his bus, claiming that he was such an experienced bus driver that he would cut an hour off the trip. Most important, he declared that children under the age of twelve could ride free.

We gratefully boarded that bus because money was always short.

I was very thin and small for my age, so there was no question that I was under age twelve. Muna was very petite and could have passed for twelve as well, but mother refused to lie about it.

We made a grave error in trusting that driver, but it would take time to reveal our blunder.

The well-worn bus creaked as we slowly pulled away from the station, and once again we weaved through the busy city streets. The bus lurched through the commercial area of Baghdad where most of the city's shopping bazaars and ancient souks and factories with tall chimneys were located. We were soon on Highway 4, a modern roadway to Kirkuk on our way north to our final destination of Sulaimaniya.

Although the bus could easily transport twenty-five people, only eleven people were on board. Mother and Ra'ad conferred about that oddity and Ra'ad queried the driver, but the man brushed off my brother's concerns with a wink.

"This gives us more room," Muna whispered with a hesitant smile on her face. She had a good point. My sister Muna was so timid and nervous that everyone in our family felt we must protect her. She was a twin to Sa'ad, who was her exact opposite in every way.

Sa'ad was dark skinned, physically strong, and personally forceful. Muna, on the other hand, was porcelain pale, fragile, and painfully docile. They were such opposites that many people accused us of mocking their intelligence when we told them that Sa'ad and Muna were twins.

I regret I was not there to witness the day when Muna and Sa'ad were born. It was such a thrilling incident that no one in our family has ever forgotten it. I had heard the tale more than once. In Mother's third pregnancy, no one suspected that she was expecting twins, not even her physician. A few hours after Mother went into labor, a noticeably disinterested nurse appeared and presented my father with a hefty baby boy. While family members were mighty pleased at the birth of a second son, everyone soon grew worried when Mother continued shrieking from behind a pair of closed doors. When Mother's cries finally subsided, the same nurse, no longer indifferent, but suddenly possessed with so much energy she was wheezing from excitement, rushed from the delivery room and straight to my father with yet a second baby!

Everyone present gaped at the sight of a tiny bundle in the nurse's hands. The nurse loudly declared the new baby a twin to Sa'ad, who was a brother twice her size. No one could believe what the nurse was saying. Several Kurdish relatives from up north accused the nurse of playing a spiteful joke on our family just because Mother was a Kurd.

But they were wrong. Muna was *not* a joke. My sister was real, although she was such a miniature package that she had to remain at the hospital for several weeks. Even when Muna was discharged, the doctor refused to guarantee her survival. Mother was told to swaddle the baby's little body in strips of cotton for the first few months of her life to protect her translucent skin, so delicate that it bled when stroked. Swaddling was necessary for a second reason as well: there were no baby clothes in all of Iraq to fit an infant much smaller than a doll.

As the years passed, Sa'ad grew manly and forceful, his opinions known to all, while Muna was so bashful she rarely uttered a word.

I felt enormous affection for my sister from the beginning, comprehending that I must shield her from the cruel world, despite the fact I was younger by four years.

As soon as we left the city behind us, the passengers napped or gazed out the windows, but I was born with an inquisitive temperament, so I made it my business to inspect all the passengers.

Two Kurdish men were sitting quietly at the front of the bus. Their traditional costumes of turbans and distinctive baggy pants made them identifiable as our own kind. I wondered if they could be part of the romantic Kurdish freedom fighters, known as Peshmerga, that I had heard such stories about. But of course, even if they were, they would have to conceal that fact. It was an automatic death sentence to be a Peshmerga in Iraq.

I couldn't stop staring.

The younger of the two was a gigantic man with the broad shoulders and thick arms of a weight lifter. But his wide dreamy eyes and kindly mien belied his physical power. A fringe of black curly hair escaped from under his turban at the nape of his neck.

The second man was small and wiry. I stared at his unusual sagging, creased eyelids. Nevertheless, he looked jolly, glittering with life.

The other four passengers were a couple and their two small children. By their attire I knew they were Arab. The husband was dressed in a dishdasha, a long shirtlike white robe worn by many native Iraqi men. His wife was wearing a black cloak over a blue dress. The children were dressed in Western-style clothing, and they stared in an unfriendly way at our Kurdish costumes.

Although Mother and I were the only two members of our family who routinely wore traditional Kurdish costumes, on that day all of us were wearing our best Kurdish clothes.

Ra'ad and Sa'ad looked dashing in their voluminous Kurdish blouses and wide trousers belted with sashes. Typical Kurdish caps, called *klaw*, were perched on their heads, and they wore sandals known as *klash* on their feet. The three females in the family were decked out in brightly colored Kurdish dresses. I was in my favorite shade of deep pink, Muna was in bright blue, and Mother was in sunny yellow. Our girlish heads were bare, while Mother's black hair was covered with a dazzling golden scarf with clinking silver coins sewn to the edges.

To be friendly, Mother offered the Arab children some of our date cookies. But their parents reacted as though the cookies were poisoned. They yanked on the hands of their children, telling Mother a curt, "*La! La!*" meaning "No! No!"

My surprised Mother fell back against her seat.

I was shocked by their rudeness, despite the fact I was old enough to understand a fact of life: most Iraqi Arabs hated Kurds.

Mother quickly recovered and offered her own children a few of the sweets. I felt so insulted by the strangers' reaction that I took enormous pleasure in munching on the cookies, loudly announcing to everyone how delicious they were. I felt vindicated when I saw the Arab kids stare reproachfully at their parents.

In contrast, the older of the two Kurdish men looked around smiling and offered pieces of hard candy to all the children. The two Arab kids moved their little hands so rapidly that they blurred. They grabbed the candy, removing the wrapping and popping it into their mouths with such speed that their parents couldn't stop them that time.

I laughed out loud at the parents' surprised faces, and the two men laughed with me, even the one who was so quiet that he had not spoken one word during the trip.

I knew that the trip would take nearly nine hours. We were the only passengers traveling all the way to Sulaimaniya. The family of Arabs, we learned, would be leaving the bus at a small Sunni village an hour or so outside Baghdad, and the older of the two Kurdish men said that they would disembark at a village outside Kirkuk.

The day was miserably hot. A large fly buzzed around the bus, and I feebly swatted at it. Just as I drifted off, I was startled awake by the angry voice of the Arab bus driver. He had been so friendly before, I could only assume that the unbearable July heat had brought on a bad temper.

He shouted, "You! Kurds! Be quiet back there! Noisy kids give me a headache!"

I felt personally affronted. We hadn't made a sound. I arched my neck proudly and glanced at the Arab family. The husband and wife exchanged a calculating look.

I dug my fingers into my palms, itching to react, yet knowing I could do nothing with Mother and my siblings around. I looked hopefully at the two Kurdish men to see if perhaps they might defend us from this unprovoked attack, but their profiles were frozen stares, studying the landscapes we passed, obviously unwilling to get into an altercation with the driver. I was disappointed, but told myself that if they were indeed Peshmergas in disguise, surely they must protect their cover.

Before leaving on this trip we had been warned that life for Kurds in the north had become extremely difficult, even dangerous. The Kurds were always suspected of fostering dissent and civil unrest. New draconian laws had been passed by the government: If a Kurd was found with a pair of binoculars, he would be hung. If a Kurd owned a typewriter without special permission, he could be arrested and tried. Cameras had always been suspect, but a camera with a zoom lens could cost a Kurd his life. Kurds could be arrested on a whim. An Arab might report a Kurd for criticizing the regime, and even if the report was untrue, the Kurd would be automatically punished.

My mother and older siblings shifted uncomfortably in their seats, but because we were Kurds and the discourteous driver was an Arab, no one dared to speak back.

The trip had lost its luster for me.

We soon arrived at a modest cluster of brown-brick houses on the outskirts of Baghdad where the Arab family took leave. They gathered their belongings, which consisted of two old carrying cases, and scurried past us without a glance. But they were effusive with gratitude to the bus driver.

My soul burned for revenge.

They lived in a modest neighborhood, typical for poor Iraqi families, where one-story concrete homes were the same color as the sand. Flat roofs exposed drying clothes and an assortment of rusted metal chairs.

Although I was pleased to see those unfriendly Arabs leave, I was disappointed that they left without knowing that my father was of the famous Baghdadi al-Askari family. Even years after the revolution, strangers we met were always awed by our family name.

We soon made another quick stop at a small, dirty gas station. As we neared Kurdistan, the gas would become scarce because as a collective punishment the government limited gas supplies to Kurds. The driver would have to look for roadside stalls where young Kurdish boys sold gas out of plastic jugs.

When the bus got back on the road, everyone dozed until lunchtime, when Mother and Muna woke us passing out chicken salad sandwiches and the Fanta orange drinks Mother had purchased at the gas station.

Both Kurdish men were grateful when Mother quietly insisted that they share our sandwiches. But the bus driver refused Mother's offer. He acted as though the sandwiches were contaminated, although Mother was the most fastidious housekeeper in all of Iraq.

Soon afterward the flat earth fell away from us when we passed over a metal suspension bridge that spanned a gorge. For the first time I could see the green beauty of a rising mountain range. We would soon be in Kurdistan, the one place on Earth that always made me feel confident and happy.

Even at that young age, I knew that I belonged there, and not in Baghdad.

"I love Kurdistan!" I announced to no one in particular, winning smiles from the two Kurdish men. The Arab driver produced a disgusted grunt but made no comment.

It was illegal to call northern Iraq by its proper name, Kurdistan. But I felt confident and brave because it was unlikely that a young girl like me would be punished. Besides, I knew that soon we would be at Grandmother Ameena's house, and this troubling trip would be behind us.

The bus driver became less cranky once we were in the cool of the Kurdish mountains. To my surprise, he turned on a tape recorder that filled the interior of the bus with rousing Kurdish folk songs and urged us all to sing along. Everyone knew that it was illegal to sing Kurdish songs that invoked nationalistic feelings, yet on occasion Kurdish folk songs could even be heard over Baghdad Radio. The oldest of the two Kurdish men pretended to sing along with the music, but I forgave him because I knew he was faking to keep the peace. But I certainly wasn't going to perform at the command of that rude man.

Within an hour the bus came to a stop and the two Kurds took their leave. Holding their hands over their hearts, they said their farewells, scrambling happily from the bus. They rapidly walked in the direction of a settlement clinging to the side of the mountain, the tops of the houses so low and close to one another that I believed that if I tried, I could use them as stepping stones up the mountain.

The bus moved on. By then we had been on that hot bus for over six hours. Weariness was setting in. But then the vehicle made an unexpected turn off the main highway, and the bus driver announced that we were stopping.

Mother quickly shouted a protest in Kurdish, "What? Where are you going?" Her question was ignored.

Ra'ad repeated Mother's words in Arabic.

The driver wobbled his head and lamely announced, "A pickup. A regular. He needs a ride to Sulaimaniya."

Ra'ad translated for Mother. Her lips turned down in a scowl. She was not pleased with the turn of events.

The road was unpaved, and the dust flew from under the wheels and into the open windows, causing everyone to choke and cough. Just as Ra'ad got out of his seat and moved toward Mother to confer further about the troubling situation, there was a shocking noise, a rattle of gunfire.

My forehead struck the seat back in front of me when the driver slammed on the brakes. Ra'ad stumbled backward but caught his footing. He fell back on the seat and gave an involuntary gasp.

I was frightened. I looked at Mother, who motioned, "Come, Joanna."

I rushed to her side, peering through the window. I spotted a group of armed men moving stealthily down a winding path. What was happening?

We heard shouts: "Off! Off the bus!"

The bus driver was the first to disembark, but we were quick to file out and follow him.

Ra'ad looked at Mother, whispering, "Bandits."

Bandits! Were we being robbed? My heart started beating hard and fast.

When we filed off the bus I saw five armed men. They looked at us angrily.

Many people in Iraq were living in hopeless poverty. Desperate bandits materialized from every part of society. Even Kurds could be guilty of highway robbery. But the men holding us at gunpoint were not Kurds.

Arab bandits would never have pity for us, even if they knew Father was a full-blooded Arab. In fact, such information would most likely make them hate us all the more, since we were dressed in Kurdish clothing.

One of the bandits started shouting at the driver. We quickly understood that he was in league with them. It was his task to travel around Iraq for the purpose of luring unsuspecting passengers to board his bus. Then he drove them to prearranged, secluded areas to be robbed.

But it was clear by their chatter that we were a disappointment. They were expecting more affluent-looking passengers.

For certain, those men were going to rob us. Suddenly, I could think of nothing but my beautiful black doll, brought back from London for me by my auntie Fatima. Auntie Fatima was the younger sister of my father, a brilliant woman who held a high government position. None of us had ever seen such a doll. She was made of black porcelain, with a perfect face and long lashes. Her dress was light green silk. Best of all, she even had matching underpants. The doll was so precious and unique that Mother said she was a collectible and put her in a box, saving her, she said, for "special occasions."

I had pleaded for days before Mother agreed I could take her to Kurdistan, to show her off to my Kurdish cousins in Sulaimaniya. Would the bandits take her from me?

I glanced up at Mother and from her worried expression I knew that she was anxious over more important things than my doll. Mother was frightened for our safety. She pulled Muna by her arm, moving her close to her side.

Ever since Muna was a young girl, many people praised her for her beauty, with her honey-blond hair, light skin, and perfect features. Perhaps Mother was worried that those men would want Muna for a bride, even though she was still very young.

Holding one arm firmly around Muna, I saw Mother throwing a meaningful look at Ra'ad and Sa'ad, signifying that they were to remain calm.

The bandits might well have believed my brothers a threat and capable of fighting back, especially Ra'ad, my older brother. Although he was not yet an adult, he was over six feet tall, towering a full head above the bandits. There was no way for them to know that my older brother was not a fighter and would much prefer to sit in a corner and study.

On the other hand, Sa'ad could create a problem. He was a big boy, too, but he was hotheaded and hardheaded. Out of the corner of my eye I saw him flexing and tensing his muscles.

But the bandits were preoccupied. They were furious with their partner, the driver, for delivering such a poor lot of passengers.

The shortest bandit, who was the obvious leader, suddenly had enough of our driver's smart mouth and menaced him with his gun. The cowardly driver spun around, then made for the high bushes edging the dirt road. Recklessly, the bandit sprayed the road with bullets, terrifying everyone.

When the driver heard the popping gunfire and saw the bullets rising from around his feet, he skidded to an abrupt stop, swirled around, and shouted, "Hey! Hey!" Making conciliatory signals to his bandit friends, he slunk back.

I was so shocked that I stood with my mouth open. We were being robbed by a gang of comedians. Unfortunately, the situation was deadly serious.

The leader cursed him with a threat. The driver pointed out our luggage, eight crammed bags lashed to the top of the bus. "Perhaps you will be satisfied with those." He looked fiercely in our direction. "Surely these Kurds will have *something* of value."

My worst fears came true when the leader ordered two of his men to retrieve our luggage. They leaned their guns against the bus frame. One of the bandits then boosted the other on top before climbing up to join him, and they began tossing our bags to the ground. They leaped on the ground and opened the bags one by one, quickly searching for valuables.

I glimpsed at Mother to see her holding her hand to her mouth. My brothers and sister looked stricken as well, watching our personal items being strewn on the ground.

But nothing pleased those men. They were so disgusted at our meager belongings that they began to fling them aside.

The driver shrugged his shoulders. "They're Kurds. What do you expect? Precious jewels?" He glared at us as if we were to blame for the displeasure of his partners, as though we were poor on purpose.

One of the men demanded of Mother, "Where is your money?"

Mother fumbled with her bag and a few coins tumbled to the dirt. She never took cash to Kurdistan. Our family in Sulaimaniya always took care of all our needs.

Just at that moment my precious black doll was hurled to the ground. A cry escaped my lips as I rushed to pick her up, despite my mother's warning shout, "*Na!* Joanna! *Na!*"

I examined the doll. She was still in one piece. Other than a few scratches on her face and a little dirt on her clothing, she was as good as new.

The driver made an alarming movement in my direction, his hands outstretched, but I screamed, tucking the doll behind me. The leader of the thieves briskly ordered, "Leave her."

I slowly backed away until I was out of sight behind Mother, peering cautiously from her side.

After selecting the best of our clothes and the gifts purchased for our relatives, all six criminals piled in the minibus, complaining loudly about our poverty. We were a waste of their time.

I pulled on Mother's arm. "Mother?"

We were dismayed to see them preparing to drive away, leaving us on the side of the lonely road, abandoned to our fate. The driver sniffed at us one final time. "Stupid Kurds!" he yelled, mocking us for being so trusting.

I stared at the departing bus, the spinning wheels covering me in road dust. When it faded into the distance, I began to sob, just for the pity of it all.

Mother was so relieved that her children had escaped unharmed that she appeared unperturbed that we were deserted without transport, food, or water, in the middle of a dangerous mountain region where there might be wild animals.

Through my sobs, I studied the foliage surrounding us, fully expecting to see wolves, foxes, and wildcats coming for us. And snakes. Surely that rugged landscape was crawling with countless poisonous snakes. Since a mischievous cousin in Kurdistan had chased me with a snake two summers before, I had been terrified of them.

My mother and siblings stared at our things strewn across the dirt road. The bandits had left our three most worn bags, so we moved together like robots, repacking the few items left behind.

"Perhaps there is a village nearby," Mother offered, breaking the stunned silence.

"The main road is not far down the road," Ra'ad said softly, pointing in the direction from where we had come.

Sa'ad was so angry he could hardly speak. He grunted.

Muna, like me, began to weep.

Ra'ad and Sa'ad hoisted the three bags on their shoulders, and we formed a perpendicular line, walking in the middle of the roadway, avoiding the sides where the hard ground was stony and overgrown with tall grass and thistles. Convinced there were poisonous snakes lurking on the side in those bushy stalks, I kept in the middle of the road, with two people on either side of me.

Soon, Muna stopped crying and sweetly volunteered to carry my doll, which was getting heavy.

The July sun was shining, so thirst quickly set in. My tongue was swollen and my lips parched dry. Our water supply had gone with the bus. There were plenty of mountain springs in Kurdistan, but no one volunteered to make their way through the thick undergrowth to locate one.

My mind began to play tricks on me, and I could think of nothing but the delicious grape juice Grandmother Ameena often served at her home in Sulaimaniya. It was poured over the pure mountain ice that was cut and delivered daily all the way from the tallest mountain peaks. Nothing in the world tasted better than that icy grape juice.

The chicken sandwiches long forgotten, I was hungry as well. I longed for just one bite of my grandmother's fresh baked bread and cheese stuffed with herbs.

Just when my legs started to tremble and I felt that I could not go one step further, we heard the noise of an engine. Were the bandits coming back?

Thankfully, we were in for a bit of good luck. A red tractor popped over the top of the hill. A farmer was perched on the driver's seat. Quickly, I recognized from his clothes that he was Kurdish.

The farmer appeared puzzled at the sight of us. He slowed without coming to a complete stop, idling his tractor engine. His eyebrows raised, he stared at us suspiciously. He demanded to know, "What are you people doing here?"

Ra'ad stepped forward to explain our situation.

The farmer's skeptical expression changed into sympathy. He questioned Ra'ad about our family background. It only took a few moments to discover the most marvelous coincidence: that Kurdish farmer was the uncle of Hady, the man who named me as a child and who had married Alia, my oldest sister. We were practically related!

The farmer jumped to the ground. "Come. Let me help you. Get on the tractor and I'll take you to my home." He kindly offered, "You'll spend the night as my guests." We were saved!

The farmer, Ra'ad, and Sa'ad found places to stack our luggage before the farmer said, "Everyone, find a safe seat."

How diversely we settled on that tractor. I twisted into a circle to curl next to Mother while Muna and Sa'ad sprawled on the tire covers. Ra'ad volunteered, "I'll sit on the tractor engine."

I knew my brother well. He wished to spare the rest of us from balancing on that hot place.

The farmer started the engine and we were off. Although the sun remained warm on our backs, there was a light wind on our faces as we rode splendidly away from that dangerous place.

I laughed aloud when I turned to look at Ra'ad. My brother was leaning forward like a horseman about to win a race.

Happy at last, I felt the breeze stirring my long hair, and as I tilted my nose high in the Kurdish air, it smelled like freedom.

2

Martyrs Hill

SULAIMANIYA, KURDISTAN
July 1972

After our miraculous rescue, we gladly accepted the farmer's generous invitation to spend the night at his home. He lived in a tiny house hidden in the shadow of a grove of tall trees. It made me think of a fairy tale.

When the tractor pulled into the dirt drive, I saw faces peering from behind lavender-colored curtains of lace, the fabric billowing through glassless windows.

Hady's uncle confided that he was a fortunate man with a good wife and three obedient daughters. At his urging, his family coyly stepped onto the large front porch, beckoning us with welcoming gestures.

I was the first off the tractor, executing an impressive leap before quickly walking onto the porch and through the front door. I noticed that the family had few visible possessions. As in all Kurdish homes, whether simple or grand, the rooms were garlanded with freshly cut flowers.

The family welcomed us as honored guests, the farmer claiming, "Guests bring good luck with them."

His wife cheerily escorted us to the back porch, where she pointed out a bucket of fresh spring water and urged us to take a drink, wash up, and take a seat so that she could serve us food. She told us warmly, "A visitor comes with ten blessings, eats one, and leaves nine."

She poured us each a glass of *dow*, a cold yogurt drink, before calling for her three timid daughters who, to my hungry delight, had already arranged large platters loaded with freshly baked flat bread, white cheese, and figs. Then we were urged to eat some *kubba*, a popular dish of mashed cracked wheat mixed with minced meat, onions, and almonds.

While we ate, Ra'ad narrated the complete story of how we had been tricked into being brought to the farmer's neighborhood to be robbed.

The farmer was garrulous, gusting numerous Kurdish proverbs. "Do not worry. Many will show you the way, once your cart has overturned."

Trying to hide my giggles at his homilies, I feigned choking with my hands cupping my mouth, but Mother silenced me with a secret nudge.

That dear man insisted that we take their cotton mattresses on the front porch while his family slept in the garden under the juniper and willow trees. There was no finer host than Hady's uncle.

After our night's rest, we woke up to a tasty breakfast of hot tea, boiled eggs, fresh yogurt, and more fresh bread, while the farmer kept his word and arranged for a trusted cousin to transport us on the final leg of the journey to Sulaimaniya, to Grandmother Ameena's house.

The cousin's car looked worn and aged, but the engine was fine-tuned, and we gathered an impressive speed as soon as we left the farmer's house. I was so excited that the trip seemed much shorter than the two hours necessary to cover the distance. The car climbed a hill and rounded a bend before barreling down into the valley that was thick with green grass and colorful flowers.

In a splendid blaze of color, picturesque Sulaimaniya burst into view. Built by Süleyman Pasha the Great in 1780, the city stands nine hundred meters above sea level in an emerald, bowl-shaped valley nestled between two mountains.

Sulaimaniya was a purely Kurdish city, the place where my mother was born and raised. Baghdad might have been the place of my birth, but my love was reserved for Sulaimaniya.

Grandmother's grand old home was situated in a neighborhood with large, open houses bordered by flourishing gardens and ancient shade trees. For me, Grandmother's home was the most beautiful house in the world. All the rooms opened up into a central garden courtyard that had a large fountain in the center. The roomy bedroom balconies above were shaded by the leaves of a thick grapevine.

Mother was lucky to have grown up in that house. She was born in 1928, the fourth daughter. Her father, Hassoon Aziz, was an Ottoman army officer from a well-known family, a mix of Turks and Arabs, and Grandmother Ameena's family was Kurdish. While Grandfather did have one son from a previous marriage, his marriage to Grandmother Ameena had produced only daughters so far.

So when Mother was born, Grandfather Hassoon was bitterly disappointed. In a desperate desire to ward off the bad luck of more daughters, he named my mother Kafia, which means "enough" in Kurdish. But his name charm was futile. Three more daughters followed Mother's birth before finally two sons were born, with Uncle Aziz being the youngest and last child of the union.

In a family with seven older sisters, it was no mystery that Uncle Aziz was greatly loved. But the daughters brought fame to the family because all seven girls blossomed into tall, slim beauties with exquisite faces and long black hair. Their celebrated good looks were a magnet for many suitors. It was said that many men dreamed of marrying one of the daughters of Officer Hassoon.

Mother was not only beautiful, she was studious as well, and she was allowed to attain the highest level of education for a Kurdish girl at that time, which meant six years of schooling. Left with a love of learning, she was an avid reader and was especially entranced by the beauty of Kurdish poetry. But Mother's happy childhood and promising future came to an abrupt end when Grandfather's appendix burst, releasing poisons into his body. No one could save him. And with his death, no one could save my mother from her fate.

During this same time, my father's mother was searching the country for a suitable bride for her deaf-mute son. While the best families in Baghdad usually intermarried, few were tempted by a

Joanna's Grandparents and Parents

Maternal grandfather
Hassoon Aziz.

Maternal grandmother Ameena Hassoon.

Maternal grandmother
Mirriam Mohammed.

Paternal grandfather Ali Ridha al-Askari,
World War I army officer.

Father Mohammed Adnan al-Askari in the early 1920s at the time he lost his ability to hear.

Mother Kafia Hassoon in Kurdish dress.

man considered handicapped, despite his wealthy family or his European education. At that time, most people erroneously believed that my father's deafness could be passed on to any children he might father.

My father's mother sent a representative across the country to report on marriageable girls from good families, and that was when the representative heard about the beautiful daughters of Hassoon Aziz.

Mother was sixteen years old, which was considered the perfect age for marriage. After several meetings, my father's family proposed that the two families be joined by marriage.

Mother, who by this time had received many marriage requests and was secretly in love with a special Kurdish boy who she hoped would one day be her husband, balked at the prospect. She did not wish to marry a man who was not only a stranger but also an Arab stranger—she was aware of the scorn Arabs expressed toward Kurdish people. She did not want to marry a man who was deaf-mute. She did not want to marry into a family that lived so far away from her family.

In those days, people rarely made long trips across the country. Mother understood the reality of the situation: once in Baghdad, she would be marooned and lucky if she saw her family once a year.

There was another problem with such a union. Unable to speak Arabic, Mother realized she would be socially handicapped and even isolated living among Arabs in Baghdad.

But Grandmother Ameena was a widow in a precarious situation. She quickly recognized the chance to unite her family with one of Iraq's most prestigious families. Going against Mother's wishes, Grandmother Ameena accepted the proposal on Mother's behalf.

At age sixteen, my poor mother had no choice but to leave the paradise of Sulaimaniya to marry a man she did not know and live among strangers in the unappealing, hot Iraqi capital of Baghdad. She was devastated, but in those days, girls had no option but to do as they were told.

And that is how I came to be born in Baghdad with an Arab Iraqi father and a Kurdish mother.

Later that day, I reclined in an easy chair in Grandmother Ameena's spacious home. Mother, Grandmother, and three aunties were involved in conversation, believing me to be asleep, with my arms wrapped around my black doll, but I was merely resting, while secretly listening in on their adult conversation.

We had been there for only a few hours, but I was still fatigued by the stressful journey. When I felt a pang of hunger, I opened my eyes thinking to persuade Mother to allow me a sweet. But just at that moment Auntie Aisha, my mother's sister who was also visiting, whispered, "Kafia. Aziz? Tell us how he is faring."

I hastily closed my eyes, feigning sleep once again, curious as to what might be said about my beloved uncle. The arrest and torture of Uncle Aziz was the one topic rarely discussed in our family. If I remained quiet, perhaps I would learn additional details of his arrest and subsequent troubles.

Mother made a noisy sigh before producing a series of clicking noises with her tongue.

Grandmother Ameena urged her. "Kafia?"

"He is as he was before," Mother finally admitted. "He spends his days playing with Joanna, or, when he is in a melancholic mood, he seeks out his *nay*."

Uncle Aziz was a talented musician and singer. He played the *nay*, a vertical flute made of a long piece of cane that had six finger holes on the front and one on the back. Although most *nays* were simple, his was beautifully decorated with ancient patterns.

Grandmother Ameena made a low humming noise in her throat, then said in a regretful tone, "If only I had not asked him to drive me on that day."

"Mother, how could you know there was a roadblock at the market?" Auntie Fatima reminded her.

"Yes. That is true. I did not know about the roadblock. But I knew there was trouble on the streets. I should have kept Aziz safe." She glumly added, "I am to blame for asking him to drive me on an errand."

Auntie Aisha, who was known in the family for her passionate religious beliefs and even stronger personality, would not allow her mother to take the blame for that dark day. "Everything happens only if Allah wills it, Mother. And Aziz was young. Young men feel invincible. If he had not been out with you, he would have been with someone else. The result of that day was Allah's will. Do not question Him."

"All young men were at risk. I knew that," Grandmother Ameena stubbornly remarked.

Auntie Muneera, who was left blind at age four when she contracted a mysterious disease that caused a sudden, horrifying deflating of her eyeballs, was busy knitting a sweater for one of her daughters, her steel needles clicking. She was a great beauty even without eyes, and after a lucky suitor won her hand in marriage, she gave him a large family. She was so dexterous that she never allowed anyone to assist her in her home. She always saw the positive of every situation. That night was no different. "Be thankful, at least, that Aziz is still with us," she reminded everyone. "We could be visiting Shhedan Gerdai [Martyrs Hill], you know."

I cracked open one eye. My mother, grandmother, and three aunties were sitting as still as stones, eyes locked onto one another, lips compressed tightly.

Like all Kurds, I had heard the story of those poor martyrs. The hill had become a shrine, a place where many Kurds visited and relatives of the dead visited every Friday, the Muslim holy day, to weep and pray for their young men, who were murdered on that hill.

Kurds were routinely targeted by the people in power in Baghdad, resulting in so many massacres of innocent people that it was virtually impossible to keep count. But the massacre known as Martyrs Hill was the most haunting in modern memory.

Soon after I was born, there had been many violent skirmishes between soldiers and Kurds. One day, the Iraqi army occupying Sulaimaniya began to round up students and other young men between the ages of fourteen and twenty-five. Thankfully, Uncle Aziz escaped that particular roundup, which would have cost him his life.

The soldiers marched the young Kurdish men through the city streets and to the highest point in the city, a hill visible to many people in Sulaimaniya. Once there, they gave the prisoners shovels and ordered them to start digging.

A great dread settled over the crowd of onlookers because they assumed the young men were being forced to dig their own graves before being shot. After the holes were dug, most of the men were told to step into the holes. Then the soldiers ordered the remainder of the young men to shovel the dirt over their friends and relatives, up to their chins. Once this confusing task was accomplished, the Iraqi soldiers shoved the remaining prisoners into the holes, where they, too, were buried in soil up to their chins. The resulting display was eerie. Nothing was visible above the dirt other than rows and rows of squirming human heads.

It was said that the crowd was mystified, but relieved. This was not the government's usual method of killing. Onlookers experienced a flicker of hope that the buried men would be left to bake in the sun for a time, then uncovered, released, and allowed to go home alive, with only their pride wounded and the tops of their heads blistered.

But then a military tank was brought up the hill.

To the horror of the crowd, the tank commander was given the order to drive his tank over the heads of the young men, to pulverize them. And that was what happened.

The scene was one of chaos and carnage. The soldiers held back the crowd by firing their weapons, as it took a long time for the tank driver to smash all the exposed heads.

The Iraqi authorities did not even try to hide that atrocity, but instead were proud of the massacre, inviting family members to see for themselves what happened to people who persisted to fight against the central government. But the Kurds were not intimidated; in fact, the event had the opposite effect.

News of the massacre spread like wildfire. That bitter sample of Iraqi injustice sent a shock wave across Kurdistan. After the brutal massacre on Martyrs Hill, there was no longer any possibility of signing a peace agreement. Incensed Peshmergas sprang from their hiding places and made several daring but unsuccessful attempts to assassinate the man who had ordered the death of the young men: Abdul Salam Arif, the president of Iraq.

The assassins escaped but the fight escalated, bringing even more Iraqi soldiers into the north. But the Kurds were victorious, for a time, and stubbornly refused to give in to the Iraqi president's demands.

That's when President Arif ordered his military to destroy Kurdish life. And it did.

The fighting became more and more desperate as the full force of the Iraqi army arrived, its numbers overwhelming. The Kurdish Peshmergas were finally defeated. Once the fighters were on the run, there was no one to protect Kurdish civilians, and so thousands of ordinary people were butchered. Soon, a conflagration of killing and destruction fanned across the Kurdish countryside: livestock were shot, wells were poisoned, and houses were torched.

After devastating the countryside, the Iraqi army turned its attention back to the cities. That's when its soldiers got their evil hands on Uncle Aziz.

His life was shattered only because he was a dutiful son. When asked by his mother to drive her around in Sulaimaniya on some errands, he rushed to do her bidding.

But after the massacre on Martyrs Hill, and the subsequent attempt on the Iraqi president's life, suspicion was cast on every Kurdish man, even young students. Uncle Aziz, while driving his mother, came across a newly erected roadblock. Although his papers were in order and it was clear that he was a student and not a Peshmerga, he was detained without explanation. Grandmother watched helplessly as her youngest child was roughed up, thrown into a military vehicle, and driven away.

Desperate months passed before a relative managed to locate him. He was found in a prison that was notorious for macabre punishments and torture. While the family was greatly comforted to discover that he was still alive, they were dismayed to think of the condition in which they might find him.

All Kurds knew that nothing good ever happened in that prison.

Frantic efforts were made to gain his freedom. Bribes were paid that finally gained his liberation.

Sure enough, the gaunt silent man released to the family bore little resemblance to the handsome young man arrested months before. Although his body bore the usual signs of torture with burn marks and missing fingernails, the most crippling damage was invisible, at least in the beginning.

For the first few days, the family believed their beloved Aziz was suffering from the trauma of imprisonment and torture when he refused to speak or leave his bed. But eventually, his catatonic behavior revealed that his brilliant mind had vanished in that prison. The young man they once knew was no more.

He was no longer the gifted math genius. He was no longer the ambitious student. He was no longer the sensitive son or supportive brother. He no longer spent hours playing board games with his friends. He no longer enjoyed sports. He was no longer interested in talk of marriage and children. Uncle Aziz was no longer connected to life itself.

No one in the family could uncover exactly what had occurred during Uncle Aziz's internment, but a student imprisoned in the same cell reported that every torture imaginable was applied to them. It was as though the torturers particularly hated the students. That was no surprise. When it came to Kurds, the Iraqi Arab government policy had always been consistent: all Kurds are a danger, but a Kurd with a pen is even more dangerous.

That cell mate was in awe of Uncle Aziz, claiming that Aziz had been fearless during his own torture sessions. But my uncle couldn't bear the suffering of others. He couldn't witness the torment of women and children, a favorite ploy of the torturers, without breaking down. According to his cellmate, my uncle's tough shell finally broke when they tied him to a chair and compelled him to watch the brutalization of a small boy.

Since the day he was released from prison, Uncle Aziz's only interest had been to entertain the youngest children in the family, to play his musical instrument, or to sing. He had reverted to being a child himself and did not work, study, or have any discipline in his daily life.

His only crime had been to be a Kurd.

I drifted off to sleep while listening to the low buzz of the voices of the women in my family, their dreadful murmurings of cruelties and perversions endured, seemingly forever, by Kurds.

3

Sprinkled by Stardust

SULAIMANIYA
July 1972

When I woke up the following morning, the sapphire sky was sunny, and fluffy white clouds were forming. Songbirds were singing. The house was filled with the sounds of children playing.

The carefree atmosphere in Sulaimaniya always felt like festival time. Grandmother's house overflowed with family. The adults slept on cotton mattresses laid out on the bedroom floors while children slept on the flat roof. The women of the household would rise early to cook a feast. All our favorite Kurdish dishes were prepared, such as *kuftay Sulaimaniya*, which was ground rice pastry stuffed with mincemeat, *doulma*, vegetables stuffed with rice, or my personal favorite, a special sweet called *bourma*, which was a very thin puff pastry with pecan nuts drenched in honey or syrup. Tea was available at all times, kept hot in enormous *samawars*, special copper Turkish urns.

Children were allowed to play all day and into the late evening. Sometimes we went on a picnic. Our preferred place was Serchenar, a place of waterfalls. While the adults chatted, the children played games. My personal favorite was a test of endurance to see who could stay in the cold water the longest; to my disappointment, I never won.

That first day of my holiday was no exception. There was more to do than one could possibly fit into the hours available. After breakfast, my sister and I received permission to accompany two of our female cousins to the central market.

Ra'ad was practically an adult so he had better things to do than hang around with children. I overheard Mother say he was going to visit with some Kurdish student activists who wrote and distributed pamphlets pressing for Kurdistan to be free from foreign Arab rule, for the Arabs forbade us speaking our language, learning our history, singing our songs, and quoting our poetry.

Several years before, my brother had joined the Kurdish Democratic Party, and his champion was Mulla Mustafa al-Barzani, the Kurdish hero and leader who fought the government in Baghdad at every opportunity.

Mother seemed pleased with Ra'ad's political activities so I didn't worry. I had no way of knowing that my brother had ventured into a risky arena that would very soon affect all our lives.

As we were leaving the house, Mother intercepted us at the front door to remind Muna to hold my hand during our excursion, just because five years earlier, when I was only five years old, my oldest sister, Alia, had returned home without me after taking me to the market.

When she was questioned, Alia said only, "The gypsies got Joanna."

Mother, Grandmother, and Auntie Aisha launched a frantic search, but I was nowhere to be found. They soon feared that, indeed, someone had kidnapped their little Joanna and that she might never be seen again. It was a family crisis. How happy they were when later in the day a friendly policeman brought me to Grandmother's door, explaining that I had been found wandering the main streets of Sulaimaniya, accosting grown-ups to buy me a lamb kebab and a cold soda.

I was always a precocious child.

Even though I was ten years old that summer, Mother demanded careful supervision anytime I left her side.

Muna clung to me as though I was a treasure. Finally, I peeled

her hand from mine, promising not to tell Mother we had dis-
obeyed and pledging not to leave her sight.

Soon, we came into sight of the marketplace. To me, it was the
most interesting place in the world. The combined scents of aro-
matic foods, exotic spices, sweet-smelling perfumes, and freshly cut
flowers were deliciously fragrant.

Everything one could possibly need was on sale in this square.
Fruits and vegetables were laid neatly on rickety tables or spread on
colorful fabric on the ground. Fresh yogurt was sold from huge
bronze pots. To keep the yogurt from spoiling, the pot top was
shielded with a white mesh cotton fabric called *melmel*, and the fabric was covered with wet loofah. After the yogurt was sold, the seller
would then sell these Kurdish loofahs, reportedly the finest loofahs
in the world.

We browsed a side section of the plaza devoted to beautiful jewelry that was handcrafted by local artisans. At one stand I spotted
three young women, who, judging by their striking physical simi-
larities, were clearly sisters. All three smiled brightly as they hovered
proudly over the colorful stones set into necklaces, bracelets, and
earrings. Those three women were so pretty that everyone walking
past paused to stare openly at them. One had styled her dark brown
hair into thick braids that fell to her waist, while the other two were
sporting matching red scarves threaded with golden ropes that were
decorated with shiny coins.

As I gawked, one of our cousins pulled Muna and me to the side
and whispered excitedly, "I must tell you a saga about those sisters.
A thrilling saga! Everyone in Kurdistan is whispering about them,"
she declared. "It's a sad story with a happy ending."

"Go on," I told her eagerly.

"Well, I will," she said with a touch of importance. "Those three
sisters are betrothed to three of Kurdistan's most revered Peshmergas. Their parents and siblings were burned alive during Qasim's
military assault in 1961 when orders were given to wipe out Kurdish villages. When the village was torched, the Peshmergas went to
that area to avenge the deaths. They arrived too late to retaliate
against the Arabs, but while there a handsome Peshmerga caught
sight of the eldest sister, who was only twelve years old at the time."
My cousin helpfully pointed her out, "That one with the braids. She
was carrying water from a spring. He was instantly smitten, struck

Joanna as a Child and Her Family

Joanna's parents in 1958 with their
two oldest children, Alia (standing)
and Ra'ad (seated on his father's lap).

Joanna in 1968
at age six.

Alia, Joanna's oldest sister.

Baby Joanna and
brother-in-law Hady
in 1962 in Baghdad.

Joanna in 1970
in the family's
Baghdad garden.

Ra'ad, Joanna's oldest brother, standing beside a photo of Great-Grandfather Mustafa, who was an Ottoman Army officer.

Muna, twin to Sa'ad, when she was a teenager.

Sa'ad in the early 1980s in the trenches fighting Iran.

by a great longing. He asked around and was told that this beautiful girl had two equally beautiful sisters. The area was in chaos, and
her parents were dead, and of course he couldn't approach such a
young girl about romantic love, so with some reluctance he left. But
it is said that he could not erase the image of her beautiful face from
his mind. After many restless months of long nights he convinced
two Peshmerga friends to return to the area with him.

"But by this time the sisters had moved away to live with
relatives."

I involuntarily turned to glance at the woman. Her perfectly
formed face was framed like a picture by those long braids of shiny,
chestnut-colored hair.

My cousin pinched my arm. "Listen, Joanna, there is more to
the story. Do you want to hear it or not?"

I nodded. "Yes! Yes! I am listening."

"All right. The brave Peshmerga was in love and he would not
be discouraged. So he and his friends searched until they found the
village where the sisters now lived. It didn't take much effort to
locate the house of the relatives because everyone in that village
knew about these three beauties. This Peshmerga was bolder than
most, so he approached the eldest male in the family and asked out-
right for the eldest girl's hand in marriage, offering to wait a few
years until she matured.

"The family called a conference. Although they respected those
brave fighters, they did not want the girl to live the difficult life of
a fighter's wife. She had suffered enough, they claimed. Also, the
girls were so beautiful and promised to grow more beautiful still,
the family was counting on substantial dowries. So they said no."

"Did she run away?" I asked, thinking that is exactly what I
would have done if a handsome Peshmerga wanted me for his bride
and my parents refused.

"No! The fighters are too honorable for that!" she snapped, irri-
tated at my ignorance concerning such matters. "Anyhow, when
the heartbroken Peshmerga was leaving the house, the girl he loved
was curious about this fighter who had followed her from one village to another, so she slipped from the garden and walked past him
as he was leaving the house, just to have a look for herself.

"He was too handsome to ignore. When their eyes met, she,
too, was infatuated.

"The rest is history. In the face of young love, the family relented when the braided one said she was going to jump into a well and drown herself if she could not marry her brave hero. The two have been betrothed since that day and the wedding is to be soon."

I turned and gazed at the beautiful sisters once more. "What about her two sisters?"

"The fiancé's Peshmerga friends accompanied him and they met the two younger sisters, and they, too, caught the love fever. As time passed, the other two became engaged, as well. They will all marry Peshmerga fighters," she said with such a satisfied air that one would think she had personally negotiated the marriage contracts.

"When are the weddings?" Muna asked in her girlish voice.

I stared at Muna with pride. Muna looked especially lovely that day with her luminous skin and big eyes, the color of deep caramel. In my eyes, she was as pretty as those three sisters. Truthfully, I was desperate to be as lovely as Muna, but I was not, and probably would never be.

My cousin replied, "Soon, I have heard. And once they marry, they will live with their husbands in the mountains. They are heroines, too. For the rest of their lives they will live for Kurdish freedoms."

I stared at the young women. They were living my dream. Ever since I was a small child, I carried the feeling that I would not live an ordinary life, that I would not be the usual bride, the girl who married the safe and respectful government clerk while draped in wedding white.

My only wish at that moment was to be grown up, to be so beautiful that, I, too, would catch the eye of a brave Peshmerga. After one glance at my face, my hero would fall in love instantly and implore that I marry him. If my parents refused, I would run away to live with my warrior in the mountains, where I would fight by his side.

My legs trembled, and I did not even follow my cousins and Muna, who had walked on until she noticed I was missing. She retraced her steps, her white face turning red, demanding, "Joanna! You promised!"

But I could think of nothing but the three beautiful sisters, waiting to be married to join their romantic, courageous husbands in the Kurdish mountains, and I worried to myself that I was not considered beautiful. Although I had been told I was so pretty a baby that I had to be protected from the evil eye, that was no longer the case. In fact, lately I had been teased for being skinny and gangly.

There were other problems. For convenience, Mother kept my hair cut close to my head. I had rather large ears that stuck out. And it was true that I was a bony girl with legs too long for my body. My skin was dark and turned darker with each passing summer.

In contrast, my mother and sisters were extremely fair. Even Grandmother Ameena, an old woman, had very beautiful white skin. Other women were always complimenting their white complexions. I was a dark-skinned person living in a country where lily-white skin was greatly prized.

In that instant, I resolved to grow out my short hair. I would also start protecting my skin from the darkening rays of the sun. I would carry an umbrella! Even so, I knew that it would be years before there was the slightest chance that I would catch the eye of a brave Peshmerga.

I leadenly followed my sister back to Grandmother's house.

That evening should have been fun for me, with the women and girls wearing their most colorful dresses and the men and boys in wide pantaloons, called *sharwual* in Kurdistan, with broad sashes wrapped around their waists.

As soon as the sun dipped to the bottom of the sky with its display of reds and pinks, everyone gathered in the courtyard. The garden was as colorful as the sunset, with borders of red poppies and white narcissi. Our mothers had prepared a feast, and we began the meal nibbling on figs, apples, pears, almonds, and walnuts. Steaming bowls of hot rice caught my eye and soon the family was being served several main courses, including *kubba* stuffed with meat, dolma made from stuffed vine leaves, barbecued chickens, and kebab.

Trying to fatten myself up, I ate more than I wanted. I was tired of being the skinny cousin. It did not improve my mood that my teenage female cousins appeared to have grown stunningly beautiful in only one short year. For the first time, I noticed that most of them had fair skin. With the wildest jealousy, I watched three of the prettiest girls swinging their heads as they spoke, purposely show-ing off their shimmering black hair that hung to their waists. Or so I thought.

It didn't help my mood that no one seemed to notice or even care that I was not my usual self. I was but a gawky ten-year-old, I realized, no longer tiny or cute, yet not old enough to be assessed for female beauty. The rejection stung.

There was a nervous knot in my throat and my eyes began to water, but I refused to let anyone see me cry. So when asked my problem, I pretended to have something in my eye.

After everyone had eaten, there was a call for music. Ra'ad found some tapes of Kurdish dancing music and soon the backyard came alive with the sound we all loved. Before long most of the teenagers and young adults were on their feet.

There is a saying: One who cannot dance is not a Kurd.

And that is so true.

Soon, a circle was formed, with everyone holding hands, men and women together. The music grew loud, and my brother Ra'ad was a leader because he was known for his talented dance moves. Despite encouragement from their cousins, Muna and Sa'ad refused to join in, for Muna was too shy and Sa'ad was too serious for such frivolity.

No one invited me to join the circle that was forming, but that was fine with me because I was newly ashamed of my short hair and long legs. I was content to sit next to Mother and merely observe.

The music was loud and the dancers held hands, swaying, pulling themselves close together, and pressing their shoulders against one another. The leading and trailing dancers began to wave colorful kerchiefs in impressive intricate gestures. Changing direc-tion, all the dancers managed to complete the complicated moves without breaking their original hand hold.

When the dancers were exhausted, the evening finally broke up and I quietly followed my cousins to the flat roof where we slept. Normally, my favorite treat was to join my cousins on the roof, but on that night I was too disheartened to take pleasure from anything.

The oldest boys and girls hauled up our bedding of lightweight cotton mattresses, pillows, and thin blankets. After everyone settled down, the older cousins talked quietly while we younger kids listened to the sounds of night, making a game of guessing whether it was frogs or crickets creating the interesting noises.

Slowly, the night grew peaceful and the youngest children fell asleep. I bedded myself down without words, pulling the flimsy blanket up to my chin and staring up to see a sliver of the moon that cast a faint light in the star-scattered sky. Already in low spirits, I felt even more depressed and insignificant under that infinite Kurdistan sky.

Just as I started hearing the heavy breathing of sound sleeping from some of the older cousins, there was a terrifying burst of noise that brought me to my feet. I knew from our experience with the roadside bandits that I was hearing gunfire. Before I could dash down the stairs to get off the roof, I was tackled and brought heavily to the floor. The breath was knocked out of me as I tumbled backward.

My brother Ra'ad was protecting my body with his own. He had me in such a tight grip that I could not wiggle.

He said loudly enough for everyone to hear, "Stay down." Then to me, "Shush, Joanna. Don't move. Don't make a sound."

Several of the younger cousins began to whimper and call for their mothers, but I heard an older cousin hiss a word of warning that it was too dangerous for anyone to stand upright.

Ra'ad instructed, "He is right. Do not stand up. You are in no danger if you stay down. It is our fighters who are being tracked and attacked. No one knows that we are even here."

I overheard a multitude of shouts coming from the thick of the tree line, as though orders were being given, but I could not clearly understand anything being said.

I stared into my brother's face as he whispered, "Joanna. Listen but do not be afraid. Something has happened. Some of our fighters have appeared in the city. Obviously, their presence has been discovered by the army. But they will never find the Peshmergas. No one who lives here will give them up. Besides, these city streets are unfamiliar to the Arabs."

Just then a lone bullet whizzed over our heads. I quivered with suppressed excitement. *This was war!*

Everyone hugged the floor with intense urgency.

There was further volleying of shots and shouts in the darkness, mixed together in what sounded like the wildest confusion.

We didn't move for the longest time, until the sounds of gun-fire grew faint as the soldiers moved away from our area. Then there was silence.

There were sighs of relief while my younger cousins leaped to their feet and fled down the steps and into the house to be with their mothers.

I remained on the roof even though Ra'ad suggested that I should go down. I did not respond, wanting him to forget I was there.

The incident aroused the ire of older male cousins, several of whom claimed they were going to join the Peshmergas as soon as they graduated. They believed they would be the generation to finally lead the Kurds to victory. "By God we will soon be tapping on Baghdad's gate," one of them boasted.

"Me, too," I whispered to myself, smiling faintly. "Me, too."

That day was a turning point in my life. As surely as I recognized my own name, I knew that I, Joanna al-Askari, would one day live the life of a Peshmerga. It had been decided.

Ra'ad, who had recently become active in Kurdish causes, con-gratulated the expectant Peshmergas, and the talk naturally veered to the injustices perpetrated against the Kurds.

As I looked intently at the starlit sky, I listened carefully to all that was said. I wanted to know everything about my country and the Kurdish people I so loved.

The first significant Kurdish revolt of the nineteenth century occurred in 1806 when armies from the Ottoman Empire gained control of our lands. This was followed by repeated waves of fight-ing against the Turks. Rebellions and wars were so frequent that they began to merge into one another.

In 1918, a mere ten years before my mother was born, the British occupied our land. When we resisted, they attacked us with their modern weapons. On the order of Winston Churchill, who labeled the Kurds "primitive tribes," the Royal Air Force dropped poison gas on the Kurds, the first time our people were massacred by chemical weapons.

In 1923, my Kurdish family supported Sheik Mahmud Barzinji when he led a rebellion against both the British and Faisal, the new Iraqi king. Barzinji defiantly declared himself king of Kurdistan, but in 1924 Sulaimaniya fell during battle to the British soldiers.

Kurdistan was occupied yet again.

Mother was born in 1928, and she once told me that she had no memory of a time when her world was *not* dominated by war. She had only the dimmest memory of the 1932 uprising, but well recalled the 1943 uprising, when Kurdish forces won control of large areas of land.

In 1946, there was a serious rebellion, after which the Kurdish leader Mullah Mustafa Barzani was exiled by the Iraqi government and fled to the Soviet Union. Kurdish calls for freedom grew weaker after his loss.

But in 1951 a new generation of Kurdish nationalists revived the movement, and Mulla Barzani was elected president, even though he was still in exile. In 1958, after the overthrow of the Iraqi royal family, there was yet another revival of calls for Kurdish rights, and our hero Barzani returned from exile, bringing renewed cries for freedom.

Kurdistan was attacked once again, but the Peshmergas were masters of guerrilla tactics. They won battle after battle, stunning the Iraqi government when they occupied and controlled the main road into Baghdad from Khanaqin, only 140 kilometers from the capital of Baghdad, something that had never happened before. Within a few years of these victories, however, we had to endure yet more hated defeat.

And on that night, in 1972, the tension was increasing once again.

I overheard a male cousin, who was close to Ra'ad's age, whisper, "You know the truth, don't you? The crime is to be born a Kurd."

Ra'ad made a small noise in his throat that seemed to signify agreement.

So, I had committed a crime merely by being born? I had no doubt that when I was finally old enough to hold a weapon there would be plenty of battles left for me to fight. Our battles were eternal, the only change being the face of our enemy.

Just then Ra'ad discovered that I was awake.

He leaned in toward me, and as I admired his handsome face with its high, broad forehead hooded over sensitive brown eyes, I was reminded that my older brother has always met the censure of being part Kurd behind a mask of serenity. He was imbued with bravery unknown by most, and even then was fighting the occupation in his own clever way.

Gently, Ra'ad reminded me, "You must sleep, little Joanna. Tomorrow we are going to the mountains, to picnic and swim under the waterfalls."

A happy image of plunging into the transparent waters of mountain waterfalls flashed through my mind.

He encouraged me again, "Joanna. Go to sleep."

"I'm not sleepy," I replied.

"Joanna," he told me, "look up at the starry sky."

"I am."

"Do you see the stars?"

"I do."

"Joanna, would you like to know a secret about the stars?"

I shivered in anticipation. I've always loved secrets. "What?"

"I will tell you a scientific secret that few people know. Joanna, anytime the stars shine this bright, there is a reason. And the reason is: the brightest stars are showering stardust. As you sleep, you'll be sprinkled with stardust." Smiling, he gently stroked my face. "Stardust, Joanna. Stardust. Just imagine it. Stardust all over your pretty little face."

I was still young enough to believe him. Besides, for me Kurdistan had always been a land of dreams. So I turned to my side and closed my eyes to sleep peacefully through the night, my dreams shimmering with sprinkles of stardust.

The following day we were awakened to news about the truth of the previous night's attack. The battle we had heard waged between the Iraqi army and the Peshmerga revolved around the three beautiful sisters we had seen selling jewelry at the market. A nest of Arab spies in the city had notified the Iraqi security about their romance with Peshmergas. At the end of the day, as the three sisters were riding in a donkey cart back to their village, there was an ambush and they were arrested by Iraqi soldiers. The beautiful brides-to-be were used as bait to draw in their three handsome Peshmerga fiancés.

The moment the fighters heard that their betrothed had been detained, they slipped into the city to rescue the women they loved, but the three sisters had already been taken to a prison in Baghdad. Entering the trap, two of the three warriors were killed during the fighting while the third escaped. The ultimate fate of the sisters was predictable. They would be tortured, then executed.

I grieved for the young lovers.

As for so many Kurds murdered over the years, their dreams of love and marriage would never come true. I felt tremendous hatred for the men who had destroyed their dreams of love; my anger hummed like slow, angry bees inside my head. I plodded steadily onward toward my fate.

Perhaps a sprinkling of stardust would light my way.

4

Baathist Terror

BAGHDAD
Thursday, July 4, 1974

The years always passed slowly in dreary Baghdad. Nothing good ever happened there. Even my growth was stunted. I had hoped that by my twelfth birthday I would see a physical miracle, that I would grow as beautiful as my Kurdish teenage cousins, but my body failed to blossom. I was still teased about my long legs, skinny body, and flat chest, a cruel reminder that I still looked like a child.

Against Mother's wishes, I grew my hair long. At least no one could deny its beauty. It was long, thick, and shiny black, hanging to my waist, although I often wore it braided into two thick ropes, just like the braids I saw worn by the tragic Kurdish fiancée I had so admired in Sulaimaniya.

An image of those sisters often flashed before my eyes. As had happened to so many Kurds, patriotism caused their deaths. Although my full heart was in the Kurdish cause, as theirs had been, I wanted to live, to feel the full pleasure of surviving the fight.

While my family still considered me a child, I no longer thought or acted as a child. My awareness of Kurdish troubles made me older than my years. I was more knowledgeable about the politics and geography of Kurdistan than many adults I knew.

During that particular summer, when I was twelve years old, our trip to Sulaimaniya had been delayed because Father was bedridden with a mysterious illness. He suffered weakness and a loss of appetite. His illness disturbed and confused all of us, because other than his inability to hear and speak, Father had always enjoyed exceptional health. But Mother assured us that if he continued to improve we would leave for Sulaimaniya only one week late.

I was desperate to return there, to Kurdistan, to paradise.

But we never made it to paradise during that summer. The trip was canceled altogether by a shattering event that changed all our lives forever.

That tragedy erupted on a day in hot July, when Baghdad was hushed and strained for more reasons than the heat. Our Baathist government was becoming more repressive. People no longer felt free to speak carelessly. There was hushed talk over unprovoked arrests with rumors of many innocent people disappearing. Tempers were not improved by the unbearable heat.

Although we lived under the shade of large palms, the swelling heat of the day crept like a haze silently and insistently through the rooms of our little home, infiltrating every corner until it became unbearable. I could not stay inside for very long or the sweat running down my body darkened my clothes.

Only my father's shaded bedroom had the benefit of cool air, and none of us begrudged him. For longer than most Iraqis could remember, dwellers of the hot Mesopotamia region had utilized an ingenious method of air conditioning, which consisted of twisting palm tree reeds into frames. Those frames were crisscrossed with additional reeds, and then a layer of desert thorns called *agool* was sandwiched between the reeds. The palm tree frame was secured over windows. Every six hours we children would pour water over the branches and reeds. With each passing breeze, the ancient apparatus cooled the interior room. Although few Iraqis at the time still used the antiquated method, Father clung to the old ways in this instance, enjoying the chilled air.

Everyone else sought the cool of the night, either on our roof, in the back garden, or on the covered porch. Sunset found Mother, Muna, Sa'ad, and me gathering on that covered porch, sorting our bedding and preparing for sleep.

Only recently had the number of people living in our little home diminished. Uncle Aziz was away visiting another sister. Ra'ad no longer lived at home since he started his freshman year at the university. He now resided with our older sister, Alia, and her husband, Hady, on the opposite side of the city, in the posh Mansur district. Alia's home offered Ra'ad two advantages: he was closer to the Baghdad University of Technology and he had more privacy. Alia had given him his own room, saying that Ra'ad needed a quiet area to study.

Ra'ad was studying to be an engineer, just like Father. Nothing was more important in the Arab and Kurdish worlds than for the eldest-born son to be educated, for one day he would be responsible for the well-being of the entire family.

Once our bedding was arranged, we slowly settled in for the night, although we did not immediately fall asleep. Despite the severity of summer days in Baghdad, nights held a certain thrill and charm. That night was no exception.

After the reddish-pink disk of the setting sun dropped from sight, the nighttime slowly broadened with a full moon shining through the grove of palm trees. Their branches were waving from the gentle breeze like long arms. The gleaming, golden eyes of a large owl who had made his home in one of the palms seemed to be watching us. Seeing that owl, I suddenly ached for Ra'ad's companionship, for many times he had pointed out that very owl, talking me out of my old-fashioned fear that owls bring bad luck.

The sounds of voices wafted through the silence of the trees: I recognized our neighborhood's night guards, called *charkhachi* from times long past. The guards dressed distinctively in their ankle-length army coats with brass buttons. They wore colorful turbans on their heads and were armed with obsolete rifles, courtesy of the British. Their ancient rifles might have ceased functioning, yet those men provided a sense of safety from thieves.

The sights and sounds of the Baghdad night slowly disappeared into a black nothingness as my thoughts floated to Sulaimaniya. My cousins were most likely on the roof of Grandmother Ameena's house, their eyes drawn to that same magnificent moon.

I would soon be there with them. Basking in that pleasant thought, I rolled up in my bedding and soon was soundly sleeping.

A few hours later, my lovely dreams of Sulaimaniya were breached by an alarming noise. Someone was attempting to break down our front door!

Sa'ad's eyes widened, and he jumped to his feet. My brother was only fifteen years old, yet he was larger and stronger than his age suggested. In the face of possible danger, he ordered us, "Stay!"

Since Ra'ad moved away, Sa'ad considered himself the protector of the women of the household, to my dismay, for I was a rebel child and not mentally equipped to take orders.

Muna meekly obeyed and remained where she was, covering her face and head with the bedclothes. But Mother, like me, was a bit willful, so as Sa'ad rushed from the back porch, we both jumped up to trail behind him through the kitchen and hallway that opened into the large living room. There we paused, standing shoulder to shoulder, listening.

Was a thief loose in the neighborhood? Had the guards come to warn us?

My father had not made an appearance, but that was not a surprise. Even if he hadn't been weakened from illness, his deafness would make him oblivious to the commotion.

When Sa'ad yelled, "Who is there?" the response was a series of strong kicks at the door. Perhaps burglars *had* targeted our home!

I gasped in bewilderment as the heavy wooden door began to crack in various places, before bulging out in the center and then splitting. A powerful force was coming for us from the outside.

Two large pieces of the door fell haphazardly on the living room floor, leaving jagged edges hanging from the frame. Whoever was kicking created an opening sizable enough for a large adult to enter. Three men dressed in Iraqi security uniforms jostled one another as they pushed through the jagged gap, trampling over the splintered sections of what remained of our front door. They were in such a rush to get to us that one man lost his footing and tumbled to the floor. In their haste, the other two men stepped on him.

The largest of the three had a red face cratered with pockmarks. He confronted my brother, screeching, "You! Spy! Where is your radio?"

Sa'ad was never afraid of anyone, not even that monster. With a sarcastic expression, he retorted, "Spies? Spies? There are no spies here!"

"We have proof this is a house of spies."

That man's tongue darted out between his lips two or three times like a serpent. I shivered with repulsion.

He shrieked, "For the Israelis!"

The *Israelis?* I could not believe what I was hearing. If not so panicked, I would have laughed at the man's preposterous claim. As far as we knew, no one in our family had ever *seen* an Israeli. In fact, few Arabs or Kurds in Iraq during those days gave much thought to the Israelis. We struggled with too many uncertainties with our own insane government to become invested in the faraway conflict between the Palestinians and the Israelis.

The man continued with his mad rant. "This is a home that supports Mullah Mustafa al-Barzani!"

While his Israeli allegation was blatantly ridiculous, this latest charge caused me a nudge of anxiety. Mulla Mustafa al-Barzani was the most famous Kurdish leader and fighter. Undeniably, he was considered a hero in our Kurdish home.

I suddenly remembered the poster hanging in Ra'ad's room. The hero's image was hanging there for these men to find. Although since 1970 we had been given the legal right to support our Kurdish heroes, such as Mulla al-Barzani, I had lived long enough to understand that mere laws were no protection for Kurds. Something told me that poster would doom us all.

The men were preoccupied with Sa'ad, so I slipped away and walked rapidly to Ra'ad's old bedroom. The poster of Mullah Mustafa al-Barzani covered the wall over Ra'ad's bed. That poster had been a part of Ra'ad's life since March 1970, when the Iraqi government finally concluded that it must negotiate with the Kurds, who were militarily defeating the Iraqis on the northern front. An agreement was reached that granted Kurdish autonomy. The accord promised to recognize Kurdish as an official language. The amendment to the constitution stated that the Iraqi people are made up of two nationalities, the Arab and the Kurd.

From that time, we were given the right to support Kurdish parties. But in reality, the Iraqi government broke the agreement from the first moment it was signed. Kurds who took their newly granted civil liberties seriously were targeted for imprisonment and worse. In their naïveté, many Kurds had since been murdered for showing their support for Kurdish leaders.

Perhaps they would murder Ra'ad.

I well remembered the day Ra'ad brought home the poster and hung it. My brother was the proudest boy in Baghdad as he measured for the perfect spot for his hero Barzani. On the bottom of the poster Ra'ad had joyfully inscribed: "The Lion of the Mountains, and the Father of the Kurds."

Regretfully, I climbed on the bed and began pulling at the edges. Breathless with nerves, I ripped Mullah Mustafa al-Barzani's likeness into small pieces, pulling up my nightgown to poke the fragments into the waist of my panties. I was not a minute too soon because I heard the men stomping through our house. I overheard the leader order one of his men to guard the front door and the stairway to the roof so that anyone trying to flee the house would be apprehended.

I froze in place when a gravelly voice loudly announced, "We are looking for the spy Ra'ad al-Askari. Where is he?"

I anxiously looked around the room for any other incriminating materials, but I saw nothing. I wanted to check Ra'ad's desk to see if any flyers or brochures promoting the Kurdish cause might be in those desk drawers, but there was no time to investigate.

The men were coming down the hallway in my direction.

I was horrified to feel tiny pieces of the poster sliding down my legs. I looked down. Gravity was doing its work. If I could not find a solution, my deed was bound to be discovered. My young age would not save me. I was struck by a dreadful thought: perhaps I would end up like Uncle Aziz, imprisoned and tortured until I lost my mind!

With no time remaining, I snatched up the poster pieces on the floor, then jumped on the bed and wriggled under the sheets, pulling the bedcover up to my chin. I simulated sleep.

Two of the men were on me before I could inhale, and I opened my eyes, affecting surprise at their presence.

I caught a brief glimpse of Mother and Sa'ad on the heels of the security men, and no one was more astonished than Mother and my brother to discover me sleeping in Ra'ad's bedroom. I watched their faces as they both glanced at the wall over my head. I was rewarded by their reactions. A triumphant gleam flashed in Sa'ad's eyes, and visible relief washed over Mother's face.

As the men tore apart the room, Mother lightly slapped her own

face, something Kurdish women of her age do when they are distressed. But she did not shriek or cry. Mother did not understand
Arabic very well, yet she knew enough to realize what those men
were after.

Their only goal was to collect evidence to indict her oldest son.
If they found anything incriminating, all would be lost.

To give myself courage, I silently recited a few of my favorite
verses of the Kurdish anthem:

> The Kurdish youth have risen like lions,
> To adorn the crown of life with blood
> Let no one say Kurds are dead
> Kurds are living
> Kurds are living; their flag will never fall.

Perhaps because I was small for my age and childlike in appearance, the men ignored me. Whatever the reason, the men paid me
no heed as they stomped around the room, dramatically holding
books up in the air and thumbing the pages before tossing them to
the floor. They crouched on knees to peer under the bed and
pounded the curtains with their hands, as though they believed a
grown man might be hidden behind the nearly transparent fabric.
One man tapped on the walls. Not to be outdone by his partner,
the other man climbed on the desk chair and began to knock on the
ceiling.

It was unsettling, even at my young age, to know that such dim-
witted men held our fate in their hands. Their tactics would have
been comical if not for that daunting fact.

I watched my brother carefully. His dark eyes flickered between
anger and despair. His lips were puckered with the effort of keeping quiet.

How I hoped Sa'ad could suppress his famous temper; otherwise
he would use his fists to stop these men. Everyone in our family
would be arrested if that happened.

Mercifully, Sa'ad maintained perfect control, the traumatic day
proving a new quality in my brother's temperament: restraint.

Soon, I hoped, they would leave. Then we could warn Ra'ad.

After searching every inch of Ra'ad's bedroom, the men moved
on to the rest of the house. When I heard them in the kitchen

throwing heavy pots and pans, I took a moment to gather all the pieces of the poster from under my clothes and from the bed and placed them under some papers the men had already examined and thrown to the floor. Satisfied that my secret was safe, I scampered from the room to join Mother and Muna, who had finally come in from the porch.

We formed a semicircle at the door and watched as the soldiers wrecked Mother's orderly kitchen. Mother kept slapping her face while Muna took sharp gasps with every dish that was hurled and every glass that was broken.

The men theatrically emptied bags of salt, flour, and sugar across the table and cabinets and floor. Those stupid men even broke the four eggs sitting on the cabinet top.

Such actions puzzled me. Would any spy hide evidence *inside* unbroken egg shells? And, if so, *how?*

It was the wildest confusion, their actions coupled with curses and threats as to what they were going to do to the Israeli spy Ra'ad al-Askari.

There was a dreadful moment when Mother's treasured tray of tea glasses was dashed against the wall, the thin shower of broken glass tinkling like delicate bells dropping to the floor.

Muna's face paled. She swayed as if she was about to faint. She couldn't take the drama. I was afraid my sister was losing her mind.

The leader of the gangster troop followed, brusquely ordering us to sit in a corner of the room. We did as told, clinging to one another as the men worked their way through the house and up the stairs to the roof and back down to the back porch and into the garden. Mother and Sa'ad trailed their steps, Mother sad and Sa'ad sullen, watching the destruction of our home.

It was strange to me that the men did not challenge my father. I supposed their offices had a full security file on our family and knew there were two reasons my father could not be a danger to the regime: he was not a Kurd and he had never participated in any Kurdish political activities. His deafness further ensured that he could not be a threat to the government. Or perhaps it was the simple matter of the sleeping pills Mother gave him at bedtime. He was probably in such a deep slumber that they couldn't easily rouse him.

Whatever the reason, I concluded that being deaf had its advantages on that night. While we were all frightened out of our wits, my father was enjoying a splendid sleep, unaffected by the most traumatic event of our lives.

A few hours later the men finally departed. As they made their way back through the broken door, they hurled curses and threats at us, but their hands were empty. They had found nothing in our home on which to hang their ridiculous accusations.

I joined Mother and Sa'ad to watch from the front porch as the three thugs stomped down the pathway to jump into their car and drive away, their tires spinning as if they had been called to a fire at the president's palace.

For me, that night was the first time terror had a face.

I listened quietly as Mother and Sa'ad discussed the best action to take.

Sa'ad told mother, "I will go to Alia. Ra'ad must leave Baghdad. Go to the north. He can wait there while we find out the source of this trouble."

Sa'ad's words excited me. Perhaps Ra'ad would become a *real* Peshmerga. Rather than distributing flyers and putting a gentle face on our struggle, he would become a warrior. I made up my mind in an instant: if he did, I would join him in those mountains. I would be the youngest Peshmerga in all of Kurdistan.

I squirmed with pleasure when Sa'ad turned to me and said, "You were very crafty, Joanna. That Barzani poster would have fed their anger *and* given them evidence against Ra'ad."

Sa'ad then hurried to change into street clothes. When he rushed back past us to leave the house, he took a few dinars for the taxi fare from Mother's open hand.

My entire body trembled with anticipation as I contemplated the new danger stalking my family. The night's event had been a personal test for me. If I was going to be a fighter, then I must be cool and calm in times of crisis.

Mother drew me into her arms, tucking her fingers under my chin, pulling my face up to face hers, and praising me. "Joanna. You were a very clever girl."

Yes, I passed my first test. Peshmergas must react quickly even when under pressure of investigation.

My mother and sister sat quietly while I fidgeted, looking around our destroyed home.

Mother grimaced. "We must clean this up. Your father must *not* know about this night. There will be big problems if he discovers Ra'ad is in danger. We must keep this night a secret from your father. And Aziz."

Mother was right. If told of the night's threats, my father would rush to the local Iraqi security office to settle the score. He had never been afraid. Never. A physical fight would ensue, and he would end up in prison. And even though I was young, I knew that times in Iraq were more dangerous than ever. The current government was not a joke. My father might not survive prison if the Baathists got him.

And what about Uncle Aziz? He had to be shielded as well. Otherwise, he could easily relapse to a dark and unreachable place.

"Joanna. Your father is feeling stronger. He might be the one to make the morning tea tomorrow."

Since I could remember, up until his recent illness, my father always arose with the sun to make a pot of morning tea. He must have tea with his bread and jam in the mornings, a civilized habit brought from France.

Mother's voice trailed off to a weak sigh. "We must straighten this mess."

I jumped to the task.

Mother took Muna with her to the kitchen.

As I was placing items back in their rightful positions in the sitting room, I heard thundering feet racing up the path and onto the porch. I turned to flee, believing that those men had returned.

To my relief, it was only Sa'ad, but his face was puffy and his eyes were dark with fury. He pushed past me looking for Mother.

I threw down a sofa pillow and followed him into the kitchen where Mother was scooping sugar off the floor.

"We are too late."

"Too late?"

"They have taken Ra'ad. And Hady."

"Taken?"

"Yes! We should have known. The searches were coordinated. At the same time those security officials were here, five men from the same unit appeared at Alia's house. They wrecked her home, searching for evidence to use against Ra'ad. They claimed to have found incriminating documents and when they left they forced Ra'ad *and* Hady to go with them."

Muna cried out.

Mother faltered for the first time. She sagged, her knees buckling, but she broke her collapse to the floor when she gripped the back of a chair. "They have my son?"

I was frozen to the spot. Ra'ad? In prison? Uncle Aziz had been in prison. Unpleasant thoughts flickered. Would Ra'ad return to us mentally impaired, too?

And Hady. What would happen to Hady?

Hady, a relative even before marrying Alia, was a gentle man. My brother-in-law was so in love with Alia that he was teased by other men for pampering his wife, which was uncommon behavior in our culture. He and Alia were the parents of two small boys: four-year-old Shaswar and two-year-old Shwan. Those boys would be miserable without their father.

Mother quickly regained her composure. "Go, Sa'ad. Go to Fatima. Tell her what has happened. Then go to Othman. He can help us."

Father's sister, Fatima, the woman who had given me my black doll, was an influential woman in Iraq and was married to a prominent man. Uncle Othman was Father's younger brother. He, too, had important connections.

Mother lightly tapped Sa'ad on his arm. "Before he went to sleep, your father said he was going back to work tomorrow. While he is there, we will visit the security officers in this area." Her voice was fiercely protective. "We must keep this secret from your father."

Sa'ad understood without further explanation.

After Sa'ad left a second time, Mother and I cleaned the house more rapidly than I would have believed possible. Muna followed us, wanting to be of help, but she was so upset she was useless.

The sun was rising when Muna and I returned to bed. It seemed a lifetime had passed in only a few hours. We had been frightened out of our wits. Our home had been wrecked. And Ra'ad and Hady had been arrested.

Yet, Sa'ad was already working to get them freed. Mother and I had restored our home to its normal impeccable condition. No evidence remained of our terrifying evening, other than the smashed front door. I had no idea what Mother would tell Father about that door.

Not surprisingly, Mother could not sleep. When I closed my

eyes, she was spreading her prayer rug, facing Mecca, lowering herself to her hands and knees, and praying.

When I awoke a few hours later, Muna was still sleeping beside me. Our home was gloomy and quiet. I was thankful to discover that Father had returned to work for the first time in ten days.

I found a scribbled note from Sa'ad under a heavy pot on the kitchen table. My brother instructed us to take care of ourselves for the day, although he had written a bold line of caution that we were not to leave the house.

Muna and I barely exchanged a word. I searched for food and found some dry bread and a small chunk of cheese to nibble on, but it was difficult to swallow.

Unaccustomed to being alone in the house, Muna and I wandered aimlessly. We saw that the destroyed sections of the front door had been removed, but the splintered gap remained. I was glad I slept through my father's reaction when he saw the condition of that door.

I paced, trying to escape our troubles, but the image of Ra'ad's face followed me. I felt hollow and frightened about his fate. My older siblings had always pampered and protected me, and none more than Ra'ad. There were good reasons for this.

It's difficult to believe, but Mother tried to kill me when she discovered she was pregnant with her fifth child. She had been overwhelmed with troubles and felt incapable of enduring another pregnancy. Shortly after Mother gave birth to the twins in 1953, Father's furniture factory had been destroyed during the revolution. My parents were suddenly very poor. Mother did not know how they could afford yet another child. She was so distraught at my coming that she embarked on desperate measures to stop me. She threw herself down stairs and jumped off the dining room table. When she failed to accomplish her goal, she even swallowed poison pills that the doctor claimed came within a few heartbeats of killing us both.

Mother gamely admitted those acts.

When the doctor informed my father and older siblings about Mother's objective, they were horrified and shocked. So they kept guard over Mother to ensure my safe arrival. When I was born healthy, everyone was so relieved that they indulged me.

Ra'ad had been the most commanding presence in my life. Since I was a toddler, I was a small shadow to him, even following him out of the house and over to the Tigris. I would often sit on the sloping banks to admire his swimming; he was so sleek in the water that onlookers affectionately called him the "crocodile of the Tigris."

Ra'ad, the brother I so loved and admired, had been taken from me. Images of the torture my brother might be enduring followed me miserably. Tears filled my eyes and then made crooked tracks down my face, which was dirty from the previous night's housecleaning.

Had I known that Ra'ad and Hady were at that very moment confined in an earthen pit, trapped in a death struggle with the hot Baghdad sun tearing at their brains, I could not have endured the agony. But we knew nothing. So we were left with only our imaginations.

Slowly a month passed, then another. And still their fates remained unknown to us.

Summer faded.

The heat lifted.

Mother's prayers filled the cooling air.

And more agonized waiting filled our home.

5

Ra'ad and Hady Return

BAGHDAD
October 1974

Mother always said that true joy is an answered prayer. So I was not surprised that Mother was the first to see Ra'ad and Hady stumble out of a taxicab parked a short distance from Alia's house, because she had been praying continually since they were taken. Mother produced shrill, piercing cries of joy that could only mean one thing. At the sound, Alia and her two boys, Sa'ad, and Muna came running from inside the house.

But Mother's joyful cries paused, then ceased altogether.

My brother didn't bear the slightest resemblance to his former self. He was so white that he looked like a ghost. He was so bent over that he appeared to be crawling. The last time I saw Ra'ad he bore himself tall and strong, but his lean, muscular body had greatly diminished, and his clothes were so tattered that I could not identify what he was wearing. Was he swathed in a ragged sheet? Or were those shredded rags the last of the pajamas he was wearing when he was arrested? It was impossible to tell.

Sa'ad finally reached him, and Ra'ad clung to his younger brother's arm, moving tentatively, like many of the cripples or old men I had seen shuffling through the streets of Baghdad. But those pitiful men would have appeared healthy and prosperous matched against my brother.

My eyes followed a slow movement behind him and there was Hady, who looked much the same as Ra'ad. His face was ashen and listless, absent of his usual broad smile.

Despite their pitiful condition, my sister Alia was overcome with happiness. She broke loose from Mother's arms and rushed to her husband. I wanted to shout a warning that Hady was too frail to touch, but I could only choke out a croaking sound.

Tears formed in my eyes when Mother ran to her eldest son and reached out to hold his face between her hands. She pulled him close. She had not seen him in nearly three months, and during much of that time she feared that he was dead and buried.

Those long months had been an excruciating wait as Mother, Alia, Sa'ad, and other relatives struggled to discover Ra'ad and Hady's whereabouts. They were finally found in the prison system. Negotiations had commenced and earlier that day many thousands of Iraqi dinars that our relatives had pooled were paid to gain their freedom. Although there was no guarantee given that they would be released immediately, we felt compelled to wait with Alia just in case.

And that is where they returned, finally. Alive, but barely.

When Ra'ad finally stepped onto the porch, he was panting like a man who had competed in a long race. Everything about my once impeccable brother was in a tangle. His hair was long and disheveled and his beard sprouted shabbily. His lower lip was so cracked that it was bleeding and hanging open, exposing his teeth, which once sparkled white but were now coated with the filth of three months' imprisonment.

I could not bear to look at him, but I did glance at Hady, whose bloodshot eyes were focused on Alia. His once slim face was now hollow and gaunt.

Both men drank a small glass of water offered to them by Muna, who was so shaken by their condition that her hands visibly trembled. Mother and Alia led the two young men into the house, where they could have some privacy to take a bath, eat, and have a short rest.

Muna and I stared at each other, unable to speak. Muna finally went inside, but I sat alone on the porch for nearly an hour, nursing my grief and anger.

Later in the afternoon our moods lifted slightly and everyone gathered in Alia's living room. A celebratory atmosphere was overtaking the house, as a number of relatives had been told the good news that Ra'ad and Hady were back and had popped in to see the freed prisoners for themselves. Most important for me, Auntie Aisha had arrived. When Ra'ad was first taken, she traveled from Sulaimaniya to support Mother and had endured every waiting moment with us. I loved that auntie most of all and cuddled contentedly next to her.

Mother sent a cousin to our home to tell Father that Alia was not feeling well and that we could not return until later in the evening.

Amazingly, and despite all the activity involved with finding Ra'ad and Hady and gaining their freedom, Mother had succeeded in her goal of keeping news of their arrest and imprisonment from Father. Our daily life had been a confusing trail of lies, with Father believing that poor Alia was often ill, which explained our frequent visits to her home, and that Ra'ad had been lucky enough to gain permission to travel to Europe, which explained his long absence. But living such a lie was stressful, because we constantly worried that someone would accidentally slip, and I was looking forward to the day when Ra'ad regained his health so we could behave normally with Father once more.

After everyone had settled on and around the sofas, the once humorous Hady was strangely silent while Ra'ad began to speak. "I will share the details."

I squeezed Auntie Aisha's hand. She lightly patted my head.

It was distressing to hear Ra'ad talk in that strained, rustling voice, no longer rising and dropping in timbre as I remembered.

"The night we were arrested, everyone had gone to bed. Alia, Hady, and the boys were sleeping outside in the garden, but I was on the roof, not yet asleep. I was listening to Monte Carlo radio while watching the full moon through the swaying palm trees. Suddenly, I felt there was someone with me on that roof. I thought perhaps Hady had remembered something he must tell me, but to my shock, when I looked up, I saw five men I did not know, all wearing civilian clothes and holding assault rifles. I had no idea how or when they entered the house because I had not heard any unusual noise.

"There was no time to speak. Three of the five men jumped on me and started hitting me while pulling me to my feet. One man grabbed my radio and smashed it. They were screaming curses and ordering me to point out my bedroom. They practically threw me down the stairs. They already had Hady. Poor Alia with her two babies were terrified witnesses.

"As I was being hustled into my bedroom, I overheard Hady asking them who had done anything wrong in the house. That's when I heard the first of many baseless charges: The leader of those men said that I had been seen spying for the Israelis! And for the Kurds!

"I replied that if he was talking about my membership in the Kurdish Student Union, it was legalized by the March 1970 Agreement.

"Nothing I said registered with those crazed men. I had recently heard that other students had been targeted for being Kurds, so I assumed they were rounding up all the members of the Kurdish Student Union.

"Then I remembered that a few days before I had been approached for membership by the Baathist Student Organization. Of course, I had refused to join. Perhaps my refusal had triggered the investigation.

"Those men started trashing my bedroom while I stood help-lessly watching, still in my pajamas. They refused permission for me to change clothes or put on my robe, although I managed to slip my feet into my slippers."

I nodded along with Ra'ad's telling. We had endured the same indignities.

While Ra'ad drank a cup of hot tea, Hady spoke tentatively. "There was nothing illegal in the house. They found a pamphlet Ra'ad had been writing, telling the history of Kurds and praising the government for allowing Kurds to start speaking the Kurdish language and studying Kurdish history. Yet, when they began to wave around that paper, I knew we were finished.

"Out came the blindfolds. First Ra'ad. Then me. Alia cried, pleading that they not take us." Hady shook his head. "Those men appeared as deaf as her father, Muhammad.

"We ended at the security intelligence headquarters in the Mansur area. I've seen that place many times. It's located in a huge old house there."

Hady was struck by a coughing spell so severe that he had to leave the room, so Ra'ad resumed the story.

"I was pushed into a chair and the blindfold was removed. I was facing an aggressive interrogator. He was cruel and stupid. He claimed I had been reported transmitting from a wireless radio. I was racking my brain, trying to think where they could have gotten such a false impression. Then I remembered that one day Hady had loaned me his automobile to drive to visit Aunt Fatima. When I came out, I noticed that his automobile aerial was loose so I removed it from the car to repair it. When I was standing there with the aerial in my hands, a neighbor kept walking past, staring first at the aerial and then at me. Looking back, I know now that he must have been a Baathist who drew false conclusions.

"The interrogator said that while I was holding that aerial that I was overheard speaking Hebrew to the Israelis! Then he claimed I moved the aerial to a different spot in the yard and spoke Kurdish to the Barzani Party headquarters."

Several family members laughed loudly at the idea of a spy so clever that he spied for two such dissimilar groups, yet so stupid that he boldly spoke in foreign languages in plain view of witnesses.

Ra'ad smiled thinly. "The accusations were so absurd that I asked the man why they didn't arrest me on the spot, which is what I would have done if I were a security official and witnessed such a busy spy. Indeed, I told him that if I was a spy, I was a most inefficient one! I asked him to tell me exactly the day and time all of this occurred.

"The man named a certain date. It was not even the same day I had visited Auntie Fatima. Then I remembered exactly where I was on the day he was claiming I had been spying. I had been swimming in the river and afterward played a game of football with a group of friends. There were twenty-two swimmers and football players who could attest to what I was saying. I insisted that he check out his facts.

"When he called out for an assistant to take down the names, I instantly regretted my words. When I was recruited to join the Kurdish Student Union, I was told that should I ever be detained I should *never* reveal names of anyone I know. One of the more experienced student members gave wise advice: part with your head, but not with your secret. I decided it was best for me to shut up.

"When I grew silent, the interrogator furiously rang a bell. Two strange men entered the room and clumsily testified that they had seen me on the very day I was claiming to be swimming and playing a football game. They claimed I was lying, that I was seen transmitting with an aerial and speaking first in Hebrew and then in Kurdish.

"I said I had never even heard Hebrew being spoken and would not recognize it if someone starting speaking it at that very moment.

"Just then they pulled poor Hady into the room and questioned him as to his relationship with me. He confirmed that he was my brother-in-law. They accused him of being a Kurdish sympathizer. Hady admitted he was a Kurd, but said that he was a peace-loving husband and father, working as an engineer.

"Those men knew that Hady's brother was a Peshmerga, though, and that Hady had recently gone up north to drive his brother's car back to Baghdad for safekeeping.

"Just then we were blindfolded again and taken out of that building and put into another car. I could think of little besides Uncle Aziz and how he had been tortured and in particular how he was hung upside down from the ceiling and beaten for a full week. I expected something of the same. I was dreading such a beating.

"Soon the car stopped and our blindfolds were removed. We were pushed into a dark area surrounded by a high wall. I presumed we were in a prison yard. Hady and I were ordered to stand side by side, so I assumed they were preparing to shoot and bury us.

"The full moon cast light on the scene. By that dim light I could see that we were standing next to a large metal cover. Then one of the guards walked our way, struggling with a ladder. When the metal cover was lifted off the ground, I looked down into a deep, dark pit.

"One of the guards lowered the ladder into that pit. Hady and I were ordered to go down. I thought they were going to throw us in a pit of snakes."

Hady had returned to the room by this time, and he spoke in a wearied voice, "Snakes I would have preferred. It was like going into the grave."

"Exactly."

Mother looked shattered. She walked over to Ra'ad and rubbed his neck and shoulders. "Perhaps you can tell us the rest later, son."

Ra'ad looked up. "I must tell this while my memory is fresh. Perhaps one day the world will be interested in knowing what innocent Iraqis and Kurds have endured under this insane government.

"There we were, alive in the grave, standing in a dark pit. Then, true terror. The metal lid was closed on us. That was the blackest black you can imagine."

Hady interjected, "But that was not the worst of it. I am already terrified and what do I hear? Ragged breathing. I shouted, 'Who is there?' It was so black that I could see nothing. But I could hear. And I could smell. Ah! What a stench! Something or someone was coming at us. I believed that we had been put in a pit with wild animals! I put up my fists, ready to fight, man or beasts.

"Then some poor man spoke, telling us, 'Do not be afraid. I am a prisoner, too. I have been alone in this hole for many weeks. I'm from Al-Najaf.'"

We knew about Najaf, a large city south of Baghdad. It was the seat of Shiite political power and considered a holy city by the Shiites. It was where the tomb of Imam Ali was located, the Prophet Muhammad's son-in-law. The Shiites had bravely struggled against the Sunni powers in Baghdad, but the current Baath government was the most repressive government of all. Obviously, my brother's pit companion was of the Shiite sect.

Hady continued, "I was so relieved that the owner of that stench was human that his smell no longer bothered me. In fact, I felt like embracing that man."

Ra'ad laughed hollowly. "He quickly related his story. His brother was a politically active Shiite, belonging to the Al-Dawa Party, which as we all know has recently become even more active against the Baathists. When the brother heard he was going to be arrested, he fled to France. Our poor companion in the pit, who had never been political in his life, was arrested and held hostage in his brother's place. He had been told that if his brother didn't return to accept his death sentence he would die in prison in his stead.

"We talked all night, partly to take our minds off the misery of being in that hole, but that man's spirits were so low that he didn't make us feel any better. He kept repeating that it was written that the three of us would die in that pit.

"He predicted that I would be the first to die. He said students were not accustomed to hardships and that students always perished rather quickly. He reasoned that he would be the second to die, because he had become so weakened by his ordeal. Hady, he decided, would survive for several weeks before he died.

"We thought we knew true torment, but that came with the morning sun. We were fried under that sizzling metal top. The heat intensified the toilet stench. Our pit was a toilet. It had never been cleaned out. The smell was indescribable.

"I realized then that, indeed, the prisoner from Al-Najaf was absolutely correct. We *were* going to perish. I didn't think I could last a day.

"I was the lowest on that first day, because I still had enough intellect to think. I believed that my life was basically over, one way or another. I knew that once arrested in Iraq, my future was doomed. I would forever be in the shadow of the intelligence officials, never again uninhibited to move freely.

"Later in the morning they opened the metal lid to lower a plastic pitcher of warm water. The pitcher was tied by a rope. Most of the water spilled out on the way down. We were given a single loaf of bread to share, but I couldn't eat anything, at least not on that first day. Hady tried to eat, but couldn't, so our fellow prisoner happily ate our share and his.

Hady interrupted, "That man no longer had any teeth. His interrogators had pulled out his teeth as part of his torture."

Ra'ad added, "They had extracted his fingernails and toenails as well. I expected the same."

Ra'ad scratched his head. "Lice," he confirmed in an apologetic tone.

I gasped and looked at Auntie Aisha. Lice? On Ra'ad?

"One day turned into the next and we lost track of time. The heat and the stench never ended. And the waiting. *Nothing* was more upsetting than the waiting."

Ra'ad glanced affectionately at Hady. "Truthfully, I was most concerned for Hady. Every day I thought: This will be his last day."

Hady laughed sadly. "And I thought the same of you."

Ra'ad grimaced and said, "But I was the first to collapse. One day I just lost it. We faced constant hunger, so I grew weaker by the day. One minute I was sitting there plotting how we might get word to everyone where we were being held, and the next minute I passed out."

Hady told us, "Ra'ad crumpled. He looked dead. I shouted for the guards, and our pit mate took one look at him, felt his neck, and pronounced him dead. That was the worst moment in the pit. I couldn't get the attention of the guards, so I took a few pebbles I had gathered from the ground and started flinging them against the metal lid.

"The guards soon appeared and I yelled at them that Ra'ad al-Askari had died. They pulled him up and out. They threw water on him. Soon I heard them exclaim that he was still breathing. With that, they put the lid on us again. I didn't know what would happen to Ra'ad after that."

Ra'ad continued, "As it happened, it was the fourteenth of July celebrations for the revolution that had brought the Baathists to power. The guards were drinking beer and arrack and dancing together. They dragged me into the middle of the festivities and chained me to a palm tree. I sat and watched a bunch of fools drinking alcohol and dancing."

Sa'ad grunted in disgust. He was the most religious of my siblings, never missing a prayer and keeping guard on his sisters' morals. The idea of government officials drinking alcohol and dancing while keeping innocent men in holes in the ground rankled him mightily.

"My head was hanging to my chest, but I saw feet coming in my direction. It was a drunken officer undoing his trousers, walking straight at me. He was going to pee on me. I found the strength to shout, startling him. He saw me chained and said, 'By God! I know you. You are Ra'ad al-Askari.'

"He had seen me at the Al-Aadamiya sports club where I played basketball. I told him that I needed help, that I had been wrongly accused. He replied that his rank was low and that he couldn't even help his own relatives, some of whom were in prison. I made a request that he at least call my family. He tapped his head, asking, 'Do I look insane to you? If I call your relatives, I'll end up chained beside you.'

"He disappeared, and I was left chained to the tree. When the sun came up, it was the first time I had seen that grove during the daytime. And what did I see? Hundreds of metal covers plastered the ground. Each of those covers represented the most acute human misery.

"Moans of anguish hummed from the covers, coming together as one long groan, the agonized cries corroding all confidence that a single prisoner would get out of that hell alive.

"I remained forsaken and chained for up to two days, tortured by those pleas for help, then I was finally released from bondage and taken inside the building for further questioning.

"I was faced with a different interrogator. He was a tall, dark man, who was much more dangerous looking than the first one. He was armed, and he waved his pistol around in a very unprofessional manner. Then he held it to my head, accusing and threatening, telling me, 'You are a low-down dog. You are a Barzani follower. You are a mutant. Why don't you confess and save me the trouble of making you?' He was a madman.

"He was interrupted when another prisoner was thrown through the door. The prisoner was crying out in Kurdish for help. My interrogator left. I was cautious since I had been warned that a favorite tactic was to bring prisoners together with the same loyalties. I assumed they wanted me to confide in this man, to confess that I was working for the Israelis or some such nonsense.

"I did ask the man why he had been arrested. He said he was caught listening to the Kurdish radio broadcasts. As far as I knew, listening to Kurdish broadcasts was no longer a crime after 1970, but I said nothing.

"I was not prepared for what came next.

"Suddenly, the door flew open and three muscular men rushed into the room and, without a word of warning, attacked that poor man, beating him viciously. I heard harsh breathing sounds, then nothing. I think he died. They pulled his limp body out of the room.

"Yet another officer came in. He spoke so softly that I could barely hear him. There was a window covered by curtains. He opened up the curtains. The palm grove was visible. I stared at the trees, thinking about all the men buried alive in that grove and how no one in the world knew or cared about that dreadful place. Billions of people throughout the world were carrying on with their lives, numerous foreign governments were friendly with Saddam and the Baathists, and all the while innocent Iraqis were in the grip of a mad government, thrown into holes in the ground, tortured, and killed for no reason. Where *was* everybody? Why didn't *somebody* care?

"This officer gazed at me with his strange sad eyes. He asked me, 'Why did you commit this corrupt deed against your own country? Don't deny it. We have witnesses that you had a wireless device, that you were contacting the Israelis and spying for them. Then you contacted the Kurdish rebel forces in the north, all this to harm your own government.'

"I don't know why, but I decided to appeal to that officer. I told him that I speak Kurdish only because my mother is Kurd. I admitted that I was active in the Kurdish Student Union, but only because I was allowed the right under the March 11th, 1970, treaty between the Iraqi government and the Kurds. I told him that I had never traveled out of Iraq in my entire life. I told him that I had never met an Israeli. I told him that everything he had read about me in the report was simply not true.

"I felt I was getting somewhere with him, so I said that when I told the truth, everyone got angry with me, but if I lied and confessed to the things they were accusing me of, that it was only to humor them. I told him that he seemed an intelligent man and that I doubted that he wanted to hear lies.

"I repeated what I had said before, that I had been swimming and playing football on the day in question, and that it was physically impossible for me to have been in two places at the same time.

"He didn't acknowledge a word I said. He raised the topic of Uncle Jafar, saying that I should honor the memory of the man who had been the first defense minister of Iraq, the man who had helped form modern Iraq. He claimed that Uncle Jafar would be ashamed of his nephew for engaging in such traitorous activities.

"Without waiting for an answer, he then said that the Kurdish movement consisted of criminals and Israeli spies.

"To my despair, I was sent back to the pit. Hady was afraid I was dead, so when I dropped back down into the hole, he was overjoyed. I was pleased, of course, to see that Hady was still alive, but terribly sorry to be back in that hole.

"While I was away, Hady had been interrogated, too, and slapped around. After what I had witnessed, I was grateful that we were both alive."

"Ah, praise God for that," Hady mumbled.

"For five more days we stayed in that hole. Our pit mate was near death. Then on the sixth day, they came to take us away. Although terrible days were still ahead of us, that was the last we saw of that pit, thank God."

Auntie Aisha asked, "What about that poor soul from Al-Najaf?"

Hady said, "As they were taking us out of the pit, they replaced us with three other prisoners. But that poor man had been there for four or five months already. He was no longer talking. He would just rouse himself slightly when the bread and water were delivered, then fall to the ground and hold on to his bread. He had lost control of his bowels. He is dead by now, for sure."

Mother was visibly shaken. "What happened then, son?"

"For that move, we were each forced to wear glasses with blacked-out lenses. But I discovered that if I held my head in a certain position, I could see a little from the sides. We left the pit prison and were driven west, out of Baghdad. The trip only took about an hour. I knew the direction we were going. I was hoping I was wrong, but I soon realized that our destination was Abu Ghraib Prison. I lost all hope at that point."

Although safe in Auntie Aisha's arms, I shivered in fear. All Iraqis knew the history of the notorious Abu Ghraib. The British had built the prison about the same time I was born, in the early 1960s. It was a huge prison complex, an independent city, with five large compounds. It was now a prison mainly designated for political prisoners, such as Kurds calling for Kurdish rights, Shiites demanding religious freedom, or even Sunnis who had displeased the Baathists.

Since the day the prison was built, the name Abu Ghraib had been linked with torture and death. But none of us had seen the inside of that prison, at least not until Ra'ad and Hady were arrested.

Ra'ad described the place for us. "They registered us and put us in a crowded cell block. There were Kurds, Shiites, Sunnis, and even non-Iraqis such as Lebanese and Palestinians in our block. We even met a Spanish journalist who had been there for over a year. The cells had bars so we could see prisoners in other cells and even talk to them when the guards were out of hearing range. There was no privacy. A single small bowl served as a toilet."

Hady tittered, "It was heaven."

"Yes. You are right. As terrible as it was to be in Abu Ghraib, compared to the hole in the ground, it *was* heaven, at least at first. We heard there was a dining hall, an exercise room, and even a prayer room, but that was a joke. It was not a social club. No prisoners were ever allowed in those areas, as far as we knew.

"Soon after our arrival we were told that one of three things would happen: We would be set free. We would be sentenced to life imprisonment. Or we would be executed. The decision was coming down within a few days.

"For me, those were the most torturous days of all, not knowing if we would live or die. Or ever see any of you again."

I glanced at Hady. Alia was sitting close by his side. She was holding her youngest son, Shwan, in her lap, while her oldest, Shaswar, was sitting beside his father. They were a perfect little family. I had to fight back my tears.

"After more than seven weeks in that place, we had heard nothing of our fate, while prisoners all around us were regularly being taken out to be executed. Then one day I was taken to see a doctor. The doctor gave me a courteous examination, asking me if I needed anything. I had been warned by other prisoners that the doctors often prescribed poison pills or gave deadly injections. So I told him I was just fine, that I only needed my freedom.

"I think he was sincere, though. He told me, 'Son, when people are brought to me, it is usually before their release. But there is one thing you should remember. Never tell anyone about what you have been subjected to, or what you have seen in this place. Tell no one. If you talk, you'll be back.'

"Then I was escorted back to the cell. I was upset to find out that Hady had been removed while I was away. Where had they taken him?

"I didn't have time to worry about Hady for very long. The moment the cell door closed behind me, my cell mates began to claw at me. Everyone appeared to have gone mad, all at the same time! Perhaps they had received orders from the prison authority to murder me!

"I fought to no avail. They pushed me to the floor and forced me on my stomach. They started pulling at my pajama top, or at least what was left of it, as I had been wearing it for nearly three months. I pleaded for mercy.

"One of the men clawing at me said, 'Relax, relax. When a prisoner is taken to the doctor, often the next step is release. We keep a pen hidden for this purpose. Now we are going to write our home telephone numbers on your back. When you get out, have a family member copy the numbers down from your back. Take this list and go to a public phone. Call all the numbers and tell whoever answers that you have been at Abu Ghraib, in the political section. They will know who the message is really from. Say nothing more.'"

Curious, I slipped from Auntie Aisha's arms and went to stand behind my brother's chair. When I looked down the neck of his shirt, I could see evidence of numbers scrawled in ink on his back.

"Sa'ad will write down those numbers later," Ra'ad promised. "Then we will call these people. It's the least I can do."

I stared at my big brother in awe. I loved him.

Ra'ad smiled weakly. "Little Joanna," he said, "I am very happy to see you."

My face flushed red. I longed to tell my brother so many things. I wanted to tell him about the owl with the golden eyes and that at the very moment when he had been staring at the full moon and the star-cloaked sky, I had been doing the same.

Despite the lice in his hair, I reached over and kissed him on the cheek, before sitting down to hear the end of his tragic tale.

"This happened this morning. Hady was never returned to our cell, so that is why his back was not used as a message board."

I was glad to hear Hady chuckle; he was coming back to life.

He reported, "That's because I had been taken to my place of employment. Those guards said we must have a guarantee from an Iraqi company that I would be employed if released." Hady swung his head back and forth. "You should have seen the faces of my employers when I stepped into the office. After an unexplained absence, I appear surrounded by prison guards, in torn pajamas, and bringing the stench of an unwashed body. But they signed the guarantee and told me to come back to work as soon as possible."

"Praise Allah," Mother murmured automatically, for many companies would have refused to keep on a former prisoner.

Ra'ad suddenly seemed in a hurry to finish the story. "A few hours ago, Hady and I were thrown out of the front gate of the prison. Our dream of freedom had come true. We were released." He snapped his fingers. "Just like that."

Ra'ad cleared his rasping throat. "There we were, looking like two lunatics with long beards and hair, stumbling in the streets, weak, hungry, and cringing from the blinding sunlight.

"No taxicab would stop for us. Cars actually careened away when they saw us. Finally, an elderly taxi driver stopped. We told him that we had been wrongly arrested. He believed us because he said his own son had suffered from false arrest the year before. His kind heart wouldn't let him refuse us."

Palms facing us, Ra'ad clapped his hands together. "And that is it. We survived."

Mother, Alia, Auntie Aisha, and several other aunties jumped to push tea and juice into Ra'ad's and Hady's hands. Our two men were home, safe and back where they belonged. Nothing else really mattered to any of us.

The celebration began.

For that moment, my heart was throbbing with energy and hope that our troubles were over. Strangely, though, both Ra'ad and Hady sat quietly, their eyes leaden, unable to take pleasure from the festivities.

Thinking back, I believe that my brother and Hady had looked into the abyss, and there they saw Iraq's future, and our own. That terrifying episode had been a beginning and not an end. Our troubles had only just begun.

PART TWO

Joanna Grows Up

6

Death

BAGHDAD
October 1976

Should I live a hundred years, memories of Ra'ad's and Hady's narrow escape from those Baathist thugs will never leave me.

After regaining his health, Ra'ad resumed his university studies, but he was required to submit to a humiliating security procedure every six weeks. He appeared at the security offices to answer questions and file reports, documenting that he no longer "committed criminal acts against the state." If Ra'ad still participated in the Kurdish Student Union, he did not tell us.

My law-abiding brother was mortified to be treated as a criminal.

Alia's anxiety over Hady's safety settled over her household like a fog. Hady returned to work, but looked shriveled and wan, his features sharp. Alia tearfully confided in Mother that Hady's vivid nightmares that took him back to the pit prison provoked nightly mayhem. There were constant alarms and excitements with Shaswar and Shwan as well, two little boys who once led carefree lives, but who now wept more than they laughed. The one joy was that Alia was pregnant with her third child and due to deliver.

Muna's torment was painful to witness. My timid sister was

traumatized by her brother's ordeal. She would sit in a huddle and draw her small body into a tense ball.

Sa'ad was born with religion in his veins, but since Ra'ad's arrest he had become even more dutiful and dedicated, never missing a prayer. He insisted that Alia's two boys sometimes accompany him to the mosque, despite the fact that at ages six and four they were quite restless during prayers. I believed that Sa'ad was on the path to become a cleric.

Such a decision would have brought joy to my devout mother, although I would have greeted the news less enthusiastically, for my brother's religious fervor promoted authoritarian conduct. I did not want nor need a guardian of my morals.

Although Mother strived to maintain a calm demeanor, I knew that her heart was bruised. I noticed a fresh web of worry lines bordering her eyes and mouth. Living in Baathist Baghdad was aging my beautiful mother. Despite Ra'ad's close call, Mother did not falter in her support of the Kurdish cause.

I was relieved because I now had plans for my future. When I was old enough, I was determined to join a Kurdish cause. No one could stop me. Yet, Mother did caution that we had entered a new and even more dangerous period in our Kurdish history with those brutal Baathists at the helm. She said that each of her children must become his or her own policeman, watching every word written and spoken, cautious of every action taken. I promised Mother that when I was old enough to join a Kurdish political party, I would be careful.

Only Father was oblivious to our worries. With her sign language perfected after years of marriage, Mother had convinced Father that thieves had kicked down our door, but had fled at the sight of Sa'ad armed with a carving knife. My father, who was a master builder and craftsman, soon fitted our home with a sturdy wooden door equipped with unique locks. I had never before seen such a door. A military tank could have broken it, perhaps, but a human foot, never.

Certainly, life would never be the same for me. When an unfamiliar car turned up outside our home, I breathlessly rushed to peer from behind the drapes, poised to shout a warning for all to flee into the back garden and over the fence to safety. I even practiced for speed. I was proud that it only took me one minute to shout a warning, seize my emergency bag, which was packed and hidden under a covered table in Ra'ad's bedroom, and reach the garden wall.

I made those practice runs daily. My mother and siblings would exchange patronizing smiles, as though I was playing a childish game, but I believed that such preparation might one day save all our lives.

I was surprised to hear Mother claim that many citizens of our country supported our Baathist president, Ahmed Hassan al-Bakir, and his second-in-command, Saddam Hussein, who was known as "Mr. Deputy" to Iraqis. Supposedly, Mr. Deputy was the true power in Iraq those days, but Mother scoffed at the idea that there was any difference between the two men, saying that when one lays the eggs and the other one hatches them, it was all one and the same.

Some people claimed that Iraqis never had it so good, with new government laws guaranteeing rights for women. A new law, called the national campaign to eradicate illiteracy, had been passed, requiring that all Iraqis must be educated. Elderly villagers who had never stepped inside a school room were suddenly obligated to attend reading classes. Undoubtedly, such social reforms were beneficial, yet the repressive atmosphere and fear of arrest and torture tilted the balance against the Baathists for most Iraqi citizens.

In 1976, I celebrated my fourteenth birthday, feeling like a big girl. I sailed along during the summer but was pleased to return to school in September. The following month, in October, just when I felt the family at last might be getting over the terror of Ra'ad's imprisonment, death paid us a visit.

The moment I heard, I was struck by the most unbearable agony. For some inexplicable reason, my first reaction was to take off my shoes and fling them in the air. Shocked faces greeted my action, but I didn't care. Next I ripped up school papers and threw them to the wind. Then I heard excruciating screams, wondering where they came from, not realizing that the screams were my own. I tore off, running into the house and racing from room to room, overturning chairs and small tables. I sprinted through the kitchen, pushed through the back door, and dashed into the garden. I shrieked so loudly the neighbors called out over our garden wall in alarm, asking what was the trouble, shouting for someone to alert the police that a massacre was occurring at the al-Askari home. I didn't care!

I concealed myself behind one of the largest date palm trees in the garden. With open palms I struck my forehead as I leaned against the prickly bark of that old tree. When I stared upward through the branches at the blue Baghdad sky, I could not believe that everything still looked as it did the day before, that the earth was still revolving around the sun that was still shining brightly while white clouds floated past. The sky, the sun, and the clouds should all be draped in black, in mourning.

My backside slithered against the trunk of the tree as I slowly collapsed to the dirt. In my anguish, I rolled around on the ground, feeling sand grind into the pores on my face. But I didn't care!

The loose sand edged toward my lips when I choked out the unbelievable words, "Daddy! Daddy! Daddy!"

Ten days before, he had collapsed at the railroad offices and had been rushed to the hospital. When word came, Mother, Sa'ad, Muna, and I sped across the city in a taxicab to the Al-Numan Hospital, located in Adhamiya, Mother staring straight ahead, praying, Sa'ad dark and still, and Muna pale and trembling. I was in an unmoving stupor, yearning to cry but unable to shed a single tear.

Alia was there to meet us, despite the fact she had given birth to her third son only a few weeks before, a precious little boy named Shazad. I had never seen my sister so distraught, not even after Hady was arrested.

When we were led to Father's bed, his features were drawn taut with pain, one side of his mouth drooping and sad. He was restless as he tried in vain to shift his partially paralyzed body.

A new and horrible side of life was suddenly revealed to me. My parents could get sick, die, and leave me. I reached to grasp Father's hand but Mother pulled me away, telling me, "Later, Joanna. Later." I then tried to catch my father's eye, but he was in too much pain to even notice me.

Shattered, I huddled behind Mother, waiting impatiently for a doctor while listening to the sounds of tired toddlers crying from the nearby hospital corridor. Finally, a short, stout doctor with heavy jowls appeared.

Father *would* live, we were assured. But in the next moment we also learned the frightening news that he had suffered a serious stroke and that he was disoriented and possibly in severe pain.

I told myself that if he could only live I would spend every spare moment by his side, doing whatever he needed. No task would be too difficult, no burden too heavy.

I longed to stay at the hospital but the decision was not mine to make. Mother remained there at Father's side while Sa'ad, Muna, and I were sent home. Auntie Aisha would soon make the trip from Sulaimaniya to stay with us.

Although I never had the comfort of making contact with my father before leaving him, to pass a secret message of my love, I did kiss his hands and face and touch his shoulder. I left the hospital with the naive belief that soon all would return to normal.

But the doctor had lied to us. He knew that my father was not going to recover.

Those days, at least in Iraq, doctors thought it best not to reveal the saddest truths.

That night at the hospital was the last time I saw my father.

Ten days later, as I hurriedly walked from school, my steps slowed when I saw large numbers of sad-faced relatives congregating at our home. My heart told me that the gathering crowd was connected to my father's illness. I knew then that nothing would ever again be the same.

Wanting to avoid the news obviously awaiting me, I considered hiding in a friend's house, but a relative saw me and came running, pulling me aside to tell me that my father was dead. Dead!

No one could make me stop screaming, not even my dear uncle Aziz, his worried face looming over my own, calling my name repeatedly, "Joanna! Joanna! Joanna!" With tears rolling down his face, he lifted me from the ground, carrying me to my room to gently put me down on a bed and cover me with a blanket.

There was a deafening commotion with everyone speaking at once, all offering advice as to what should be done with me, a brokenhearted girl who was screeching to see her father one more time. I called out for my mother, but she was still at the hospital where Father died. She would go from there with my brothers to the grave to make plans for the funeral for the following day because Muslims must be buried within twenty-four hours. So it was uncertain when Mother would be home.

Auntie Aisha had arrived from Sulaimaniya. She rushed to sit by my side. She was the only one who could comfort me. She ordered everyone to leave my room.

Yes, I wanted to be alone with my memories of my father.

Although my father could never tell me anything of his life because of his inability to speak, I had learned much about him from Mother, Ra'ad, and Alia, as well as from older relatives who knew him from the time he was born. My thoughts brought him back to life, if only in my own mind.

Unlike us, my father's childhood was privileged. The al-Askari family was very powerful in 1914, the year my father was born. Later, the family became personally and politically aligned to Iraq's royal family, which ruled the country from the end of World War I until the revolution of 1958.

My father grew up in a large home in the Aiwadiya area in Baghdad, a gracious villa shaded by swaying Iraqi palm trees. My father and his younger brother Othman spent many hours lazing on the banks of the ancient Tigris, a place of dreams for men since the beginning of civilization. There they would watch the river craft drifting by, two young men dreaming of the days when they would take their rightful place in Baghdadi society. But my father's dreams ended when he was only seven years old.

The first sign of trouble came quickly. One morning his throat was so painfully sore that he could barely swallow. A high temperature followed. His parents then noticed a red rash that developed on his neck and chest. It was said that his rippled red skin had the rough texture of sandpaper. His tongue became swollen and red. He soon slipped in and out of consciousness. He recovered, but when his parents came to assess his condition, he cried out, "I cannot hear you!"

Although father was suddenly deaf, he had not yet lost his ability to speak, and he began to sob softly, his panicked cries gaining momentum until harsh sounds of despair exploded throughout the house. His gentle father, a physical giant of a man, clasped his son's small hands in his own and wept with him, while his mother stood still and silent, a wooden figure, her brown eyes glowing dark, her very white skin fading whiter still.

Father's parents were wealthy, and every medical specialist in Baghdad was consulted. None offered hope.

Father's anguish increased when he began to lose his ability to articulate properly, for when children go deaf, they generally lose their ability to speak as well. He was so ashamed of his infirmity that he withdrew into isolation.

In 1921, the year Father was stricken, Iraq was not a country equipped to deal with such medical problems. Most children struck by similar calamities were abandoned to a hidden area in the home and ignored by their families, who felt that a handicapped child was a shame and a burden.

But Father was more fortunate than most. His family was wealthy and highly educated. Most important, he was the nephew of the renowned Jafar Pasha al-Askari, an admired military genius of World War I, a budding diplomat, and a treasured friend of many leading Europeans and Iraqis. I never knew that uncle because he died twenty-six years before I was born, but it was an accepted fact that he was exceptional.

Jafar Pasha announced that his handicapped nephew must be educated and trained in a productive career. And so my father's future was magically arranged.

When he was eleven years old, he was sent to a special school in France for the deaf-mute. He prospered there, becoming a master wood-carver and earning a university degree in engineering. He was so contented in France that he remained there for twelve years, reluctantly returning only at the request of his family when his beloved uncle Jafar Pasha was assassinated in 1936.

His uncle's assassination was only the first in a long line of family sorrows. On March 22, 1937, approximately five months after the death of Jafar Pasha, Father's own father, my grandfather Ali Ridha, killed himself. In a spiraling bout of depression over his brother Jafar Pasha's assassination, he shot himself in the head.

His death was a terrible blow to everyone in the family, and especially to my father. The next big setback to my father's happiness happened on July 14, 1958, when the royal family was massacred. During the same upheaval, his booming furniture factory was destroyed. At the destruction of his business, my father was doomed to be forever poor.

The following morning my father did come home from the hospital, but not in the manner I had hoped or imagined. He came to us in a wooden coffin that was placed in the middle of the living room.

Our home was overflowing with many grieving relatives, friends, and acquaintances, as my father was a well-respected gentleman. But the only thing I could see was that coffin. Father's face was not visible since the coffin was kept closed, but my imagination took me in there with him.

I could not bear the idea that my athletic father was so tightly encased in that small box. I refused to leave him, so I lingered around the periphery, watching everything through a soupy haze, seeing the faces of well-wishers, distinguishing the movement of lips as mourners spoke of their sorrow, but not hearing exactly what they said.

Alia was inconsolable. When my sister saw that wooden box, she completely broke down by throwing herself on the coffin, crying, and pleading for Father to come back to her. It took both Hady and Sa'ad to pull her off the coffin. Mother and several aunties followed to comfort the grieving Alia.

I stayed with my father. I moved closer, staring at that small box, whispering, "Daddy," under my breath, willing him to reclaim life, open his eyes, and use his strong arms to push the coffin cover away, to look at me, to smile at me, to open his arms and pull me to him.

But he did not. He stayed in that little box.

I remained in the living room until the men designated to carry the coffin came in to take my father to the Sheikh Maroof al-Karkhi cemetery.

Women in my country did not attend actual burials, although we could visit the grave later. Yet I knew exactly what would happen: at the cemetery, they would lower my father into a hole in a ground and then cover him with dirt.

Although discouraged by my aunties, I followed the procession down the street, watching the coffin until my father was out of sight. And my darling father was gone, just like that, never to return.

7

My Mother and My Father

BAGHDAD
October–November 1976

My father's kindly heart was filled with riches, yet he died a pauper.

After his death, apprehension about the future kept our home in turmoil. The urgency for money was so great that soon after the funeral, Mother, Alia, and Auntie Aisha searched through Father's possessions. They found a mere sixty Iraqi dinars. For me, they found other, more important items that revealed what my father truly treasured. There was a stack of grainy photographs of his children and of his parents and other dead relatives, all delicately wrapped in wrinkled tissue paper. Under the photographs he had amassed cherished notes that his children had written him over the years. Since he could not hear or speak, we often interacted by writing notes.

Sixty dinars would last us but a few weeks. Mother had four children still in school. Only Alia was married and no longer looking to Mother for her well-being. With money problems looming, our Kurdish relatives urged Mother to return to her childhood home in Kurdistan, so that we might benefit from our large and loving family there.

Of course, I pressed for Kurdistan. But because of my young age, no one cared about my opinion.

Alia heard me pleading, but cautioned me not to wish for such a move, saying that our lives would be very different in the north. The Baathists were becoming even more brutal with the Kurds in Kurdistan. Violence was escalating in our torn land, with government raids, sieges, and the murder of many innocent Kurds.

I had a lot to think about. Suddenly, I was discovering that nothing about adult life was easy.

Mother was anxious that the government would order us to vacate our home, as we were living in a house that belonged to the railroad; it had been assigned to my father only because of his employment.

Before the revolution, my family had enjoyed living in a lovely large house in the Salyiya district, but after the revolution in 1958 my parents lost everything, including their home and my father's modern furniture factory. They were fortunate when Father was quickly appointed as a mechanical engineer for the Iraqi Railroad. A benefit of his job had been assigned housing in the unpretentious district where I grew up.

Although in our teeming family life there had never been any privacy, I enjoyed growing up in our crowded, modest, yellow and brown–brick bungalow. It was built during the 1940s by British officials. Many British had lived in Iraq during the years when they ruled the country through their puppet king, Faisal.

Yet when the British finally quit the country, they were thoughtful enough to leave behind our cozy bungalow with its front garden hedged in by *yass* bushes with a citrus fragrance that, when in bloom, perfumed the entire area. It had a small front porch that opened into the sitting room, with sofas arrayed around the walls, three bedrooms, and a bathroom. A tapered, tight stairwell gave us access to the roof, which was handy because during the hot summer months Iraqis and Kurds generally sleep outside on the roof. Mother did most of her cooking in the small kitchen that adjoined the most popular room in the house, a sizable veranda furnished with large tables and plenty of chairs. Best of all, the house was situated in the heart of a vast palm garden with trees so tall that they blocked out the hot rays of the Baghdad sun.

We were worried about being evicted, so it was a pleasant

surprise when government officials told us we could continue to live there during Mother's lifetime and that Mother was entitled to a small pension from the railway company. We would have just enough money for food and clothes. In a few years, Ra'ad would graduate from college and as the eldest son, he would automatically assume responsibility for our well-being. Suddenly, our future seemed less bleak.

With all this good news, Mother decided we would remain in Baghdad.

After the funeral, our closest Kurdish relatives remained with us for many days. One night after dinner when the women of the household gathered in a morose group on the back porch, Mother's sister Fatima became unusually animated and began to tease Mother, saying, "Kafia, it is time for the weeping to stop and the living to begin!"

I was dazed by this kind of talk, as I could not envision finding joy in life then or ever. My fatherless heart was wounded raw.

Auntie Fatima had an impish smile on her round face, and her brown eyes were sparkling as she peered at Mother and asked, "Kafia, have you ever told your girls how much your husband loved you?"

Mother shifted uncomfortably in her chair, frowning at her sister, refusing to acknowledge her improper question.

Mother possessed many exceptional qualities: she was a selfless mother, a devoted wife, a devout Muslim, and an accomplished cook. She was so welcoming to visitors that our home was always filled with visiting relatives, people who would rather be at our home than at their own.

Her children had always been proud of her in other ways, too. She was a regal beauty: her skin was fair, her eyes dark and lively. She was tall and had a mane of shimmering black hair that was the envy of her sisters and daughters. Even her hands were exquisite, with slender fingers and perfectly formed nails.

It was no surprise to me that she had won her husband's affection, despite the fact their marriage was arranged.

Auntie Fatima looked around at the large circle of women and said, "Why, Muhammad was so captivated by Kafia that once he even threw himself under the wheels of a bus!"

I perked up. I had not heard this story.

Mother glanced at Alia, Muna, and me, cupping her hands over her mouth, embarrassed, I supposed, for her daughters to think of her as a desirable woman.

Auntie Fatima slapped her hands together. "If Kafia won't tell this story, then I will. Girls, I'm sure you have heard about Muhammad's mother, Mirriam. Everyone in Baghdad knew that she was malicious to all her daughters-in-law, but that she hated Kafia most of all, making her life miserable. When Kafia became pregnant, what did Mirriam do? She *threatened* Kafia that she was going to forbid a doctor to assist her in her first labor!"

Auntie Fatima looked round the circle. "Tell me now, what kind of woman wishes for another woman to suffer needlessly during childbirth?" A murmur of horrified disbelief went round the room.

"Sixteen-year-old Kafia was terrified of having her first child attended by her cruel mother-in-law, a woman capable of almost anything. Mirriam often expressed her hatred of baby girls, so Kafia had good reason for concern, thinking that Mirriam might go so far as to harm her child if it happened to be a girl.

"So one day, while Mirriam was napping, Kafia slipped from the house and posted a letter to Mother in Sulaimaniya, saying that if Mother didn't send someone to rescue her from her mother-in-law she was going to throw herself into the Tigris!"

I glanced at my sister Alia, thinking that she, as I, had been in great peril while in our mother's womb. Alia had been threatened by drowning and I had been poisoned. It was a miracle that we both existed.

"As you can imagine, Kafia's letter created the greatest uproar in Sulaimaniya. Because the envelope postal date was indistinguishable, Mother became frantic that it was already too late.

"Without time to pack, Mehdi and I boarded the first bus to Baghdad. We arrived while Muhammad was at work. You should have seen Mirriam's face when we told her that we had come for Kafia. She vehemently protested, determined to keep her hated daughter-in-law within her sphere of influence. But Mehdi, our wise brother, was diplomatic. He didn't accuse Mirriam of cruelty, which is what I wanted to do, but instead stressed Kafia's youth and inexperience, saying that it was only right for such a young bride to be with her mother when she delivered her first child. Mirriam reluctantly relented.

"Certain that Mirriam would change her mind and prevent her from leaving, we were so rushed to leave that Kafia forgot about Muhammad."

Auntie Fatima burst into laughter.

"When we left the house, we saw one of those red city buses conveniently passing by Mirriam's house. I took it as a sign and said, run! The three of us ran as fast as possible, with the very pregnant Kafia hiking up her dress, scurrying like a duck.

"As fate would have it, just as we were boarding the bus, Muhammad turned the corner and caught sight of us. I suppose he believed that Kafia was leaving him, never to return.

"Now, don't forget, this was a man who couldn't shout, stop, or wait. Instead, he did the only thing he knew to make his point: he dropped his parcels, ran to the front of the stationary bus, and threw himself under one of the front wheels."

Auntie Fatima laughed lowly, shaking her head. "That poor man went so far as to perfectly position his head under one of the bus tires!

"There was instant bedlam. The angry bus driver was blowing the horn. We were pushing to get off the bus. A crowd gathered. Everyone was shouting. None knew that the would-be suicide was deaf, that he couldn't hear a word they were shouting.

"It took us a few minutes to push through the crowd, but finally we could see Muhammad. Girls, it was the strangest sight! Your father was flat on his back. His arms were crossed over his chest. His eyes were closed. Like this," Auntie Fatima demonstrated for us.

Everyone laughed. Even Mother did not look displeased. She had a dreamy, faraway look in her eyes.

"By now Mirriam had heard about the excitement. Someone must have recognized Muhammad and run to tell her. That woman was like a tank, forcing her way through the crowd like a strongman from the circus, lifting and throwing people aside."

Auntie Fatima jumped from her chair and said, "Like this!" My breath shot out of my body as she pulled me from my chair and tossed me across the room. Everyone but me thought that was funny.

"When Mirriam realized that the potential suicide was indeed her son, what did she do? That crazy woman began yanking on his arms!"

I hurriedly moved a safe distance from Auntie Fatima, not wishing to be victim of yet another demonstration.

Auntie Fatima carried on, "Kafia squatted as best she could, considering her big belly. There they were, the wife and the mother, both women pulling on Muhammad. Oddly, he refused to open his eyes. His lips were moving slightly. I suppose the poor man was saying his final prayers! Preparing to meet his God!

"Well! Mirriam didn't hesitate a second. She reached with those strong fingers of hers and forced open Muhammad's eyelids.

"When Muhammad saw that that his wife was there, too, he gave her an accusatory stare. After all, he thought she was leaving him.

"Kafia knew enough sign language by then to explain what was happening, that her departure was not permanent. That she was just going to her mother for help in delivering her first child. That she would return. A suddenly hopeful Muhammad pushed himself on his elbows and leaped up.

"Of course, that incident made Mirriam even more bitter and jealous. It was obvious Muhammad was very much in love with his wife if he would rather die than face living without her."

Auntie Fatima's story had fulfilled her purpose.

I forgot, if only for a brief time, that my father was gone from me forever. I felt cheered by reflecting on the happiness my father and mother had derived from their marriage. When I retired later in the evening, it was the first time since my father's death that I did not cry myself to sleep.

I was not yet mature enough to understand that the winds of fortune veer continuously, or that soon I would have a meeting that would be the most pivotal event of my life.

8

Love in a Torn Land

BAGHDAD
1977

It was a Thursday evening when Alia telephoned Mother to complain about her life. Mainly, my sister was exhausted. With two rambunctious sons close in age, and a third son a toddler, Alia was becoming haggard at a young age. Of her three daughters, Mother loved Alia most of all, so she quickly promised Alia that she could "have" Muna and me. We were to be gifts! Mother said we must go and babysit for Alia for the next few days, even though we would miss two days of school.

The following afternoon my three nephews were taking a nap when I heard loud voices. I was frightened. My first thought was that the security police had reappeared to apprehend Hady and Ra'ad. My heart thumped loudly as I leaned against the wall to listen. Three loud voices echoed. One was Hady's. My brother-in-law was arguing about the increasing tensions facing Kurds under the Baathist regime. I heard Alia's cheerful voice break through what seemed to be an affable dispute.

The two men and Alia were in Alia's kitchen. With a rush of relief and a spark of curiosity, I walked down the short hallway to see for myself the owner of that other loud, almost strident, voice.

I stopped a few steps short of the doorway. I knew the visitor. It was Hady's nephew, Sarbast. I had seen him hovering around the perimeter of our family life in Kurdistan since I was a little girl, yet I had never really noticed him until that moment.

I was suddenly struck by his good looks. As I stared, I became captivated. My face felt flushed, my stomach took a dive, and my heart was beating faster than normal. What was happening?

A memory flashed through me of the handsome Peshmerga in love with the beautiful Kurdish girl, a tragic love story that ended in imprisonment and death. I felt a weird but wonderful kind of foreboding.

I tried to remember everything I knew about Sarbast, which was not much. I had seen him infrequently during our summer holidays in Sulaimaniya; he had grown up in Kurdistan, and he was older than me by five or six years.

He was so *very* handsome. He was not very tall, but tall enough. His body was compact but well built, with a large chest and muscular arms. His face was handsome, his skin olive, and his mustache full for a young man, masking his upper lip. Most striking, his chiseled face was framed by abundant curly dark locks. His hazel eyes were animated but earnest under a furrowed brow.

Sarbast was expressing his ideas loudly and emphatically. Hady, on the other hand, responded calmly. Sarbast seemed unreasonably obstinate with his uncle, but I found his passion strangely charming.

He waved his hands for emphasis and said, "I am *not* afraid of the Iraqi government. Listen, Hady, the trick is to *expect* to die. Then if you live, your life is a bonus. I *will* fight them to the death!"

My entire life transformed in that instant.

Yes! Here was a true Peshmerga!

Suddenly, my happiness depended on a man I barely knew.

It was then that I saw my sister smiling at me with a perceptive expression. I decided to beat a hasty retreat, but before I could turn to my bedroom, Alia held out one hand. "Joanna. Come. You have not even said hello to Sarbast."

The men ceased talking. I sensed Sarbast turning to glance at me.

I patted my hair with my hands. It was hanging long and straight without any style to it. My fingers tugged on my skirt. It was not one of my favorites. I had no desire to talk to Sarbast, not in such a disheveled condition.

Alia was persistent. "Joanna?"

Sarbast broke in, his unthinking words plunging into my heart like a dagger. "Alia. Your little sister?" He looked at me and smiled, "Oh? Yes! Joanna! Is *this* the *same* Joanna who was always so naughty?"

He studied me closer before laughing. "Little Joanna is still skinny!" Amused, he glanced at Alia. "Don't you feed this child?"

Tears started forming. Although I was fifteen years old and felt quite the adult, I was often teased by relatives who told me that I looked no more than twelve or thirteen, even though I was very tall and slim.

Sarbast not only thought of me as a child, he thought of me as a *skinny* child!

Alia laughed along with him, saying, "Joanna is naturally bony. She will always be skinny."

I looked accusingly at Alia. I *hated* her!

Tears spilled out, but no one seemed to notice. Thankfully, Hady was so caught up in the conversation that he was wholly oblivious to me. He dragged a chair from the table, advising his nephew, "Consider my suggestion, Sarbast. First you finish college. Then, if there is still no peace, you can fight. But if there is an acceptable treaty with Baghdad and no longer a good reason to wage war, at least you'll have a profession. Think about it." He lifted both shoulders in a shrug. "You'll be better prepared to help build up Kurdistan."

Sarbast turned his attention back to his uncle and slapped him on the back. "You old men have given up the fight," he said loudly, although affectionately.

Hady laughed merrily, glancing at Alia. "Wife, there is no wild beast like an angry young man."

For once in their married life, Alia ignored her husband. Instead, she gazed at me, to Sarbast, and then back at me. She drew me close with a hug and wiped my tears away with the back of her hand. "Come, Joanna."

Reluctantly, I allowed my sister to settle me at the table, in front of Sarbast. She softly stroked my shoulder and smiled as she turned to prepare a pot of tea. Afterward, she arranged sweets on a platter, her hands busy but her eyes locked on me.

As for me, I could not stop staring at Sarbast. Even his hands were perfectly formed. They were resting on the table, only inches from my own.

I could have touched his hands, if I dared. But I didn't. Instead, I listened attentively to everything that was said.

Sarbast had grown up in Hady's small village, Qalat Diza, in northern Iraq. He was the son of one of Hady's sisters. He had graduated from high school in the spring. He scored such high marks in school that he had been admitted as an engineering student at Baghdad University. Yet, he declared that he would rather be fighting the government in the mountains with his childhood friends than sitting in a classroom.

It was then that I learned the most exciting news of all: Sarbast would be moving in with Alia and Hady soon. Within the next week! My mind raced with the possibilities his move presented to me.

Alia was really too busy. She needed assistance with her three young sons. I made plans to work harder during the week to maintain my high school grades. Mother would be pleased if I volunteered to continue to help my sister with her boys.

Wanting to gain Sarbast's attention, I gathered my courage to announce that I would one day go to Kurdistan and become a freedom fighter myself. But before I could say the words, Sarbast jumped up to bid farewell, saying that he had an assignment to finish. Before walking away he selected two of Alia's cookies and slipped them into his trouser pocket. "I'll be back in a few days, with my clothes and books," he said with a friendly nod to Hady.

My emotions were in a whirl. I ached for him to notice me, to say good-bye to me. Yet I was thinking it best he not look too closely, not when I felt so untidy, even ugly.

But he surprised me when he turned back at the doorway, first glancing at me and then at Alia. "She's a child now," he announced unexpectedly, "but she'll prove to be a splendid woman."

Grinning, he turned to wink at me, then jauntily walked out the door, vanishing like a marvelous mirage. Tiny prickles erupted over the entire surface of my flesh.

Hady walked rapidly after his nephew, their conversation ongoing.

I jumped up from the table and whirled giddily. "Splendid! Splendid! One day I'll be splendid!"

Alia shook her head and laughed. "What is going on, Joanna?"

I continued dancing and twirling, refusing to confirm what my sister had already guessed. I had fallen in love!

Thankfully, Alia was a loyal sister. As far as I knew, she never told my secret to anyone, not even to Hady.

Over the next two days I cross-examined Alia, and she willingly told me everything she knew of Sarbast.

He was one of twelve children. The reason he was so passionately devoted to the Kurdish cause was that his family had suffered terribly for being Kurds. They had even lived in exile in Iran for several years, after the Baghdad government napalmed their village. Most important, he was not engaged. Alia comforted me with the news that Sarbast's family had not yet begun the matchmaking process, a routine procedure of our Kurdish culture once a man graduates from high school. Thankfully, it had been decided that Sarbast should concentrate on his studies first. I also learned that he was very artistic, that he sketched portraits and composed poems. He was perfect.

The remaining days dragged by. The image of Sarbast hovered in my mind. How I wished he would make a return visit before I left to go home and resume school.

But should he make an appearance I was desperate to look my best. So I made a point of getting up early, putting on my best clothes, arranging my hair, and biting my lips to keep them pink. When I was alone, I walked into my sister's bedroom and examined my image in the mirror. Admittedly, I was too skinny, but for the first time I happily noted that there was a hint of breasts rising under my blouse. Soon I would be a woman.

I did make one undeniable discovery about romantic love: love was a disturbing passion. One moment I was limp and miserable with hopelessness, believing that Sarbast would never see me as a beautiful woman, that I would forever be Alia's little sister in his eyes. The next moment I would be energized by hopeful certainty that one day I would develop into a beauty, and when that happy day arrived, Sarbast would pursue me to be his bride. It *must* happen!

I became so irritable and unpredictable that Alia teased me, "Joanna, watch out or your condition will be fatal! If you *don't* win Sarbast, you will die of grief. If you *do* win Sarbast, you will die of happiness."

Not realizing that Muna was busy tidying the pots and pans in the nearby pantry, I brashly made a bold confession. "Alia, I will be what I have to be, and I will do what I have to do, to capture Sarbast's love."

Metal pots and pans crashed to the floor. Muna stood, her face distorted in astonishment, her eyes wide and wild as she looked first at Alia and then at me. She cried out, "What? What?"

Alia chuckled. I smiled, too. It was clear that Muna believed that her younger sister had gone quite mad. But then Muna had never been in love, so how could she understand?

I pinched her flushed cheek, teasing her, "Love is surely wonderful, Muna," before prancing out of the room.

Love *was* wonderful, but it was *not* easy, for I was in love with a man who didn't love me in return.

Although my plotting to help Alia with her boys meant that Sarbast and I often saw each other at my sister's home, he always treated me as a child, despite my efforts to appear older than my fifteen years. I even tried to butt into his political discussions with Hady, determined to alert him to the fact that my young mind was as stubborn and determined as his own.

If I was not with him, I was daydreaming about him, reflecting endlessly on his handsome face and powerful personality. His intensity often created unpleasant scenes, for Sarbast never ran out of reasons for a good political argument. I even saw him shake his fists in anger at Hady, a man who would never even raise his voice. I found Sarbast's political passions very appealing. But to him, I was nothing more than Alia's little sister.

Knowing that I would never love another man but Sarbast, it was exquisitely painful to realize that Sarbast might never love me in return. My only consolation came from the fact that he never referred to marriage with another woman. Despite that, an imaginary clock was ticking loudly in my mind. Sarbast was of the age at which his family would soon insist that he agree to marry. Our culture demanded marriage and children of its sons and daughters.

There was some small hope, though. The mirror was promising physical change. Even Mother offered encouragement. When I complained about my skinny body, Mother confided that several aunties had recently mentioned that I was growing out of my gangly stage. They thought I was becoming very pretty.

Perhaps I would soon be beautiful like Mother, Alia, and Muna, and when that happened, Sarbast was sure to take interest in me, as I had warily noticed that he was attentive to beautiful women.

After careful consideration, I resolved to use a different tactic with Sarbast. I would be indifferent. The next time I was at Alia's home, I faked disinterest when Sarbast entered a room. I yawned and excused myself when Sarbast and Hady became involved in their customary debate regarding the maddening discrimination faced by Iraqi Kurds. My studied apathy took the strongest resolve.

After several days, Sarbast made an unexpected request: he opened a conversation with Alia, looking first at her and then at me. "Alia, have you noticed that Joanna has an unusually interesting face?" He paused, then said, "I would like to sketch her. With your permission, of course."

I stood quietly, secretly astonished. My ploy was successful! I hummed happily. Perhaps dreams do come true.

One unforgettable day a few weeks later, Sarbast collected his notebook and sketching pencils and placed a stool in front of a blank wall. He told me to sit.

I did as I was told. He was going to sketch my portrait. For the first time, Sarbast concentrated solely on me.

I felt like I was in heaven. Never before had I held this man's full attention. I relished every moment. There were long silences broken only when I slightly moved my head and shoulders and then Sarbast chided me with soft words that I have never forgotten. "Joanna. Be *very* still." He cleared his throat and smiled. "Youth doesn't come twice, you know."

I found him to be a talented artist. My shoulder accidentally brushed him as I looked at a mysterious likeness that I found difficult to believe was me.

I smiled my approval while gazing into his intense eyes. He grinned, but his smile was brother friendly. Still, I was consumed with the greatest happiness.

But that brief happiness was quickly dissipated when word came from relatives in the north that there was renewed upheaval in Kurdistan.

Sarbast began to speak of leaving his studies and going into the mountains to fight for Kurdistan.

I was plunged into a deep depression. Living in a land torn by continuous war was not easy. And experiencing love in a torn land was doubly challenging.

9

War

The worst had happened. Baghdad was being bombed by Iran.

I was less than one year away from starting my freshman year at the University of Baghdad in the College of Agricultural Engineering and was visiting the campus when the bombing started. In a panic, I unwisely tried to make my way home, but the jostling crowds made my passage across the city a form of street fighting. Every city block was jammed with surging crowds, with dense masses of people pressing from all sides. At first, the Baghdad police tried to control the crowd, but then gave up and fled the scene. They were so unconcerned about the people they were supposed to protect that one of them even trampled me, his heavy boot crushing my toes.

When I finally arrived at our front door limping, my hair was hanging with sweat and my face was streaked with dirt and soot. To my dismay, I discovered that I had lost one of my shoes.

Breathless, I told Mother, "I was caught in the open. There were many Iranian planes." I pointed at my feet. "And I was trampled."

Mother was in shock. She began to speak incoherently. "Joanna, I tell you. These days no one in Iraq should go out without cleaning their house."

I looked at my mother and laughed nervously. The entire country was in the greatest turmoil and Mother was talking about housecleaning? What was going on? Had her nerves completely unraveled?

The country had been at war with Iran since September 22, but never did we expect our capital city to be bombed. Yet it did not take a genius to know that we were on a risky path. We were fighting a war against a country three times our population, a country governed by fanatic religious mullahs who would like nothing better than to die as martyrs.

I was puzzled and angry with our government. I felt in my heart that Saddam Hussein, who had replaced Ahmad Hassan al-Bakir as president only the year before, had fired the first shot, despite the fact that the propaganda claimed otherwise, with our media caricaturing the Iranian leader Ayatollah Khomeini in a grotesque manner. But I did not dare express my ideas or opinions, at least not to anyone outside our family circle, because any Iraqi heard speaking against the war was summarily executed. Already there were whispered rumors of Iraqi parents being put to death after cursing the government for sending their sons to die at the front.

There were many other problems with the war. The Iranians were a Shiite nation, and Iraq's army was mainly manned by Shiite Muslims. During the past few years, tensions had risen to an all-time high between the Baathist government, which was dominated by a Sunni minority, and the Shiite clerics. There was even a religious edict issued against the Baathist government by Ayatollah Sadr, the most popular Shiite cleric in Iraq. Ayatollah Sadr had ruled that the Baathist regime was not Islamic and that his Shiite followers were forbidden from dealing with the government. The Shiite Al-Dawa Party was then banned by Saddam, and many members of Al-Dawa were executed during the early months of 1980.

What motive did any Shiite have to fight for Saddam Hussein?

There were rumors that in the early days of the fighting Shiite conscripts in the Iraqi army had actually turned their weapons against their own military superiors. If such situations continued, we would lose the war.

And there was the Kurdish situation. All Iraqis had reasons to worry during that dark time, but Kurds worried more than most.

Many times in the past, Iraqi Kurds had looked to Iran for protection from the government in Baghdad. With Baghdad now fighting Tehran, there was enormous danger for Kurdish civilians. Kurdish villages and cities were mainly located on the Iranian border. Sulaimaniya, where Grandmother and our aunties and cousins lived, was only a few miles from the border, as was Halabja, where Auntie Aisha lived. With two huge armies stalking each other in the region, Kurdish civilians were in acute danger.

Once again I heard the loud noise of the planes dropping bombs, so I seized Mother's hand and we ran into our small bathroom to find Muna cowering on the floor, her face in her hands muffling her screams. We sat on each side of her. I grabbed Muna's soft little hands in my own to reassure her. There were no nearby shelters in our area, and our small house gave us only a modest measure of protection.

My thoughts drifted to Sa'ad, who had already been sent to the front and who was in an area where there was heavy fighting. He was in the oil-rich Iranian province of Khuzistan, where his division was laying siege to Ahwaz. Sa'ad was specially trained to provide wind speed and locations to the Iraqi artillery divisions, who we heard were pounding Iranian territory. Undoubtedly, my brother's life was in danger every moment.

Had I been told a year ago that I would be mumbling constant prayers for Sa'ad's safety, I would not have believed it possible. Since I was a teenager, Sa'ad and I had not enjoyed an easy relationship. Sa'ad was a young man who was simple in his habits and moderate in his desires, yet he made it his sacred duty to watch over the honor of women. My conservative brother was like so many Iraqi men, very controlling when it came to the females of his family. Because I often refused to obey his orders, we had often clashed.

For years, Sa'ad had directed my fashions. He was so strict that he would measure the length of my dresses, forcing me to cover my arms as well as wear a black scarf over my long hair. But he couldn't watch me every moment. So I dressed as conservative Joanna when at home. But I was liberal Joanna at school. While I might depart the house with a scarf on my head and my skirts pulled right down, the moment I was out of his sight, I would snatch off the scarf and roll my skirt up from the waistline until I achieved a fashionable length.

Teenage Joanna in conservative Islamic dress at the demand of her brother Sa'ad.

Joanna at her first job, at the travel agency in Baghdad, shortly before Sarbast proposed.

College student Joanna (second from left) attending a lecture at Baghdad University.

Only a few months before Sa'ad was sent to the military, we had seriously clashed. In fact, he was so angry with me that I had to flee our home and live with Alia for several weeks.

That unsettling incident occurred when I won a high honor at school, placing second in all of Iraq in a French-language competition. The Iraqi government and the French Ministry of Education awarded the first- and second-place winners an all-expense-paid trip to France.

Never had I been so excited. I had never traveled outside of Iraq. But Sa'ad, as head of the household, forbade it, saying, "No, Joanna is too young. No females should travel without a guardian."

I could not believe Sa'ad's decision. My brother was telling me that I could *not* go to France! I was furious. I yelled, cried, and created a commotion. I had worked hard for years to maintain high grades. I deserved my award.

Mother felt so badly for me that she and Alia eventually conspired to let me go after all and that Sa'ad would be told I was at Alia's house.

I left for France on schedule, while Sa'ad didn't question my absence because he thought I was at Alia's. I loved everything about France: the beauty of the country, the people, the history, and the language. The pleasure of that journey will forever be etched in my mind and heart. But my lie was soon revealed to Sa'ad in the most bizarre manner.

Before leaving Iraq, we winners were told to pack an ethnic costume. After arriving in Paris, I was photographed in my Kurdish traditional dress. As fate would have it, it was my photo that was reproduced on the front page of several Iraqi newspapers on the very day I arrived back in Baghdad. But I knew that like most Iraqis, Sa'ad rarely read the local newspapers, for nothing was as boring as newspapers forced to print government propaganda. So I prayed for the best.

Mother, Muna, and other family members and friends were forewarned to hide that particular edition from Sa'ad's view. But it was as if God himself were conspiring against me.

On that very day, Sa'ad went for his usual afternoon swim in the Tigris and then lay on the bank to take a brief rest. Somehow, the front page of the paper came spinning down the street in the wind and actually came to rest on his face! He nonchalantly lifted the paper, opened his eyes, and what did what did he see? There on the front page was his younger sister, Joanna, proudly displaying her Kurdish traditional dress in Paris, France!

Sa'ad jumped to his feet. He was so agitated that he forgot to put on his trousers, startling bystanders as he raced home in his swimming trunks. He roared into the house, banging the front door and waving that newspaper.

I had arrived home only hours earlier. I froze, staring in terror at the expression on his face. I had the good sense to flee, calling out for Mother, who was in the kitchen. Sa'ad raced after me.

Mother and Muna came to my rescue and intervened, the two of them leaping between the two of us, stopping Sa'ad from committing an act he might later regret. It was the greatest bedlam. Sa'ad was trying to strike me, I was screaming, Muna was crying, and Mother was screeching for Sa'ad to leave me alone. I was surprised our neighbors didn't call the police.

Mother yelled, "Joanna! Run! Go to Alia!"

While they held back Sa'ad, I dashed to catch a bus and made my way to my sister's house.

Thankfully, Ra'ad had a more modern attitude when it came to women. He took my side, and Sa'ad finally calmed down, at least on the exterior, because he would never go against his older brother.

But only a short time later, Sa'ad was in a trench, facing an army of warriors wishing to kill him. All old arguments were forgotten. I loved my brother and would have accepted his infuriating bossiness if only he would come back to us alive.

After the Iranian planes finally departed from Baghdad airspace, we turned on the television to see grim-faced news broadcasters shouting their rage about those Iranian villains: "The criminals have been chased from Iraqi airspace, but we promise, every Iraqi will make sacrifices to bury our enemies!"

As I listened to their senseless war babble, I knew that Iran was not the enemy I feared most. Our Baathist government had been so brutal from its first day in power that it was a spiritually dead movement, but no one yet dared acknowledge that truth, other than the Kurds.

I believe that history will one day show that no group in Iraq fought more stubbornly against the Baathists than the Kurds. We never gave up.

In that moment, however, my main concern was for us all to survive that terrible time. I knew that other men in my family were at risk of joining my brother in the trenches.

Ra'ad had graduated as an engineer from the Baghdad University of Technology. He was twenty-six years old and not yet married, but he was running a prosperous business. He could be conscripted any day. Hady, Alia's husband, was forty-three years old and the father of three young sons, but he, too, would be considered young enough to fight. And Sarbast? He was twenty-two years old with only one more year of engineering school. Thankfully, his family had pushed for him to pursue his degree, telling him that one war or another would always be waiting for him in Kurdistan. So Sarbast had remained in Baghdad.

Our government assured its citizens that the war would last no longer than another month and that college students *would* receive a student exemption and be allowed to graduate. But no one knew when this policy might change.

I knew in my heart what Sarbast's reaction would be to a military call up. He was a man who would fight to the last for his own ideals. But he hated those Baathists too much to go to war on their behalf. If pushed to join the Iraqi military, he would take to the mountains at his first opportunity to join the Peshmerga.

Exhausted from the day's trauma, we soon retired, but I could not sleep. My thoughts were dominated by Sarbast despite the fact nothing between us had changed. Although I could not match my mother or my sisters in beauty, I had finally left my childhood behind. I was eighteen years old and had developed into a woman whom many people found attractive. I was tall and slim with thick black hair and had an interesting face that Sarbast still found beautiful to sketch. Despite my physical changes, though, he remained distantly friendly and had never once broached the topic of love.

Sadly, I could never tell him of my feelings. Although I struggled against many things in my conservative culture, I could never make the first move. Such an action on my part would ruin my reputation forever. And so I waited.

Thankfully, I did have some memories to cherish. It was true that Sarbast once told Alia that I "motivated him," that my pretty face and lively manner tempted him to pick up his sketching pen. It was true that Sarbast often drew me into political discussions, finally understanding that I shared his love of Kurdistan. It was true that we spent treasured moments together discussing books on various topics, for at his behest, I had become an avid reader. It was true that I witnessed a flash of pleasure in his eyes when he learned I had been accepted and had enrolled in agricultural engineering school.

It was true that even after years of unrequited love I still felt the same about the man.

Alia believed the situation to be hopeless, admonishing me, "Joanna! You have marked yourself! Marked yourself as a woman with a heart to be broken. No good can come from this."

It was easy for her to say. My lucky sister was married to a man who worshipped her.

10

The Trenches

AHWAZ BATTLEFIELD
Spring 1981

Ghastly screams woke me in the middle of the night. I was so startled that it took me a few moments to comprehend that the screams were coming from Muna. Muna's bouts of depression rarely left her in those days. Her mental health had been noticeably deteriorating since the start of the war the previous year.

I jumped from bed to meet up with Mother at Muna's bedside.

Mother pulled Muna's head into her arms to soothe her, but my sister could not stop shrieking, calling out for her twin, "Sa'ad!" Her hysteria increased until she cried out, "Sa'ad can't breathe! Sa'ad is suffocating!"

A chill ran through me.

Mother was visibly shaken. She cautioned Muna, "*Na! Na!* You had a bad dream, Muna. *Na! Na!* Sa'ad is not suffocating."

Nothing calmed my sister. She trembled, wept, and repeatedly called out, "Sa'ad! Sa'ad!"

Her hysteria continued throughout the night until I began to think she was going insane from grief.

Muna was imbued with an uncanny "twin connection" to her brother. She had always felt his joys and sorrows as strongly as if they were her own. Since Sa'ad had gone to war, Muna had suffered so dreadfully I often reflected that she might go to the front and climb in those trenches with him. I felt so sorry for poor Muna.

Morning finally came and Muna slept at last.

I paced back and forth from my room to Muna's bedside, silently watching her chest rise and fall, reassuring myself that she was still breathing. I stood beside her quietly, lifting a few locks of her loosely scattered hair and letting them slip through my fingers, thinking about my sister and admiring her beauty. Already twenty-three years old, Muna was still a delicate beauty with her doll-like sweetness. Although her skin was pale like porcelain, it glowed softly, with just a hint of pink at her cheeks and on her lips. Muna had many physical charms, yet she was so fragile in spirit that I had obsessed over her well-being since I was a young girl.

In our culture, Muna was considered old to be unmarried, yet she was so pretty and sweet that she had received more marriage proposals than most. She was also known to be submissive, and our culture greatly valued obedient wives.

No proposals had been accepted because Muna was shy of marriage and wanted to remain living with Mother. But relatives and neighbors were beginning to talk, saying that if Muna did not marry soon, she would be a spinster and eventually be dependent on her siblings.

Even Mother was expressing doubt about the wisdom of allowing Muna to postpone marriage. But I was of the opinion that Muna should never marry.

From what I knew, while most Iraqi men were loving and kind during their courtship, they were often transformed into selfish and difficult, or even abusive, husbands soon after marriage. I did not want such an arrangement for our darling Muna. No one could love, protect, and pamper her as we did. There was so much to worry about.

Later that day we received a terrible shock. We heard that there was an atrocious battle at Ahwaz that produced thousands of casualties. My heart skipped a beat. The last letter we received from Sa'ad came from that place.

In a state of panic, Mother and I stared at each other. Mother's eyes told me that she and I were thinking the same thing. Had Muna's dream been a warning, a premonition? Was it true that Sa'ad had been suffocating? We scrambled to discover all we could about the battle at Ahwaz.

Built on the banks of the Karun River, Ahwaz was part of the oil-rich borderlands along the Shatt al Arab. That strip of territory had been contested between Iran and Iraq since Iraq was formed as a country. On the first day of the war, six Iraqi army divisions had attacked Ahwaz and several other cities across the border. Then they quickly pushed inland and occupied over a thousand kilometers of Iranian territory. After those first few victorious days for Iraq, though, there had been a stalemate. Neither side had been able to achieve a decisive military breakthrough.

That was why Sa'ad lived in a trench. Thousands upon thousands of young Iranian and Iraqi men were crouching in parallel trenches, waiting to kill one another.

Human life had become cheap to our government. As a matter of fact, families were paid off for their dead. Saddam Hussein decreed that a life was worth two months' salary and a pension, as well as a plot of free land and a television set. Later, as the war continued, Saddam increased the payoff to include a Toyota and a $15,000 cash payment.

But as poor as we were, we had no desire for any of those benefits. We only wanted our Sa'ad back.

But had his luck run out? He had survived that mud hell for six months while many of his friends had perished before his eyes.

Sa'ad was a frequent letter writer, but all communication from him had lately ceased. We had not received a letter in several weeks.

His silence followed by Muna's vivid nightmare and the news of a terrible battle had alarmed everyone in our family. Had Muna's nightmare really been telepathy?

When Ra'ad was summoned to the Al-Rasheed Military Hospital where military casualties were taken, I nearly collapsed. The family gathered to wait nervously at Alia's house.

After a miserably long interval, Ra'ad returned with bad news, good news, and amazing news. The bad news was that Sa'ad was a patient at the hospital and was in serious condition, having nearly died in the trenches. The good news was that Sa'ad would live. The amazing news was that Muna's dream had been, in fact, telepathy.

As Ra'ad related Sa'ad's story to us, his smooth pale hands moved from side to side. "The frontline battle at Ahwaz became so intense that Sa'ad could not abandon his trench, not even for a call of nature. His boots, soaked from the muddy trenches, began dissolving on his feet. His toilet was a metal milk box. His food supply was depleted.

"During one intense bombing, a good friend of his who was squatting only inches away received a direct hit. He was decapitated. The shells were falling so heavily that no one in the trench could risk raising their heads to shove the dead body from the trench. Sa'ad lived shoulder to shoulder with a decomposing corpse for many days.

"After nearly a week of this horror, everyone in the trench was dead except Sa'ad. He alone was alive. There was no holding the Iranian soldiers back. Sa'ad was startled to hear Farsi being spoken by enemy soldiers close to his position. One of the Iranian officers ordered his men to kill every Iraqi soldier they saw.

"Sa'ad realized he was cut off, accidentally left behind the enemy lines, an enemy who had resolved not to take prisoners.

"Sa'ad closed his eyes and crumpled into a distorted position, tricking his Iranian enemies into believing him dead. Luckily, the Iranian soldiers only gave his trench a cursory glance before rushing past in pursuit of fleeing Iraqi soldiers. He jumped from his trench to escape, but then saw human movement at his back.

"Escape was impossible. There was no option but to hide.

"Tall pyramids of dead bodies caught his attention. Slain Iraqi soldiers had been piled into heaps. Sa'ad made a quick decision to take cover under the decomposing bodies."

My thoughts flashed back to the night Muna woke us, screaming that Ra'ad could not breathe.

"I told Sa'ad something of Muna's nightmare. Sa'ad confirmed to me that he had fought for breath, fearing he was going to suffocate."

At his words, Mother and I cried out simultaneously. I gasped, holding my hand to my throat, feeling myself suffocating as well. *Never* would I understand the eerie link between the twins!

"Sa'ad said he would have died there, underneath those corpses, and we would have never known his exact fate but for our soldiers fighting desperately to retake the territory they had just lost. By the time Iraqis reached his position, however, Sa'ad was so weakened he was unable to make his presence known.

"After a time, bodies were pulled from the mound to be buried. An alert Iraqi soldier noticed a slight movement. It was Sa'ad, struggling to breathe. He was pulled free, seconds away from being dumped into a mass grave. An ambulance took him from the battlefield to be transported back to Baghdad and the Al-Rasheed Hospital."

We learned from the doctors that Sa'ad's health had been severely compromised. Upon receipt of Sa'ad's medical report, the Iraqi army released him from further duty. While relieved that Sa'ad would not be returning to the trenches, we had the worry he might die young.

Before we could fully absorb that troubling information, however, further bad news broke.

Now Ra'ad was our center of concern. He had received orders to report for a military physical examination.

11

Ra'ad Leaves Us

BAGHDAD
1982–1983

My hands trembled as I packed my suitcase. Ra'ad, Mother, Muna, and I were leaving Baghdad for Europe. Our upcoming trip could prove to be our undoing.

The rising tempo of the war with Iran had increased Iraq's internal instability. Iraqis were forbidden to travel outside the country. But the country was so corrupt that a generous bribe paid to the appropriate official temporarily loosened the restriction on our family. Most Iraqis wanted to flee our dangerous land but could not, so our approaching "holiday" created envy and suspicion in the minds of our neighbors and friends.

Our skeptical neighbors and friends were right. Indeed, we were *not* going on vacation as we had claimed during our interview with security forces. We were traveling for an illegal purpose. And if our plan was discovered and we were apprehended while departing the country, we could be executed.

Ra'ad was fleeing Iraq, possibly never to return. My brother had made plans to seek a new life in Europe. That new life of his required a certain amount of money. Iraqi law allowed each family member making the trip to take out the equivalent of 1,500 U.S.

dollars each. With four travelers, Ra'ad would have 6,000 U.S. dollars to live on until he could find work or gain permission to begin schooling.

There was to be nothing pleasurable about our nerve-racking voyage. We would endure a tiring flight, disembark in Europe, pass Ra'ad the cash we were transporting, and then return to Iraq to face potential problems with Iraqi security.

How would we explain our abrupt return without one of our traveling party? Yet despite the danger to ourselves, we were all willing to take any chance to help Ra'ad escape Iraq.

There were two good reasons my brother was fleeing Iraq. The most urgent was to do with the war.

When Ra'ad reported to the military, he had made known his desire to be a pilot. He had heard enough about the trenches from Sa'ad to avoid being a foot soldier. During his medical exam, however, an undiscovered problem with his spine was revealed. He received a medical exemption that distressed him while his family rejoiced.

But the danger had not passed so easily. As the war ground on, soldiers became scarce. Young men previously considered unfit for service were soon called up. Unable to qualify as a pilot, we knew that our fastidious Ra'ad would eventually be sent to the front to live in a muddy dugout to face hordes of enemy soldiers.

Imagine our surprise to learn that many of our Iranian enemies were extremely young and advanced into battle without traditional firearms. Their only weapons were of a spiritual kind: keys to paradise draped around their slender necks.

We could not help but feel sorry for those pretend soldiers, some as young as nine years old, children who had been wrenched from their mothers' arms to be recklessly thrown at the battlefront. There they were gutted by machine-gun fire or marched through minefields, their small bodies used as cannon fodder and shredded into raw meat.

As cruel as our government was, at least it did not stoop so low as to send young children into battle. Thankfully, we Iraqis did not live that particular horror.

The second reason Ra'ad wanted to leave was his business. After graduating from college Ra'ad taught at the university for one year. He then went into partnership with four former college classmates to set up a cable company in the city of Ramadi, a city in central Iraq, about 100 kilometers west of Baghdad. My brother had learned his organizational skills from our father, who was European trained, so Ra'ad impressed his partners by winning many contracts. It was rare for anyone to succeed in Iraq without influence from one of Saddam's cronies, but my brother and his partners accomplished the impossible, at least in the beginning.

When his four partners were drafted and sent off to the front, their fathers became involved in the business and proved themselves unworthy of their honest sons. Soon, they began plotting to steal Ra'ad's shares. When Ra'ad refused to relinquish what was his, his new partners went to Saddam Hussein's notorious uncle, Khairullah Tulfah. After Saddam rose to his high position, Khairullah used his nephew's position as protection to rob and murder Iraqis. Khairullah did not ask nicely. Ra'ad was instructed to sign over his shares or have them taken by force. Ra'ad was made to understand that to refuse would win him a prison sentence or even execution.

I will never forget that day when Ra'ad came home in despair and doubt as to how he might save what was rightfully his. He paced along the banks of the Tigris, a place he had loved best in all of Baghdad, and found that he lost his belief in his country. Iraq was no longer a place for a principled man. He eventually made the heartbreaking decision to leave Iraq, possibly forever.

Our family unit had begun to splinter. After losing my father and nearly losing Sa'ad, I did not want to lose Ra'ad as well. I feared it was my destiny to lose all the men whom I loved.

Even Sarbast was gone. I had not seen him in over a year, since he had fled north to Kurdistan. Just as I had feared, the college graduate was summoned for his military physical and was found to be in perfect health. There would be no medical exemption for Sarbast.

While he was unable to avoid doing his military training, *nothing* could force him to join the ranks of his hated enemies on the battlefield. He slipped from his army unit to flee to Kurdistan. There he joined the Patriotic Union of Kurdistan (PUK), an organization formed by Jalal Talabani, a former member of the Kurdistan Democratic Party (KDP), the first political organization for the Kurdish Peshmerga.

But he did leave me with one sweet memory that sustained me during the forlorn days of his absence.

Before departing Baghdad, Sarbast startled me with a request. Passing me in Alia's hallway, he called me aside. The always solemn Sarbast was surprisingly jovial, as though he didn't have a care in the world, despite the fact he would soon be a fugitive from the government in Baghdad and putting himself and his family in danger. But his brave family encouraged Sarbast, as well as his brothers, to battle against Saddam and was willing to lose everything to further the Kurdish cause.

But on that particular morning Sarbast was as happy as a child.

"Joanna," he murmured softly, "I must leave very soon. Before I go, though, I must tend to some business at the university. Would you go with me?"

His eyes were shining large and dark, and he had a playful smile on his face. His dark hair was long for a man, with those winsome curls looking wild, as though he had just run through a strong wind.

I stared for a time without answering, one hand guarding the other to keep from pulling on those curls. This was too good to be true, I thought, as a shiver of anticipation shot from my head to my toes. I was certain that Sarbast was finally going to open the topic of marriage.

"Yes! Yes, of course," I agreed.

Together and alone after years of girlish longing, that magical day unfolded as the fantasy I had dreamed about for many years. We laughed as we ran for one of the many street buses. While riding to the university he bent forward, peering from the bus windows, packing the moment with his sharp observations and opening my eyes to the vitality of Baghdad street life. Never had I noticed the absurdities in the gallery of contrasting Baghdadi characters: the portly street merchants hiding their money, the harried housewives shrieking at their disobedient children, the young boys balancing their fat bundles, the shy lovers giving their discreet signals, the old women with astonishingly round bodies, or the elderly men sitting in the heat, opening and closing their mouths like the gasping *masgouf* fish that was such a delicacy at special Baghdad riverbank cafés.

Sarbast made me laugh until tears rolled down my face, our mirth creating a camaraderie with strangers on the bus who gazed at us with affection. They probably thought that we were newly-weds just returned from our honeymoon.

Sarbast's every action made me joyful, and I was smiling even as I waited alone while he tended to his final business at the university. On our way back to Alia's house, we were both looking to prolong the day, so we slipped into a bookstore. We paused in front of the fiction section, my fingers lightly brushing the spines of books, my eyes on him. His voice was so seductive and sweet that when he disclosed that he liked my hair long and loose I believed for a breathtaking moment that he had fallen in love with me.

Baghdad was not a place where one might speak openly, so he drew close and whispered, his face so near that I had never seen him so clearly, his gaze thoughtful and the full fire of life in his eyes directed at me. I heard him whisper that he had no fear of dying, yet he wanted to live, to work, to have a comfortable home, to know what it was to marry a beautiful woman, and to hold a son in his arms.

If such a thing as complete happiness exists, I was living it.

Breathless, I leaned in closer, waiting to hear words that I was sure were forthcoming. Surely he was about to say that he could not live without me.

Of course, my answer would be yes. Already my fevered imagination had me saying good-bye and packing a small bag and fleeing Baghdad with him to Kurdistan. I would go with him to live in a Peshmerga village. I would support this man in whatever it was he needed to do.

I smiled so widely that he paused in his musings, but I encouraged him, "Go on. Go on."

Admittedly, ours was not the usual method for becoming engaged in our culture. But our family connections, I believed, made everything less complicated. Unlike most women, I had years of knowing Sarbast behind me. I had already discovered that I loved him.

I kept waiting for the magic words. I waited. And I waited.

Finally, Sarbast seemed to grow weary of talking. Nodding toward the door that led to the street, he said, "We must go. It is getting late."

In a sort of mild insanity, I followed him from the store, unsure what had just happened, so anxious that I almost blurted that I loved him, that I could not bear for him to leave Baghdad without me, that I wanted to marry him.

But I could say nothing. To keep my honor intact, I knew that I had to restrain myself. Although Kurdish girls can be bold in many things, when it comes to love, we cannot push ourselves forward.

I had done all I could do to let Sarbast know my feelings. I had spent the day with him. I had listened intently to his every word. I had smiled. I had laughed. A Kurdish girl could do no more.

My thoughts were swirling. In a last desperate hope, I concluded that Sarbast might be planning to abduct me instead, a not uncommon method to speed up the process of marriage. My spirit soared anew with that expectation.

I considered telling Sarbast that he did not have to go to the trouble of abducting me. I would go willingly, if only he would ask. But I didn't, and he didn't.

Instead, his mood was subdued, almost surly, on the return bus trip. What had happened? Nothing I could say or do could shake his altered mood. He stared at everything but me.

What was he thinking? Had he believed himself in love but during our outing concluded that he did not love me after all, that I was less worthy than he had first believed?

I slumped forward, my chin in my hand, in a special kind of uncertain agony. My thoughts tumbled, one over the other. He was leaving the following day. I might never see him again.

He must ask me to marry him. He must! But he didn't.

In the silent hours of the night, my anxious heart drove away sleep. The next morning Sarbast left Baghdad after saying a breezy, unfeeling good-bye.

I did not see him after that. I did not even receive any letters from him. During that time there was sporadic but vicious fighting between the Peshmerga and the Iraqi army. I had no way of knowing if Sarbast was alive or dead. Nevertheless, my love for him never waned.

12

The End of Hope

BAGHDAD
1984

At least all had ended well with regard to Ra'ad and his escape from Iraq. None of us was arrested on our return from Europe, only forty-eight hours later, without him. Iraq was in such turmoil after four years of war that our risky escapade was unobserved. We were lucky, for one of the few times in our lives.

In only one short year, Ra'ad was prospering in Switzerland. He was employed by a prestigious company and was on his way to attaining Swiss residency. His meticulousness, so like our father's, perfectly suited the Swiss, who everyone knows are famous for their precision.

Although I missed Ra'ad, I finally realized it had been best for him to leave our mangled country. The continuing military stalemate meant that no one knew for certain who would be the ultimate victor. The Americans had supported Saddam within the first year of the war, mostly due to U.S. outrage and bitterness over the taking of American hostages in Iran. Many Iraqis took comfort from their belief that the Americans would never allow the Iranians to win. But the war raged on.

Sarbast was still alive, but he had slashed my heart into pieces.

My hope that we would one day marry and live the warrior life and raise children together had finally died. Everything with Sarbast had unwound quickly and unexpectedly.

I was still in college, and even after more than a year of not seeing Sarbast, I had never stopped mourning his absence. My love for him endured, despite the fact that during my college years my family had received more than one marriage proposal on my behalf. The men were handsome, pleasant enough, and pledged prosperous futures, but to the alarm of my family, I turned each suitor down.

Everyone but Alia and Muna was mystified by my stubborn refusals. Only my two sisters were privy to my secret, that it was impossible for me to marry one man while in love with another. Defying the marriage customs of my country and culture, I spent my college years waiting.

And then one afternoon I arrived at Alia's house and there he was!

It was clear from his physical appearance that life in the mountains had been challenging. He was as handsome as I remembered, but he was thin, and he had deep lines around his eyes and mouth.

But I was so happy to see him that I couldn't stop smiling. My attraction for him was as strong as ever.

I quickly noted that Sarbast had undergone other changes. His personality was more subdued. He was friendly enough, but not too friendly, vaguely claiming that he was in Baghdad for political reasons.

During our long war with Iran, many Kurds had linked with the Iranian fighters, so detesting our own Iraqi government that they preferred the Iranians, a people Iraqis were fighting against for their very survival. Saddam Hussein found the situation humiliating and unbearable. Trying to find a settlement with the Kurds to prevent them from allying themselves with the Iranians, Saddam had authorized a rare cease-fire with the Kurds in late 1983 that lasted through most of 1984. During that cease-fire, Peshmerga fighters received amnesty, which meant they could leave the mountains and travel into the cities. That was why Sarbast was able to visit.

Despite his offhand manner, I was certain that Sarbast had traveled to Baghdad for only one purpose: to come for me. Obsessed with wringing a marriage proposal out of him, I made my plans.

I would not allow Sarbast to leave Baghdad without a serious conversation as to our future. I was nearly twenty-two years old and set to graduate from university. I was ready to marry, but only if my husband could be one particular man. Of the 4,770,104,443 people living in the world in 1984, of whom nearly half were men, only *he* would do.

First, I tried to draw him into conversation, asking to hear about his fighting adventures, but Sarbast remained oddly remote. Love covers many faults, so I explained away his reluctance to speak by assuming his fighter's life was so harsh that he could not speak of it.

One afternoon when he settled at Alia's table with a cup of tea, I saw my opportunity. I joined him without an invitation and probed, "Sarbast, if this peace process fails, will you go back to the north?"

Reserved, he responded, "Yes."

There was a long silence.

He drank his tea and stared at his hands, which to my dismay looked grimy with numerous scratches. What kind of work had he been doing with those beautiful hands?

Looking away, I reminded myself not to get distracted. I took a deep breath. The moment had come. I would say anything to get what I wanted.

I declared, "I want to go, too. I can fight. I *want* to fight." Although I knew that throughout Kurdish history only Turkish women, not Iraqi women, had fought side by side with their men, I had decided that given the chance, I would learn to shoot a firearm and volunteer to carry messages, that I would make myself useful.

Sarbast's curls lightly lifted when he threw back his head and laughed. When he saw that I was serious, he gestured with his index finger and said, "You don't know what you are saying, Joanna. It is a dangerous life. Every moment we are running to a fight, evading the soldiers, or hiding from the Jahsh. Death is all around us. Already I have lost good friends."

I knew the Jahsh were Kurdish turncoats, men who, to avoid Iraqi military service, accepted bribes from Baghdad to spy on their Kurdish brothers. Those were the most contemptible Kurds, causing the capture and deaths of many of our fighters as well as civilian sympathizers.

I refused to give up easily. "Sarbast, ever since I was a little girl I knew I would one day support the Peshmerga."

His words were edged with irritation. "*Na. Na*, Joanna. It is not a fit life for you. You are a city girl, accustomed to all of this." He lightly gestured at the modern conveniences in Alia's Baghdad home. "The mountain life means nothing but sacrifice. Listen," he said, "I eat the same food every day. *Bad* food, I might add. I often sleep in the open, in the cold, without a blanket. Planes drop bombs every day. There is always shelling. We are often wounded. Doctors have been forbidden to treat us. Many people die from treatable injuries because we have so few doctors."

When he tilted closer to make a stronger point, it took my full power to keep my hands steady on the table. I was fighting a desire to caress his face.

"Joanna," he admonished, his voice rising to nearly a shout, "this is the simple truth: joining the Peshmerga means that many bad men do everything in their power to *kill* you."

"I do not care," I retorted stubbornly, sensing I was losing our argument and that soon he would be gone and once again I would go back to that yawning void of unbearable waiting. "I do *not* care!" I repeated, banging my fist on the table.

"*Na*," he said, "*enough!*" before thrusting his chair back and stomping to the sink to fling free the last drops of tea. He set the cup down so vigorously that it cracked. He left the room without even glancing back at me.

As I had feared, the cease-fire fell through. The Kurds felt they were dealing with a leader so beset with problems that they believed Saddam would soon be unseated. There was no reason to give in to his demands. He would soon be gone. Confident of Saddam's removal, Kurdish leaders tucked their victory plans in their pockets and waited.

Sarbast rushed out of Baghdad to return to the fighting. He failed to bid me good-bye.

I returned home to Mother. My love for Sarbast was a form of madness. Despite his hurtful behavior, I didn't know how to *stop* loving him.

Three days later, Alia left her three sons in the care of a trusted neighbor and traveled across the city by bus to see me. I was home alone, for Mother was at the vegetable market and Muna was visiting a friend.

The television was blaring in the background as I ironed a dress for a college class the following day, but I was not concentrating on the broadcast. Baghdad television was unbearably repetitive in those days, for all the programs focused only on the war and Saddam Hussein. I do recall that the show was a repeat of a speech by Saddam calling for Iraqi soldiers to "cut off the heads of the Iranians." He was sternly advising our soldiers to "strike as powerfully as they could because the necks they were striking were collaborators with the lunatic Khomeini." He called our boys "Allah's swords on Earth."

I glanced up at the television screen to see Saddam sitting behind a desk. How I hated that man. He was the reason Ra'ad was no longer with us. He was the reason Sa'ad still suffered from health problems. He was the reason Sarbast was living the Peshmerga life, so far away from me.

Many times I prayed that Saddam Hussein would ease our situation by dying. I stopped ironing to study his image for a few moments. Unfortunately, our persevering dictator looked a picture of perfect health.

That's when Alia came into the house without knocking.

I smiled a greeting, but my smile quickly faded. The grim expression on my sister's face gave me a fright. Worst-case scenarios flashed through my mind.

Sarbast! Was Sarbast dead?

"Joanna. Sit," Alia told me as she pushed me backward until the backs of my legs were brushing the sofa. She gave a gentle push on my shoulders. I sat.

"Joanna. Sarbast . . ." My sister was finding it difficult to deliver the message.

I couldn't take the uncertainty another moment longer. I shrieked, "Is Sarbast dead?"

"Dead? No. Oh, no. He is alive." Alia paused, looking thoughtfully at me. "Very much alive, in fact."

"Is he injured, then?"

"No, Joanna."

Alia bent forward and grabbed my upper arms in her hands and looked straight at me, her unwelcome words tumbling forth. "Joanna, listen to me. Sarbast has asked someone else to marry him."

I tilted my head to the side. Surely I had misheard.

"What did you say?"

"That is the reason Sarbast came to Baghdad. He came to ask another woman to marry him."

"What?"

"Sarbast wants to get married, Joanna, but not to *you*."

I stuttered, "Who?"

"You do not know her, darling. She was with him in class, at the university."

"Her name?"

"Joanna, I do not know her name. I only know that he asked a former classmate, a Kurdish girl, to marry him."

My mind was in such a whirl that I could hardly comprehend what Alia was telling me.

"Joanna? Are you all right?"

I was *not* all right! I tried to get up, but my legs appeared to be tangled.

Alia hugged me, saying, "Perhaps this is best. Since the moment you met him, Sarbast has been a torment. Now you know it was not God's plan for you two to be together. You can choose another now."

I muttered, "Sarbast *is* dead, in a way."

Ali pulled back to look at me, an anxious smile shadowing her face, "You are very beautiful, Joanna. How many marriage proposals have you turned down, now? Five? Ten?"

Tears were falling one after the other, blurring my sight. But I found the strength to pull myself to a standing position, swinging my shoulders and slinging Alia until she turned me loose. I ran out the front door and down the street.

I stopped running when I reached the banks of the Tigris. I threw myself down on the grassy knoll. Without bothering to wipe away my tears, I stared at the rippling green waters of the Tigris as it made its tortuous way through a tortured city. A group of young teenage boys were out for their daily swim. When they looked at me with curiosity, I turned away.

Sarbast was going to marry another. He did not want to marry me. He had never wanted to marry me. I meant nothing to him. I had *never* meant anything to him. That's why he was so distant when he was last in Baghdad. He was involved with her, even as I was pushing myself at him.

I cringed in shame, remembering that day in the kitchen when I had practically asked him to marry me.

Who was this woman he loved? How did she capture his heart? When had he fallen in love with her when he could have me?

I felt a flash of anger. He was supposed to be studying while at the university. So now I knew. He had really gone there to meet potential brides!

I was filled with the wildest jealousy. Who was she? Who was she? Who was she? Did she love him?

I knew one thing for certain. Whoever she was, she would never love Sarbast as I loved him. She would never know him as I knew him. Over the years, I had studied him, his every mood, his every dream. Sometimes, when he started a sentence, I silently finished it. He was a man memorized. By me!

I slumped forward, my head on my knees. I groaned. He didn't love me! He loved another. I sat up, utterly still, destroyed.

I felt overwhelmingly lonely, even with the sounds and sights of Baghdad city life carrying on all around me.

An old woman shuffled by with a puckered face. She glared at me with disapproval, and I could read her mind: a young woman alone on the riverbank is surely looking for mischief. I glared back at her, my palms itching with the desire to jump up and slap her for her unfounded suspicions. Young men walked past the river, their white dishdashas flapping in the breeze. I was furious that they were not at the front, fighting for their country. Donkey drivers noisily urged on their overloaded beasts. I wanted them arrested for mistreating those poor animals. A group of schoolgirls filed past like ducklings, their school uniforms still fresh even after a day of school. They glanced shyly at the cute boys in the river, but turned their heads and giggled when the boys took an interest.

Those young girls were fools, just like me! I hated everyone in my sight.

Only when total darkness threatened and the Tigris reflected the yellow of the moon did I have the strength to move. I wearily pushed myself up from the bank and slowly retraced my steps.

Walking into the house, I found Mother, Alia, and Muna waiting anxiously.

Alia had informed Mother, I presumed. She had told Mother that her youngest daughter had been in love with a man who did not love her in return.

I was a woman scorned. But it no longer mattered.

I fleetingly glanced at the three women who loved me most in the world. "I cannot discuss this matter today," I whispered as I glided past, holding my finger to my lips. Over Alia's disappointed cries and Mother's objections, I retired to my room, closing and bracing the door with a heavy metal trunk. I stood staring at my reflection in the mirror.

I looked extremely pale, as white as Muna, something I had always yearned for. But while her porcelain white face was lovely, my white face had a mottled, unhealthy appearance. There was nothing of beauty reflected in that mirror.

Still, I stared at my pitiful image, knowing that everything was lost. I had no choice, I must bear the unbearable. The irrefutable fact was that Sarbast had asked another woman to marry him. My hopes and dreams of winning Sarbast's love had been the driving force of my life since I was fifteen years old, seven years ago.

I could lose nothing more.

13

The Secret Police

For two years, nearly everything of my life was a perfect misery. Although I was a young woman of twenty-three years in excellent health, had graduated from university, and was the focus of attention of a number of young eligible bachelors, nothing led to happiness. In fact, I was so melancholy during those two years that there were times that I actually prayed for death.

The hellish war with Iran was unending. With each passing day, it grew worse. Our young men died in such shocking numbers that the entire country was saturated with coffins.

There were other losses that were almost as tragic. One of my favorite cousins from my father's side of the family, Uncle Othman's son Sadik Osman, was reported missing in battle. We feared he was a POW.

Iran claimed to have over 50,000 of our young men imprisoned in their dungeons, while we held fewer than 10,000 of their men. There was a reason the POW figures were so unbalanced. It was whispered that the Iranian soldiers refused to surrender, smiling ecstatically as they charged moving tanks with empty hands held to heaven, seeking certain death.

Hatred of President Saddam Hussein inspired so many enemies at home that attempts on his life became commonplace, motivating Iraqi security to turn the whole of Iraq into one tyrannical gulag. Nearly every Iraqi lived in terror of his or her government.

And in March 1985, Iran and Iraq unleashed the War of the Cities on civilians. Baghdad, Kirkuk, Basra, and corresponding Iranian cities were hit by bomb raids and by surface-to-surface missiles. Retaliation was the order of the day and we innocent civilians were trapped under angry skies raining death.

As far as Sarbast went, I was full of disappointment and anger. I knew that no woman could ever love him as I loved him.

By the sheerest chance, I had seen the object of Sarbast's desire, which produced added torment to my misery. This happened on an afternoon when I was at the university with one of my cousins. She did not know about my love for Sarbast, but knowing of Sarbast's connection to my sister Alia, she suddenly nudged my shoulder and motioned with her head. "There, Joanna, there is that girl Sarbast asked to marry him."

I snapped to attention. My rival was a great beauty. She had lovely fair skin and beautiful long blond hair, which was rare in our part of the world. I felt a rush of hatred.

I edged closer and was startled to hear her speaking. Her voice was so gruff and deep that my jaw dropped.

I had always heard that God does not bestow all blessings on one person, and that woman's grating voice was proof. Despite her blond beauty, all feminine appeal vanished at that moment. My jealousy was replaced with wonderment that Sarbast would find a woman with such an annoying voice attractive.

It was some time later that I heard that Sarbast's marriage proposal had been rebuffed after all that. The blond beauty had refused to marry him unless certain conditions were met. She had some unexpected demands for a Kurd. She had insisted that he give up the life of a Peshmerga. She had also demanded that he turn his back on Kurdistan. Lastly, he had to gain permission to leave Iraq and seek citizenship in a European country. Otherwise, her answer would be no.

I was not surprised that Sarbast refused her selfish ultimatums, for I knew that he would *never* turn his back on the Kurdish cause. The man I loved would never leave Kurdistan voluntarily.

Although my mood was lifted by the news, for I never pretended to wish them wedded bliss, neither did Sarbast's failed proposal revive my hopes of a life together. In fact, I was determined to push Sarbast forever from my mind. Finally, I really understood that he did not love me and that he had never loved me. Never again would I humiliate myself. Never!

I had graduated from college, but instead of accepting a job in my field of agricultural engineering, I worked at a travel agency. The work was sociable, suited to my gregarious personality, and paid well. I earned double the salary of an engineer. For the first time in my life, I had money of my own, although each payday I gave most of it to my mother for household expenses. With the war raging, goods were not only scarce but extremely costly.

My job was the lone pleasure in my life, at least for a time. With the war on, tourist travel was nonexistent. Iraqis were forbidden to leave the country unless on official government business. Instead, our offices were responsible for making travel arrangements for expatriate workers who came to Iraq to fill jobs vacated by our men who were busy making war.

Then one day I received a frightening summons.

Arriving at work one morning in mid-1986, my boss met me at the door, visibly traumatized. He motioned for me to enter his office, closed the door, and whispered his ominous message. "Joanna, you had visitors. From the secret police. You are to go to their offices tomorrow."

He stood in silence with his hand over his heart, shaking his head with worry. Finally he asked, "Do you have any idea what this is about?"

I shrugged. "No. I do not."

And I was speaking the truth. I had committed no crime. I did my job. I went home. I visited with family. Occasionally, I visited a girlfriend. Very occasionally I went with my family to the cinema.

I had not even been to Kurdistan for the past two summers. The northern area of Iraq had become a dangerous war zone. There were roadblocks at every corner, and we had heard that innocent Iraqis were hauled off to prison for just traveling into the area. Kurdistan was out of bounds.

That unwelcome news concerning the secret police gave me a jolt. I was half Kurd. Before the war with Iran, I had spent much time in the Kurdish north, an area considered the den of the government's most hated enemy. My brother had fled the country to live in Europe, never to return. Through Alia, I was connected to a man considered the most heinous criminal, a Peshmerga. All these things would look suspicious if held under a magnifying glass by the secret police.

I shuddered with fear and wanted to run away, but there was nowhere to hide. There was nothing to do but to appear the next day as summoned.

My poor boss was solicitous, so anxious for my safety that he volunteered to accompany me, something few Iraqis would do. Although he was a Baathist, I knew he was a member for the same reason so many other Iraqis belonged to the party: they had no choice. I would never allow him to put himself at risk on my behalf.

"No. I will be fine," I assured him, although I was not convinced.

I warned Alia and Hady of my unexpected directive in case I failed to return. Wanting to avoid worrying Mother, I told her nothing. If I were imprisoned, there would be ample time for her to become involved.

Everyone living in Iraq had heard horror stories of Saddam's prisons. Despite my Kurdish connections, I had luckily avoided any problems with security, but perhaps my luck had run out.

I could not sleep because my mind swam with thoughts as to what the morning would bring. Perhaps it was the last night I would enjoy the comforts of my own bed. After all, there were many Iraqis just as innocent as I, rotting in one of the many prisons scattered throughout the country.

In fact, there was a large diversity of prisons. There were prisons where Iraqis were confined to holes in the ground, such as the prison Ra'ad and Hady had experienced. There were the dreaded coffin prisons, where prisoners were locked in coffins with a single air hole and allowed out only one hour out of twenty-four. There were dank dungeons where prisoners never saw the sun. There were no good prisons in Iraq. Even ordinary prisons without the flair of bizarre confinements were a horror because of overcrowding.

At best, I would be in a narrow cell crammed together with too many other women. There would not be enough room to extend my arms or to stand up straight. I would be forced to sleep on a damp cement floor without bedding. Perhaps there would be a single toilet, perhaps not, and in that case the toilet was wherever I might find a space.

I lingered on the variety of tortures I might undergo, for I had heard of the electrical shocks, the hanging hooks, and the yanked-out fingernails. There were whispers of mirrored rooms where women were violated while their male relatives were forced to observe.

I shivered. What was going to happen to me? What had I done to draw their attention? I relived everything of my life during the past few months and I could think of nothing. I had not visited Kurdistan and I had received no communications from anyone in the north.

Morning came too quickly. With a heavy heart and puffy eyes, I took a taxicab and dutifully appeared at the Sadoun Security Headquarters.

My taxi driver was middle-aged and had a kindly face. His eyes squinted with worry when he asked if he might wait for me, expressing concern for my safety. He said that he had three daughters and would not allow any of them to go alone into that building.

I asked him to return in two hours, if possible. If I failed to appear, he agreed to go to Alia and Hady and tell them that I had been taken. That sweet man watched me until I was inside the security doors, his consideration reminding me that there were still decent Iraqis.

The stench of old sweat rose like a vapor from that building. It was the odor of fear, I supposed, wrung from the bodies of the innocent tortured.

Upon entering, I gave my name to a clerk who was sitting behind a large metal desk. He scrawled my name on a lined piece of paper held by an old clipboard. When the clerk's head lowered, I peeked at the list. There were many names above mine, yet I was the only person in the waiting area. Where had everyone else gone?

The clerk busied himself with a ringing phone. He grunted, pointed to a group of six wooden chairs, and told me to sit.

I did as I was told.

The recessed waiting area was grimy. In fact the entire interior was shabby. This, in a country that had the second largest known oil reserves in the world. Making war for six years had depleted

Iraq's treasury. All the oil money was being spent on tanks, planes, and bombs.

I sighed, looking around for anything of interest. Nothing surrounding me was attractive. The dark brown plaster on the walls was peeling. The light blue plastic on the chairs was splitting, and nasty tufts of stuffing were spiking out. There was a small wooden table with one chipped ashtray that spilled over with cigarette butts.

Practically everyone in Baghdad smoked. Who could think of a reason to quit while living in a country where death already beckoned from every direction? Not me!

I longed for a smoke. I had begun the habit shortly after Sarbast asked another woman to marry him. But it was a secret habit. No one in my family knew, although Alia and Mother had accused me of slipping smokes after sniffing my long hair, which unfortunately attracted the smell of tobacco smoke.

But it was not acceptable in Iraq for a respectable woman to smoke in a public place, so I had nothing to soothe my nerves. I only hoped I would not break down under questioning. I must not!

My interrogators would be bullies, ruling by fear. After all the stories I had heard from Ra'ad, Hady, Sarbast, and my Kurdish relatives, I knew that their greatest pleasure came from terrifying innocent people.

But no matter what they did or said, I promised myself to hang on to my composure. I was worried. I had always had problems controlling my sarcastic tongue. While friends and family joked about my sharp-witted disposition, I knew that the men in this building would gleefully snap my skinny neck.

I turned my thoughts to the reception clerk, wondering how he justified to himself working in such a place, trying to imagine whether his family was pleased with his station.

He was interesting to watch, though, with his air of self-importance. He was far too absorbed in his clerical duties to give a visitor a reassuring look, a kind act that would have cost him nothing.

Just then a small round man in a rumpled security uniform came into the room and called out my name. I took a deep cleansing breath, straightened my back, and followed him without a quiver, so anxious to get out of that dismal place that I was suddenly eager to get the process started.

I was ushered into a small, dimly lit room where two overweight men were perched side by side in chairs so close that I thought they might be welded together. There was a single chair placed in front of them. They didn't invite me to sit, but afraid that my trembling legs would give me away, I literally fell back into the chair.

The security officers were a striking contrast. The mustache on the man on the left was long and thick, while the hair on the other man's lip was sparse. The man with the bushy mustache was bald, while the other showed off a healthy, full head of black greased hair fashioned in a rather elaborate pompadour style reminiscent of Elvis Presley.

Under different circumstances, I would have asked him about that wild hair.

Judging by their brutish facades and place of work, I expected them to be ill mannered, but they were unpredictably soft spoken and polite.

The bald man opened the conversation haltingly. "Welcome. We know you are an al-Askari. Welcome."

Trying in vain to control my trembling lips, I smiled widely, as though my life was not in mortal danger, that instead I was a friendly acquaintance dropping by to invite their families to a celebration.

The man I named Elvis courteously asked, "How are you doing today?"

"I am good."

"Is your work satisfactory?"

"Yes. Of course."

Elvis opened a file he was holding in his hand. "Miss Askari, we have a report on you."

I was sitting so straight against the hard chair that my back began to ache. I shifted, crossing one leg over the other.

"This file says that you are working in the tourism area."

"Yes. That is true."

"But it says here that your specialty is engineering. You are a college graduate in agricultural engineering."

"Yes. That is true."

"It says here that you were an acceptable student."

"Yes. That is true."

"It says here that you are not working in your field of study. Is that true?"

"Yes. That is true."

"Tell us, Miss Askari, is there some reason you choose to work at a job where you routinely meet with foreigners? We are curious. Why would you spend years studying and then abandon your field?"

An image of Sarbast's face flashed in my mind. I could not tell these men the truth, that I made a stupid decision because I had fallen in love with a man who was now a Peshmerga. Surely I would be arrested and held as a hostage until Sarbast reported for an exchange. Then they would execute Sarbast.

I was angry with him, but not that angry.

I could not even confess a second truth, that soon after entering my first year at the university I had discovered that I hated my choice of majors. I preferred literature. But in Iraq, once a decision was made, there was no turning back.

Knowing that they were surely taping the interview, I willed myself to clear my mind, to think quickly, and, most important, not to show my fear. "It was a simple matter of salary. The pay in tourism is better. My father died when I was a teenager. My mother does not work. I am contributing to our household."

"I see." Elvis thumbed through my file. "It says here that you have a brother, one Sa'ad al-Askari, who supports the family. Is this true?"

"It is true that my brother is still at home. And it is true that he helps us. But he has serious medical problems. And he has a wife. He has other responsibilities. I am an adult. I must help out."

"Hmmm, you were born on May 13, 1962, is that correct?"

"Yes. That is correct."

"So, you are twenty-three years old, soon to be twenty-four years old, is that correct?"

"Yes. That is true."

"Tell us, Miss Askari, we are curious. Tell us, why are you still unmarried at your age?"

"I do not know."

Elvis exchanged a look of disbelief with his partner.

"You do not know?"

"Yes. No. Yes. That is true. I do not know why I am not married."

Elvis squinted his eyes and stared me down.

I cleared my throat and lowered my head to pretend to examine my skirt, taking a swipe at an imaginary speck on it.

"Are you a Kurd, Miss Askari?"

"My mother is a Kurd. My father was an Arab."

"Do you feel yourself Kurd? Do you feel yourself Arab? Or do you feel yourself to be both?"

Here we go, I thought. Once again, having any Kurdish blood puts a person under total suspicion.

"Yes. That is true."

"*What* is true?"

I lied. I have always felt myself a Kurd, but I knew the danger of the truth in this particular case.

"I feel myself to be both."

"Tell us, Miss Askari, why is it you never joined the Baath Party?"

Ah! This Elvis was smooth, slipping in one of the most vital questions of the day as though it was insignificant.

But I knew better. I had prepared my response, knowing any question about party membership would be crucial.

"I was too busy at home. My father was dead. My mother was struggling. My sister was ill. My brother was at the front at the time when the war had gone to the trenches. I had no time for anything but school and home. I did not want to be a lazy party member, unable to participate fully. I would have been of no advantage to the party."

"Tell us, Miss Askari, it says here that your best friend at the university, a young lady by the name of Jenan, was a very active party member. Is that true?"

"Yes. That is true."

Of course, I couldn't tell them that Jenan had loathed the Baath Party, that she had joined only because she was unlucky to be pressured on a day when she didn't have a good excuse on the tip of her tongue. My dear friend was trapped and ended up being one of the thousands of reluctant card-carrying members.

Jenan and I had giggled about those Baathists, their silly "Baathist speech," their self-importance, their suspicious minds, their stiff mannerisms, their arrogant certainty that they had the right to hassle other students.

When the Baathist students assigned a member to bully me into joining, Jenan volunteered. Many afternoons after school she would catch me in the hallways and whisper, "Let's go for a coffee, Joanna. I'm supposed to bully you today."

And we would go for our coffee. While relaxing, we would discuss clothes, marriage, and relatives but with our faces posed into serious expressions, knowing that somewhere in that coffee shop there was an informer, another member appointed to watch Jenan to make certain she had indeed spent ample time recruiting me. At the next Baathist meeting, Jenan would dutifully report that I had two sick family members and had to go straight home from class to work in the garden to grow vegetables until dark and afterward had time only for my lessons. For sure, I wanted nothing more than to join the Baath Party and would do so at the first opportunity.

And so our deceptive game persisted all the way through the university.

Thanks to Jenan, I never did have to join those unpleasant Baathists.

"Miss Askari, you are working in a sensitive field with visitors to our country. You *must* join the party."

"But my mother?"

"Your mother will be fine, Miss Askari. She will be proud of her daughter, a party member."

The bald official leaned forward. "Unless she believes the party not worthy?

Elvis's black eyebrows shot up. His pompadour wobbled. He whispered, "Is your mother *against* the party, Miss Askari?"

Baldy chimed in, his voice rising in excitement, "If so, it is your duty as a loyal Iraqi to report her, even if she is your mother."

I could feel sweat dribbling down my back. Their little mind game was becoming dangerous. I must look sharp!

"No, no. My mother is not against the party. The president is a member of the party. She respects the president. And the party. But she needs me at home. She is old. She is sick."

"Your sister lives at home. Is that true, Miss Askari?"

"Yes. That is true."

"Surely, your sister can take care of your elderly mother. Isn't that true?"

My interrogators were shrewd. They were masters at entrapment, their every question a calculation, a form of trickery. And how did they know about Muna?

"It is true that my sister lives at home. But it is not true that she can help my mother. My sister Muna is, in many ways, practically an invalid."

"Your sister is an invalid?" There was a rustle of papers as Elvis sorted through the file. His voice sounded an alarm. "There is no mention of this in your file."

"Yes. It is absolutely true. My sister is unwell. She cannot take care of herself. And she has a toddler. Mother is their caretaker while I am at school, with the help of my brother's wife. But Mother is elderly and cannot be the caretaker twenty-four hours a day. I assume responsibility when I return in the afternoon."

Elvis slapped my file down on the desk, hastily picked up a pen, and began scribbling in the margins.

Oh, my. Muna's mental condition was now a matter of police records. I shifted uneasily.

Poor Muna. She had been ill omened even in the womb she shared with her twin, Sa'ad, with Sa'ad growing healthy and strong while Muna came into the world as a tiny sack of bones. There was a huge celebration in the family when Muna passed her first birthday, for it had been believed she would not survive. Over the years, conditions had not improved for Muna. In fact, she grew more physically and mentally frail with each passing year. But the past two years had been the worst of Muna's life.

My sweet sister had barely survived an arranged marriage, her mental health deteriorating further after she married and moved away to live in the home of her husband's family.

I had spoken against the marriage, but there was nothing I could do. My culture pushes marriage on everyone, even those for whom the institution would be unsuitable, such as Muna, who had been crippled by serious bouts of depression since she was a young girl. People believed that "girls must marry," that it was a great humiliation for a woman to forgo the opportunity to be a wife and mother and instead remain a spinster. And so Muna was married.

The marriage was questionable for reasons other than Muna's fragile health. Muna's husband was too old. Her mother-in-law was too cruel. Those two tyrants passed themselves off as ordinary people, then exploited my compliant sister as a slave.

Muna became pregnant within a few weeks and suffered a difficult pregnancy that produced a beautiful baby daughter named Nadia.

The marriage quickly collapsed after the birth of little Nadia. With a new baby to care for and a cruel husband, her sadistic mother-in-law insisted that Muna continue the heaviest drudgery of the housework. When Muna was unable to achieve all the duties to their satisfaction, the mother-in-law and her son began to beat her.

Muna was a gentle girl who had never once been subjected to angry voices or raised hands. One day while trying to avoid their physical blows, Muna ran out of the house. She was so frightened and confused that she fled without her child and made her way home. Mother would not force Muna to return to that place. But Nadia had been left behind. Now the husband's family claimed they had the right to keep her, because in Iraq fathers keep custody of children. But when Mother appeared at their door, she somehow convinced those monsters to give her Muna's baby.

Although Muna was back home with her child and would never again be mistreated, the painful episode had taken a toll on her. She had withdrawn almost completely, except when playing sweetly with her darling Nadia.

Elvis appeared traumatized. My incomplete file was the obvious cause. Its imperfect status appeared to work in my favor, for he abruptly sprang to his feet and sent me away with an ominous warning. "Miss Askari, you have a few months to get your affairs in order. Then you will join the Baath Party and become an active member. You cannot work in the tourist sector otherwise."

Politeness forgotten, he barked, "You are dismissed."

I nodded and said, "Thank you for your kindness," then moved as quickly as possible, away from those shady characters, out of that dark room, through the gloomy hallway, and into the sunshine, clearing that sinister Baathist air out of my lungs.

I had not been arrested. I was not going to prison, at least not that day! In truth, I felt like dancing.

I spotted the old taxi driver waiting in his car on the other side of the road.

He looked as relieved as I was happy. Although we Iraqis had learned to be especially guarded when talking to strangers, I *knew* this old man was not one of *them*, and while he drove, I opened up, sharing something of my frightening experience, confiding that they had given me only a few months before I must join the Baath Party, or face dire consequences.

With mouth open wide and stained teeth visible, he gaily said, "Do not worry. Anything can happen in three months."

He turned his head to look me in the eye, asking, "Do you remember the story of the king who offered fabulous riches to anyone who could teach his donkey to talk?"

I was so happy I laughed with him, but I had to admit, "No. I do not know that story."

"I will tell you!" he said eagerly, one hand on the wheel and the other held triumphantly in the air. "The king offered anyone willing to take on the job advance payment. Teach his donkey to speak and keep the money. But at the end of the year, if the donkey was still braying rather than talking, the volunteer would pay with his life.

"A man said to be the wisest man in the kingdom accepted the king's offer, pocketed the money, and said that yes, he would teach that donkey to talk. His friends cautioned him and questioned if he had lost his mind, because there was no evidence a donkey could ever be taught to speak.

"But he was an optimistic man. In his wise opinion, many things might happen in a year. The king might die. He might die. The donkey might die. Or, perhaps, there would be a miracle and the donkey would learn to speak."

I giggled.

The old driver glanced at me in his mirror, his face bright with a knowing smile. He winked slyly, lowering his voice to whisper, "Who knows? The president might die. Those two officials might die. The Iranians might fight their way into Baghdad. The security police building might burn down. Your family might move away. Anything can happen in three months!"

Later, I would remember every word of that conversation.

But at the time, I had no way of knowing that *everything* in my life was about to change. I would eventually leave Baghdad forever. I would never join the Baath Party. Most inexplicably of all, my fate would, in a very important manner, be linked to a donkey!

On the very day that I was riding through the busy streets of Baghdad in that taxi, a donkey was making its long steep climb over the foothills of mountainous Kurdistan, its final destination Sulaimaniya. That donkey was transporting heavy bags and bundles. Tucked carefully into one of the bags was a letter addressed to one Joanna al-Askari of Baghdad, an unexpected letter that had been written months before, a letter that would put me on a different path and change my life forever.

14

Love Letters

BAGHDAD AND SULAIMANIYA
1986–1987

The New Year

My darling Joanna,

With the arrival of a new year, I feel a certain melancholy in the air. We had a small party here in the mountains, and afterward I returned to my pen to greet the New Year. I had dreamed of welcoming the New Year while having accomplished a cherished wish, to begin my life with you.
    You are the world to me.
    Please accept my proposal.
    Please be my wife. Make me complete.

Sarbast

What?" I spoke aloud, tightening my lips as I skeptically rotated the single thin sheet in my hands, first examining the flip side of the letter, then the plain brown envelope, front and back. I could not find even the slightest indication of a postmark.

A short time earlier, Alia had darted in through the front door, loudly exclaiming, "Joanna! A letter! A letter for you! From Kurdistan!"

A warning bell went off. Sarbast had been killed and someone was writing to tell me. But why would I care?

Nevertheless, I held my hand out and ordered, "Give it to me!"

As I was ripping open the envelope, Alia continually interrupted with exclamations, explanations, and questions. "It must be from Sarbast, Joanna. It was hand delivered this morning by one of Hady's cousins from Sulaimaniya. Is it from Sarbast?

"The cousin told Hady that this letter was brought to his home in the hands of a mysterious woman he did not know. He heard a tapping on the door. He opened the door. There she was. She looked rough, he said, as though she had been hiking through the mountains. Without a word, she passed him this one letter. She then walked away. He didn't have a chance to question her. Can you believe she never spoke?

"Is it from Sarbast? She could have said something!"

"Alia! Please! Give me a moment." My sister was giving me a headache.

Alia had been troubled for some time over my well-being. Nothing I said convinced her that I had indeed successfully pushed Sarbast from my mind. Alia was certain that I would never be happy with any man but Sarbast, and I knew that she was secretly hoping we would make our way back to each other.

I read the letter again. Was it some kind of joke? Who had sent it? The letter had been written months before, at the beginning of the year.

I could not believe it was from Sarbast, although the flowery style of writing implied it could be him, for he *was* a poet. But the last time I had seen Sarbast his heart had been closed to me while open wide to another. *That* man would not have written *this* letter. Never!

After my interrogation by the secret police, I had become mistrustful. Perhaps Elvis and his bald partner had sent this letter. Perhaps our home was under surveillance? If I penned a reply, perhaps I would be arrested and sentenced to a long prison term for communicating with Iraq's enemies, the Peshmergas. I held the letter at arm's length. Perhaps it had been rolled in a toxic substance. Nothing would surprise me in Saddam's Iraq.

Still holding the letter far away, I read the words yet one more time. I had to admit that the writing in the letter did look very similar to Sarbast's handwriting.

But Sarbast had scorned me for another. And now, without a meeting, without any ensuing communication, he wanted to *marry* me?

No, I didn't think so.

If not Sarbast, who, then, was trying to bring further shame on me? Who hated me enough to want me to reply to a fraudulent marriage proposal?

It was making me very angry. I glared at Alia, feeling an unreasonable spark of fury. I felt the need to scold *somebody*. "What is going on here?"

Alia made a chastened expression as she shrugged her shoulders. "I know nothing other than what I told you, Joanna. The letter was brought to us by Hady's cousin, who arrived yesterday from Sulaimaniya." She eased the letter from my hand. "It *does* resemble Sarbast's handwriting, Joanna." She studied it more carefully, holding the page before the light, drawing it near to her eyes and then away.

"I don't see any hidden messages. It must be from Sarbast. Look," she said, indicating his signature. "He signed his name. Why would anyone else take such a risk, Joanna?"

I dropped down into a chair at the table, positioning the letter and the envelope on the table, considering the complicated journey the letter had to have made to arrive into my hands, *if* it was indeed from Sarbast. An active underground existed in Kurdistan, with smugglers constantly on the move transporting money, mail, food, and military equipment. Without the underground, the Peshmergas couldn't survive a month.

With the continued face-off between the Iraqi and Iranian armies, and with the PUK allied with the Iranians, all of Kurdistan had been whipped into a particularly vicious battleground. Although the PUK had recently gained a lot of rural territory, which was a cause for celebration, there were still plenty of urban areas held by the Iraqi army. And in those Iraqi-held regions, roadblocks had proliferated until it was almost impossible for any Kurd to make the shortest journey without risking life and limb. We had heard that Saddam was so enraged by the joint Kurdish and Iranian victories that he planned to move strong reinforcements from the south to the north. If that happened, Kurdistan was doomed.

To receive a letter from a Peshmerga in a heated war zone was equivalent to a valuable gift, for travel in the Kurdish mountains had always been treacherous. No Peshmerga would risk the life of any smuggler over a mere letter unless the content was felt to be very important.

Was it true, then? Was this letter from Sarbast? If so, what had changed to make him believe he loved me now?

And even so, I cruelly reminded myself, I was second choice. *Second choice.* I must never forget it! Still, I was curious. I lightly brushed the page with my fingertips, thinking. I knew that the letter in my hand, if authentic, had gone on quite a journey. It would have left Sarbast's hand months before to be concealed in the load on the back of a smuggler's donkey.

Smugglers were most often men, but on occasion women would transport the mail, for their sex had proven a believable cover. Iraqi soldiers, accustomed to the Arab tradition of keeping women away from the front lines, did not understand that Kurdish women routinely imperiled their lives to assist the cause.

The smuggler and the donkey would make their way through the mountains, past the checkpoints and into the cities. It was a dangerous undertaking that required steely nerves. Should any contraband, such as Peshmerga mail, fighting supplies, or even food, be detected at the checkpoint, the smuggler would pay with his or her life. His or her family would never be informed, made to endure the special kind of agony of never knowing.

Once in the city, the smuggler would seek out a chosen Peshmerga family, who would somehow arrange to deliver the letter to the addressee. Another arduous process would then commence.

Our torn land was in a major lockdown. Delivering mail from Peshmergas was a risky business.

If grime was the test for authenticity, the letter was certainly from Sarbast. The page was filthy with dust in the creases.

I lifted the envelope to my nose. "Whew!" It stank of a fetid pack animal. I had been in the company of a few donkeys and mules during my days of visiting Kurdistan and found them to be very smelly, at least to my city nose.

I mulled over it for so long that Alia finally left, saying she had to get home to her boys.

"Let me know if it is from Sarbast," she said as she closed the door behind her.

I clutched the letter in my hand and went into the garden, settling in a chair to read the letter a third time.

When Mother, Muna, Sa'ad, and his wife came home, I tucked the letter in my pocket, telling them nothing. At bedtime, I retrieved the letter and read it several more times before I slipped on my nightgown.

I sprawled across the mattress. But I couldn't sleep.

If the letter *was* from Sarbast, where was his explanation for that magical day at the university? Our hearts had met on that day. What had happened? Why hadn't he asked me to marry him then?

Where was his explanation for his coldness on the day when I made it clear I wanted to return with him to Kurdistan? Where was his explanation for asking another to marry him? He offered no explanations, only a declaration of love.

I finally accepted that the letter was from Sarbast. I knew his handwriting too well.

But I felt incredibly sad. At another time, Sarbast's letter would have made me the happiest woman in Baghdad. But I could not forget that I was second best in Sarbast's eyes. Had his blonde said yes to his proposal, then Sarbast would be married and perhaps a father by now.

I swallowed down my pain, but I found it impossible to swallow my pride. I ignored the letter and did not reply.

Several months later a poem came to me via a similar route. Only this time Sarbast did not address me, nor did he sign it.

> I might have wronged you.
> I might have taken the decision too late.
> I had my doubts
> And now I know how wrong I was
> What I am sure of, is my love for you.
> My love has no boundaries.
> And you are crushing my heart with your silence.

Don't be silent.
Don't be cruel.
You are in every page I turn
In every word I write
All the birds here chant your name.
I am nothing without you.

Now the birds were chanting my name? This was becoming very interesting.

Despite Sarbast's heartfelt pleas, I felt stubborn, unwilling to meet him even halfway.

When I glanced into the mirror, I was surprised to see stern features reflected in the mirror. I was sad to acknowledge that I was a new person, no longer the joyful Joanna I had always been.

I slipped the poem away in a secret place, along with his first letter. I did not respond.

Several months later, yet a third communication arrived, carrying the smell of the donkey express.

Dearest Joanna:

If sadness had sizes, I would wake up every day to a mountain of sadness. If yearning had a language and tunes, you would hear symphonies. I know no geography except that toward the south. From the mountain top my vision is as clear as that of Zarqa al-Yamama, and it pierces the distances toward Baghdad's gates to your window.

The north asks the south about you, the mountain tops ask Baghdad's buildings about you, the pecan trees ask the palm trees about you, but there is no answer. I cover distances, I go over mountains looking for one word of you, but words are missing, and the distances are killing me.

Tell me how to reach the road to your heart, give me a sign, and I will be there. I am ready to travel to you, only give me a sign, and I will come to you. I do not want to lie to you, but I mean it when I say, I will sacrifice my life for you.

Sarbast

For the first time in months I laughed aloud, receiving some pleasure from Sarbast's love letter. If the mountain tops and trees were beginning to discuss me, then this was becoming a very serious situation.

By this time everyone in my family knew something of my quandary, for such a secret could not be kept for long in such close living quarters. But I provided them with few details. Only Alia and Hady knew for certain the urgency of Sarbast's love campaign.

Alia told me to be happy now that I was being pursued. But I could take no satisfaction in that our situations were now reversed. For years Sarbast had been casual about me, while I had been desperate to win his love. Now, it seemed, he had fallen in love with me, while I was the hesitant party.

I felt he had squandered our chance for happiness. Yet a great misery was hanging over me.

Once again, I was reminded of the grief and pain that attaches itself to romantic love. I willed myself to be strong, not to return to that wounding place.

And then a fourth communication landed on my door.

> *Do not declare your war on me*
> *In this case*
> *I am a weary stranger in this town*
> *Do not torture me*
> *From there afar, thousands are persecuting me*
> *Your war on me is not heroic*
> *Stay with me and make me happy*
> *For I only have your eyes to make me happy*
> *Nothing is heard save the beat of my heart*
> *The mountains and the trees*
> *Have ceased talking to me*
> *Like they used to before*
> *The sun has set*
> *Another day is demolished by my loneliness*
> *I am sad and weary in these mountain tops*
> *And together with silent nature*
> *I am in mourning*

Suddenly, his dashing image came to me, and I was swept away with memories of why I had fallen in love with Sarbast in the first place. I began to weep quietly.

Mother slipped into the room and sat beside me on my bed. My hair was piled on my head, and she took out the pins and let my long hair fall down my back, lifting strands with her fingers, pulling them to her nose, and sniffing their scent. Then she kissed my cheek before raising my chin with one finger and pulling me to face her, saying, "Daughter, you look so sad."

Leaning my head against Mother's shoulder, I began to sob.

I felt Muna's presence in the room, but my darling sister stood quietly, saying nothing.

Mother and Muna had been watching me closely for several weeks. In fact, everyone in my family was suffering along with me. My wounds were reopening. Sarbast's letters and poems were getting to me. My entire body felt raw, crushed. I had become impossible, irritable. Sa'ad and his wife had begun to avoid me. My coworkers believed there was a family crisis.

Since the day Sarbast had disregarded me, an unacknowledged unhappiness had been walking with me, but I had put that unhappiness in a locked compartment, and now his letters were letting it out. Remembering the agony of love's rejection, I feared its return.

The following morning, Mother asked me to sit with her for a while. The two of us sipped tea, talking about mundane matters.

Then, with a firm look, Mother reminded me, "Daughter. There are real people risking their lives to deliver these unanswered letters. It would be a pity for some brave man or woman to be killed over them."

I cringed. I had not considered all the dangers for others.

Mother patted my knee, "Joanna, write to him with a yes. Or write to him with a no." She kissed me. "Joanna, I do not want you to marry this man and live the fighter's life. But *if* you love him, and that is what will bring you happiness, I will support your decision."

I stared at Mother and loved her even more for her offer of sacrifice.

Under the current climate, with the Iraqi army eagerly composing Peshmerga epitaphs, few families would allow their daughters to marry a fighter, even a Kurdish family supporting the cause.

Kurds were losing many of their sons. They didn't want to lose their daughters, too.

If I traveled to the north and lived the Peshmerga life, my mother would exist in a fog of endless worry, never knowing if her youngest child had been captured, was being tortured, was dead or alive.

I began to tremble. I felt a true yearning for Sarbast. I finally made up my mind. I threw myself into my mother's arms. "Mother!" I had my answer.

PART THREE

Love and Tragedy
in Kurdistan

15

Love and Marriage

SULAIMANIYA TO SERWAN
May 17 to June 20, 1987

Mine was a wedding without a groom. Everything normal was denied me. When I tilted my head against Mother's shoulder to whisper my disappointment, Mother reminded me that I should be happy that I was having a wedding at all.

It *was* true that weeks of uncertainty lay behind us. Much had taken place since that day I had tearfully confessed to Mother that I had never stopped loving Sarbast, despite my resolve to pull out the roots of the love planted ten years before.

But I had caught the fever of his letters and poems. His confessed love for me became overwhelming and regenerated my love for him. Now I was passionate to become the woman of my childhood fantasies, a woman who marries her handsome Peshmerga hero to live out her life as a freedom fighter in the mountains of Kurdistan.

Taking Mother's advice, I had finally answered Sarbast's communications. However, my message was not the love letter he was hoping to receive. Instead, I poured out my heart, telling him of my feelings, my frustrations, and my slow burning anger.

I vented my resentment over the woman he had asked to marry

him, writing hateful words, telling him that in his stupidity and blindness he had chosen an incompatible woman with selfish demands, a woman who sounded like a man. I spitefully added that had she said yes he would have found a rasping shrew in his marriage bed.

With that letter Sarbast understood there was a new aspect to his happy and sweet Joanna, indeed, a new persona that *he* had created, for my pain over his actions had created my bitterness.

Despite my anger, he was not discouraged; in fact, he became even more forceful in his efforts to sway me to say yes. Fate had altered our positions.

Unbeknownst to me, Alia slipped a brief note in with my own, disclosing that there were other men seeking my hand in marriage. I no longer had to endure lengthy silences from Sarbast.

Tortured by the idea of other suitors, another letter arrived in record time from the distant mountains. I must say yes or he would not survive.

I had nearly forgotten the intensity of Sarbast's passion for everything he loved, whether country, cause, or family. And now those passions were directed at me. It was splendid to be loved by the man I had vainly loved for so many years.

All ended as it was meant to be.

I finally said yes, that I would marry him and that I would leave Baghdad life behind to join him in the mountains, even it if meant becoming a fugitive in the process.

I was not frightened. I was excited, for with one decision two dreams were fulfilled. I was going to be a Peshmerga wife, a freedom fighter supporting her husband and her beautiful country.

I set about to leave Baghdad forever. I informed my boss at the tourist office that I would be leaving, that I was to be married. However, I did not disclose to him the full truth, that I was marrying a Peshmerga. I bade trusted girlfriends secret good-byes, friends who so loved me that they were horrified to learn that I was going to marry a PUK Peshmerga. Even in Baghdad we had heard that Saddam's soldiers no longer made distinctions between Peshmerga men and their wives. When captured, all were slaughtered. I told other, more casual, friends that I was moving to Sulaimaniya to be with my mother's family.

A worried Sarbast beckoned, sending an urgent message that I must leave Baghdad quickly, that everything in Kurdistan was changing for the worse. The fires of war were roaring out of control.

Only the year before, in 1986, the PUK had allied itself with the Iranians to fight Saddam as the common enemy. The Iraqi president became savage with rage, screeching that the PUK leader Jalal Talabani and his fighters were "agents of Iran" and vowing to destroy all members of the PUK.

Sarbast was PUK. Very soon I, too, would be considered PUK in the eyes of our enemies.

While the Iraqi military occupied all the cities in Kurdistan, the PUK Peshmergas remained strong in the outlying areas, and with new support from the Iranians they had begun assaulting the occupying Iraqi army forces in the northern city of Kirkuk. Kirkuk was a coveted city by all as it was blessed with enormous oil resources. Baghdad's answer to the PUK's newfound military offensive was extreme.

On March 29, 1987, the Revolutionary Command Council issued Decree Number 160, which granted Ali Hassan al-Majid, the head of the Northern Bureau, the power to proceed with the Kurdish final solution. Ali al-Majid was a particularly brutish man, and he was the man who would determine whether Kurds lived or died. He would see that they all died.

Two weeks later, he began the campaign of genocide that would earn him the infamous title of "Chemical Ali." On April 15, he dropped poison gas on the PUK headquarters in Sergalou and on the PUK communication center in Bergalou. While there was some loss of life, most of the fighters survived because the chemicals had been weakly mixed and the wind was not blowing in the right direction. But with chemical warfare now a reality, there was a new urgency to defeat Saddam.

The Peshmergas could not win against the invisible weapons of sarin and mustard gas, because there were few gas masks available for the fighters and none for the civilians. Saddam had made it illegal for Kurds to own gas masks. Suddenly, that ruling sparked an ill-omened implication.

With the PUK unable to offer protection to civilians, villagers would be forced to flee. If the villages were abandoned, the

Peshmergas would lose their hidden access to their secret mountain hideaways. If the mountains were overrun, the Peshmergas and Kurdistan would be finished.

An old Kurdish saying flared in my memory: flatten the mountains and Kurdistan will not last one day. I fretted about the new turn the war had taken. I was eager to be there, to share with Sarbast the escalating danger.

Three days before I was to leave Baghdad, I was jolted by another summons from the secret police, commanding me to return to their offices within the week to report on my membership in the Baath Party. Amid all the excitement of my engagement, I had forgotten Elvis and Baldy, but they had not forgotten me.

It had been quite some time since those men had given me only a few months to join the Baath Party. I had expected the summons earlier, but obviously they had been busy with other more important matters than a young woman working in a tourist office.

But now my time was up.

While the earlier summons had terrified me, I found the second directive less unnerving. I even smiled a little, recalling the kindly taxi driver's prediction that anything could happen.

"Anything" *had* happened. I was leaving Baghdad and fleeing into the mountains where Elvis and Baldy would be the hunted ones, should they be so stupid as to choose to pursue me there. I would be living in the forbidden area where only Kurdish fighters and villagers walked the land, out of reach of routine police surveillance. Or so I thought.

I prepared a letter that my boss volunteered to deliver to Elvis and his partner once I had left Baghdad for the north. The letter informed them that instead of pursuing a career, I had decided to marry and move away from Baghdad.

I assumed their interest in me would fade upon receipt of my letter.

"Cheerio, Elvis!" I gaily called out several times a day, leaving bewildered expressions on the faces of friends and family who became concerned for my sanity.

My last full day in Baghdad would be May 5, 1987. Mother and I would travel to Sulaimaniya the following day, where we would be welcomed by Sarbast's family, and we would have a week to organize the wedding. As the head of our family, Sa'ad would follow, arriving in Sulaimaniya in time for the marriage contract to be formalized.

Not having seen Sarbast for too long, and desiring to be beautiful for his eyes only, I foolishly spent more money than I should have in the finest shops located in the Mansur district and the Al-Nahir souk. My closest girlfriends helped me to select the latest fashions, the highest heels, and the sexiest nightgowns, as well as extra supplies of makeup and perfumes.

Who knew how long I would be living in a mountain village without access to anything of normal life? With blissful anticipation, I carefully packed my girlish treasures into a large bag. I was ready.

Alone at home the day before my departure, I glided along, selecting favored spots and treasured objects to wish a fond farewell to, for something inside me cautioned that I would never return to my childhood home. While much of my future was unknown, I knew I was leaving Baghdad forever.

Many family treasures sparked happy memories, but none more than my mother's clothes chest, still tucked away in her bedroom and full of fine clothes, left behind from the early days when she and my father had enjoyed prosperity and had received formal invitations to the palace.

I was such a lively child that my exhausted mother had often encouraged me to dig around in that chest, to pull out the ball gowns and high-heeled shoes. I would put on a fancy gown and slip into the red heels with the toes so pointed that I could and did inflict dents and marks on the walls. After dabbing my lips with Mother's brightest red lipstick, I would suspend a small beaded evening bag on my elbow before prancing around the house, making believe I was at a fancy ball where there were kings, queens, and young princes and princesses.

I sat in my father's fine walnut desk chair, a simple but elegant piece that along with his elaborately carved desk he designed and made at his beloved furniture factory, the factory I never had the pleasure of visiting, but had heard described by Ra'ad and Mother so many times that I felt I had worked there myself.

Many were the occasions I watched my poor overworked father sitting upright at that desk, his broad back erect against the chair, his elbows propped atop the desk, busily examining documents and adding and subtracting long rows of figures in a vain search for that elusive money to feed our large family for one more day.

Those two pieces of furniture were the only items my father salvaged from the fire that destroyed the factory during the revolution of 1958. Even an untrained eye would guess that the walnut desk and chair had been crafted by a talented furniture designer.

The pain of my father's loss felt unbearable even after eleven years. I left the house and drifted out to the garden, underneath the largest palm tree, my favorite refuge, where I had so often escaped as a child. I settled easily in a familiar spot, a furrow worn into the dirt from many years of use, leaned my head against the solid trunk of the tree, and looked up into the brilliant blue sky. "Good-bye, palm trees. Good-bye, Baghdad sky."

I bade farewell to twenty-five bittersweet years. "Cheerio!" I was happier than I had ever been, a young woman fulfilling an enduring dream.

When the following morning came for Mother and me to depart Baghdad, all our family gathered to say good-bye, the women weeping, the men quiet and solemn, as if they had just received word of my funeral.

I laughed away their fears. Mine was a happy occasion!

Had I known the mayhem and death soon to face me and the horrific massacres waiting to claim so many Kurdish lives, or that it would be years before I would see my family again, no doubt my courage would have failed me and I could not have left them, not even to run into the arms of the man I loved.

I comforted a sad Alia. "Just remember, with every end comes a new beginning. I am ready for this new beginning."

Alia smiled her knowing smile. Only Alia had been there at the beginning of my journey of love. Only Alia could fully comprehend the years of anguish that lurked behind my happy ending with Sarbast.

I wasn't sorry to see the last of the dust of Baghdad, despite the fact that we were traveling into unknown danger.

After several years of seclusion in Baghdad, we were not prepared for the stark changes in the north. The land we loved was being assaulted from the air and from the ground. Too many helicopters to count roamed like angry bees overhead. Military checkpoints dotted the main highway from Baghdad to Kirkuk to Sulaimaniya, making sure that supplies and communications did not get through to the Peshmerga fighters as well as to the Kurdish villagers.

Saddam had plans to starve us.

Mother and I endured a strange horror waiting at checkpoints, for every visitor to the area was deemed a spy. We sat watching helplessly as several Kurdish men were pulled from their cars to be taken away. Those poor men were doomed. Rumor was that Kurds were being murdered indiscriminately. But at each checkpoint, we were just two women with our papers in order and with many relatives in Sulaimaniya, so during routine questioning we were able to convince the guards we were simply visiting those relatives, and we would be waved through.

While waiting at one checkpoint Mother began clicking her prayer beads so loudly that I peered into her worried eyes and asked, "Are you trying to create a special tune with those beads, Mother?"

She whispered anxiously, "This day will seem a picnic compared to your new life, Joanna."

True. But I would not have wanted it any other way.

After my wedding, I would be going with Sarbast to live in a vital guerrilla hideaway for the PUK, the village of Bergalou, which was nestled in the narrow Jafati Valley, a long strip of difficult terrain in southeastern Iraqi Kurdistan.

Inhabited by fighters, Bergalou was a temporary village that housed the PUK radio station and a field hospital. Bergalou's importance to the Kurdish resistance made it a tempting target for Baghdad. The village was routinely bombed and shelled by the Iraqi army.

Strangely enough, I felt wholly unconcerned for my own well-being.

I stared out the window and thought about Sarbast. I was eager to begin our married life and impatient to play some small role in supporting Kurdish freedoms.

A heartfelt Kurdish welcome awaited us at the house of Sarbast's brother, Osman, who lived in Sarchnar, a residential district of Sulaimaniya. Mother and I felt at home for more reasons than one. Osman was married to my mother's niece, Nawbahar, who was the daughter of my favorite auntie, Aisha.

I was taken by surprise when Sarbast's family presented me with a lovely wedding gift of four gold bracelets.

Gold is greatly valued by the Kurds, and the groom's family traditionally offers expensive presents to the bride, usually items of gold that will always belong to her, in the event she is widowed or her husband asks for a divorce. In such tragedies, many women have found that their wedding gold kept them and their children from starving.

Yet I had been expecting nothing. After I had accepted Sarbast's marriage proposal, he wrote to ask what I wanted for a dowry. I had replied in writing, "Other than a plain gold wedding ring, I will accept nothing." I knew that his family had made many financial sacrifices for the Kurdish cause, that the Iraqi army had retaliated against the family for having two sons who were Peshmerga, and that they had lost their family home.

We would begin our marriage on an equal footing. Neither of us would possess anything of value. We would build our future together. After Kurdistan was free, we were sure to prosper. Sarbast claimed to be the luckiest man alive, understanding that I was marrying him for true love.

Although I never asked, I did wonder if he ever compared my honest emotion with the greedy dowry demands made by his first choice for a bride. I hoped that was the case, that he was glad his first proposal was rebuffed so he could now marry me.

Although those gold bracelets were only a token, I was delighted, for I knew it was a way for Sarbast's family to notify me of their pleasure that I was joining their family.

The ladies of the house were inquisitive when I unpacked my large suitcase. They gathered around me in a friendly, jostling circle as I proudly showed off my expensive new wardrobe.

I was baffled by the peals of loud laughter that greeted every item.

"What? What?" I looked at the women, my hands held aloft, my eyes wide in puzzlement.

Sarbast's mother was such a sweet-faced lady that I loved her already, but when her expression grew grave, I became confused. She guided me by my shoulders to the edge of the bed and pushed me to sit. "My dear girl, Bergalou will *not* be a party. You are going to the mountains to live the Peshmerga life. Your clothes must protect you in those harsh mountains."

She lifted the edge of one of my satin dresses, a bright shade of red. "This dress should be declared a murder weapon! You'll sparkle like a beacon." She shook her head. "The Iraqi army will love it if you wear this dress, Joanna. You would make their surveillance very easy. Everyone on that mountain will go straight to Allah if you wear this." She threw both hands in the air. "Boom!"

"And this!" She pointed at a lightweight beige blouse and lacy skirt, one of the latest fashions from Paris. "Joanna. You will freeze. And these? Is my son marrying Cinderella?"

Everyone laughed merrily when she used a finger to prod one of my impossibly high black Italian stilettos marked by a gold streak.

I was mortified. I had been so keen to excite Sarbast and look my best for him that I had temporarily lost all common sense. I bit my lip and looked around, wishing that the lot of them would evaporate.

The moment grew worse when one of Sarbast's younger sisters pulled out my most beautiful sheer nightgown and a pair of matching panties and began to dance in place. I gasped and snatched them from her hands, the blood rushing to my face.

By that time I was the only woman in the room who was not bent over laughing.

After catching her breath, Sarbast's mother appeared sympathetic. She hugged me, then became serious. "Joanna, what you will need is heavy trousers, boots, and sensible jackets. You can leave your silks and satins here, for the future, when everything settles down."

My face fell in disappointment.

She shrugged, patting me on my shoulder. "Every war ends, eventually."

That afternoon we all crowded into a dilapidated taxicab and went to the local souk. The women assisted me in selecting sensible mountain clothes, which, to my dismay, meant men's wear.

I purchased several pairs of the smallest men's trousers available, the baggy-legged trousers so popular in Kurdistan. Those pants were so wide in the waist that they drooped. I'll have to tie them up, with string, perhaps, I thought glumly, beginning to realize that I had been wrong to think I would not miss anything of my former life. I was not accustomed to dressing so shabbily. Every young bride wants to look beautiful for her husband, and I was no exception.

A future sister-in-law noticed my gloomy face and teased, "These pants will be invaluable, Joanna. You can ride donkeys, climb tall mountains, and," she added with a hearty laugh, "leap as high as my head in these trousers. And, look," she explained, "look at these long pockets. You can transport whole loaves of bread in these roomy pockets!"

Indeed, those pockets ran the length of the pant leg. They would come in handy when trekking over the mountains.

I despondently folded and put away my lovely clothes before repacking my suitcase. However, I refused to leave behind my beautiful new pink bedding, despite warnings that I would be traveling by mule at some point during my trek to Bergalou and that such elegant bedding had no place in the mountains. I even got into a physical struggle with one of my future sisters-in-law over the bedding, but I refused to turn over my quilt or pillow, determined that I would have *something* of beauty in my new mountain home.

Later, we made a second trip to the gold souk to purchase wedding bands. Everyone chuckled when I pulled a twig from my handbag, telling the shop owner, "My fiancé sent this to me. His ring finger is this exact size."

What fun I had sliding various styles of men's wedding bands down that twig while a mesmerized crowd gathered in excited curiosity.

There were several more hurdles to overcome before I could marry Sarbast. Saddam had made it a crime for any woman to marry a Peshmerga. No government officials anywhere in Sulaimaniya would risk their necks to provide us with the proper papers, and few Kurdish mullahs were brave enough to officiate at such a ceremony.

Just as I was beginning to believe that our marriage would not take place and that I would be forced to admit bitter failure and return to Baghdad, Sarbast's brother solved the problem. He arranged the paperwork and knew of a brave Kurdish mullah, Ibrahim Salih, who would agree to conduct the ceremony.

With that dilemma solved, yet another arose, making me wonder if God Himself was against my marriage.

I felt the bitterest pang when the message came that Sarbast was unable to make the journey from the mountains to Sulaimaniya. My knees buckled. As there was for all Peshmergas, there was a bounty on his head. Furthermore, Baghdad had just intensified its offensive in the area. It was impossible for any Peshmerga to leave the mountains, cross the forbidden zones, clear all the checkpoints, and enter an occupied city. Such a trip might cost Sarbast his life.

In mute desolation, I sat and brooded. But I felt better when reminded that our traditions do not demand that the bride and groom attend the marriage ceremony together. In fact, in many Muslim countries men and women are intentionally separated during the ceremony. The mullah could solemnize the marriage first with Sarbast, and then with me. Once the marriage was consummated, we would be considered husband and wife.

I was amazed and forever grateful when that brave mullah volunteered to make the perilous journey into the mountains to reach Sarbast to solemnize his side of the union.

Yet another pesky problem was solved.

I was heartbroken, though, that Sarbast could not be in attendance at our wedding. I tried to remain stoic in front of Sarbast's family, but I failed to restrain tears of disappointment.

Finally, the anticipated day arrived.

Swinging between hope and despair that at the last minute Sarbast would unexpectedly show up, I had spent the two days before my wedding in Sulaimaniya beauty salons having my long black hair styled and undergoing facials, waxings, manicures, and pedicures.

But Sarbast was nowhere to be seen.

My brother Sa'ad arrived a few hours before the ceremony reporting that he had experienced no problems at the checkpoints, which was an enormous relief. With Ra'ad living in Switzerland, Sa'ad would be the one to formally agree for me to marry Sarbast.

Finally realizing that Sarbast would not be surprising me at the last minute, I choose not to wear the beautiful pink dress I had purchased for my special day. Instead, I would wear a sensible pink and gray suit.

I pulled my long black hair back with a barrette. I put on minimal makeup. Sarbast's absence dulled the day for me. I really could not believe that after so many years of anticipation, mine would be a wedding without a groom. But it was.

Everyone gathered in Osman's sitting room. It was a warm and pleasant room, with red fabric on the walls and a wooden floor strewn with handmade carpets. There was a painting of wild horses hanging behind the sofa and interesting knickknacks scattered about.

In celebration, my cousin had prepared some homemade sweets. But I was too edgy to eat, certain that something else was bound to happen to derail the ceremony.

Perhaps the mullah had been shot at a checkpoint. Such tragedies occurred daily in Kurdistan. But that dreadful scenario did not happen, and finally Mullah Ibrahim Salih arrived. I couldn't help but notice that his thin lips were closed tightly as though he found it difficult to smile. Being a Kurdish mullah had become a dangerous calling.

Sarbast's father and brother rushed to thank him. I smiled gratefully at him.

Mullah Ibrahim said little of his mountain adventure, other than to admit that it had been harrowing. He proudly displayed a document with Sarbast's signature that confirmed his permission to conduct the ceremony in his absence.

He glanced in my direction, and with a smile told me that Sarbast wished me a safe trip into the mountains.

I took this to mean, for a new groom: bride, get here as rapidly as you can.

Just then Sa'ad noticed that my head was uncovered, which was more than he could bear in the presence of a mullah. He made a bit of a fuss until someone tossed me a white scarf.

I raised the thin scarf loosely over my head. Sa'ad grunted in irritation but managed to hold back speaking his true thoughts.

I glanced at Sa'ad and smiled. I did love him. My brother was a handsome man and incredibly sweet, at least on all things but his opinion of how women should dress.

He nodded and smiled back, looking happier than I had seen him in a long time. I had a quick thought that my brother was most likely thrilled I was finally getting married. At age twenty-five, I was old for a Kurdish bride. After the wedding, I would no longer be his problem.

The ceremony began, and my religious ignorance was soon apparent. Mullah Ibrahim read the required passages from the

Koran in formal Kurdish and I was told to repeat after him. I had enormous difficulty understanding formal Kurdish for I was fluent only in ordinary speaking Kurdish.

I felt myself in a daze, stumbling over every phrase. Sa'ad and Mother both shifted in their seats, looking uncomfortable.

Generally, the clerics I knew dripped dignity, but this cleric proved to be a lovely man, repeating each phrase several times, shortening them, trying to ease the embarrassing situation for me.

I was hopeless. I gave up and tried to suppress my giggles, knowing that Sa'ad would never recover if I laughed aloud during my own marriage ceremony. I was so pathetic that even Sarbast's sweet relatives looked at one another aghast.

Sa'ad glared at me. My brother knew the Koran by heart. He was appalled at my lack of religious knowledge.

My pink suit was damp with sweat when the ceremony finally ended. What should have been the happiest day of my life had turned into an embarrassing fiasco. And I feared I had failed the test.

What if the cleric ruled that I had botched my chance to marry?

But Mullah Ibrahim obviously regarded my performance passable, for he said nothing negative as he presented some documents for signature. My marriage was official. Sarbast was my husband. Finally!

Although a groom might not be a requirement for a Kurdish wedding, a groom *is* crucial for a successful honeymoon.

I was in a hurry to leave Sulaimaniya to find my groom. But I could not make the trip alone. Guides would be necessary all along the way. My fate would be in the hands of people I did not yet know.

After the ceremony, everyone enjoyed a lovely lunch, although we were unable to confide in any visitors who might pop in that we were celebrating my wedding. Despite the fact those visitors were Kurdish acquaintances, we could not be too careful. A careless word spoken might lead to the discovery that the mullah had broken one of Saddam's laws by performing a Peshmerga marriage. If that happened, everyone would be punished.

Late that evening word rushed through Sulaimaniya that Saddam's army was preparing for a big attack against the Peshmergas. I bade a hasty farewell to my new in-laws and to Sa'ad early the next morning.

Mother and one of Sarbast's sisters accompanied me from Sulaimaniya to the village of Qalat Diza, where I would be passed like a parcel into the hands of a female guide. Of course, we were driven by a male driver, for women in that area do not normally travel the roads without male protection.

The fertile plains surrounding Qalat Diza soon came into view. Despite the current tensions, Kurdish farmers in baggy pants were cultivating fields of wheat. Kandil Mountain rose majestically from behind the village, its rocky vaults still covered with snow, with beautifully wooded sides of the mountain sloping to frame the village.

Qalat Diza was one of Kurdistan's most beautiful villages. It was of particular interest to me for Sarbast had spent much of his childhood there, although his life was dramatically altered there.

Kurdistan had always been a hotbed of rebellions and massacres, and in 1974–1975 the unrest simmered yet again. Without a word of warning, the Iraqi government dropped napalm on the civilians of Qalat Diza, and hundreds died. Sarbast was a youthful witness to the chaos of sudden death. He had once described to me his anguish as he attempted to save neighbors and friends.

After the attack on Qalat Diza, Sarbast's family fled to Iran and lived in a refugee camp for nearly two years. By the time they returned from exile, Sarbast had formed a lifelong hatred for the government in Baghdad, a hatred that would lead to his becoming a Peshmerga.

Thankfully, Qalat Diza had survived a difficult past. I hoped the bad days were behind it. Yet, something sinister was in the air.

Arriving safely in Qalat Diza, I discovered that my guide was someone very special. She was Zakia Khan, Sarbast's cousin and the wife of a high-ranking PUK Peshmerga Qadir, a Kurdish warlord, considered royalty by Kurds. Zakia had courageously volunteered for the risky mission of helping me cross into the forbidden area of Kurdistan controlled by the Peshmerga.

It was at Qalat Diza that I bade my mother good-bye. It was a very emotional farewell for us both, for the seriousness of the situation in Kurdistan was now clear to us. Perhaps we would never see each other again.

Although saddened at the parting, I was in a rush to begin the precarious trek to the Forbidden Zone. I must get to Sarbast.

During the journey I grew to respect Zakia, finding her to be a brave and resourceful woman. While I was quaking with fright, she skillfully maneuvered us through some very dodgy situations at checkpoints.

I was horrified to discover that some of the checkpoints were manned by Kurdish traitors, collaborators known as Jahsh, men who should have been fighting on the side of their Kurdish brothers, but were in fact using their skills to betray brave Peshmergas. The Jahsh were in many ways more dangerous to us than Saddam's soldiers. They were of our kind and difficult to distinguish as they easily slipped into Peshmerga ranks as spies.

Those shameful collaborators sold out Kurdistan and the Kurds to a government that would happily murder them once they were of no more use. I could barely believe that there were Kurdish men who were prepared to kill Zakia and me if they should discover I was the new bride of a Peshmerga fighter.

But Zakia assured me that was the case.

The perilous trip was grinding and tense.

Finally, once under the protection of the high mountains and the canopy of the trees, I felt free and unafraid for the first time in days. I looked at the beauty around me, the mountains rising in lofty peaks, the luxuriant creepers that covered the limbs of gigantic trees, and the rushing streams swollen by the melting of the snows. The breathtaking vista helped me forget the hostile forces we had left behind.

At last, at the end of a six-hour drive over rocky unpaved roads, so bumpy the top of my head constantly bashed against the ceiling of the jeep, we finally arrived at the small village of Merge. By then I had terrible pains in my head, but when I was told that Sarbast was there waiting for me, I forgot my headache.

Merge, a small and extremely poor Kurdish village, was divided in two by a main road that was lined by simple houses built of concrete blocks. None of the tourist wealth that had once flowed to its close-by neighbor, Dokan Lake, a well-known vacation region in northern Kurdistan famed for its vineyards, figs, and pomegranates, had benefited Merge.

I knew that Sarbast was there, somewhere, in one of those homes, waiting for me. I wondered how on Earth we would find each other.

Impatient, I began anxiously searching the doorway of each house we passed. Suddenly, there was a flash of movement and Sarbast appeared from one of the houses. When his eyes met mine, he began running as quickly as he could, his long hair flowing, his eyes flashing, trying to catch the jeep.

I screamed at the jeep driver to stop. I reached my hands through the open side, wanting Sarbast to pull me from the jeep and into his arms. For some unexplained reason the driver sped up.

I peered out helplessly. I had never realized that Sarbast was such a fast runner. He was gaining on the jeep!

Fearing that the inattentive driver was going to race through the entire village without slowing, I decided to risk everything and leap from the jeep into Sarbast's outstretched arms. I braced myself and prepared to jump. When the driver saw what I was about to do, he finally pulled to the side of the dirt road and came to a stop. I was out of that jeep before the man could turn off the ignition.

Sarbast grabbed me in his arms and started spinning around and around, twirling me in the air. I laughed out loud. I had survived a thousand tribulations to reach that moment.

I opened my eyes to look past Sarbast's shoulder to see many smiling faces. A small crowd had gathered. It's not every day that a Peshmerga gets married to a woman from Baghdad.

One Peshmerga embarrassed Sarbast when he revealed that for the entire time I had been traveling, Sarbast was so anxious that he could not eat or sleep. In fact, he had sat up watching the road all night, dashing out to check on each vehicle that passed through the village. His comrades had added to his torture when they called out false alarms every few hours, telling him that the jeep with his bride had passed through the village without stopping. And that is nearly what happened!

I turned to look at the driver, wondering what on Earth he had been thinking. When I saw him laughing heartily, I realized that he, too, was in on the joke. But all had ended well, so I smiled happily at him.

Zakia climbed out of the jeep to stand proudly beside us, nodding at her cousin Sarbast and accepting his heartfelt thanks for bringing me safely to him.

Wedding and Honeymoon

Joanna in Sulaimaniya in May 1987 on her wedding day and without a groom. From left to right: Father-in-law Hussain Mohammed Amin; brother-in-law Osman Hussain; Joanna; Sa'ad; sister-in-law and daughter of Auntie Aisha, Nawbahar Mahmoud.

Joanna and Sarbast on day 1 of their honeymoon in Serwan.

Joanna and Sarbast on day 5 of their honeymoon.

I laughed, more excited and happy than I had ever been in my life. I knew in my heart that I belonged with these good people. I had come home.

Yet I could barely take my eyes off Sarbast. To me, he was still the most handsome man in the world. But he did look different, no longer the dashing young man I had fallen in love with. He seemed in need of a good night's sleep. He had grown a full beard. His hair was even longer, and those curls of his were completely tangled. I felt a rush of anticipation, as I thought that soon I would be free to tousle those curls with my hands. I had wanted to pull on those curls for ten years. Soon, my chance would come.

Then I remembered my own shabby appearance. Although I had planned on looking as pretty as possible, when Zakia spotted my large suitcase, she had firmly snapped her fingers, ordering that it be taken away. She explained that such a piece of luggage would create dangerous curiosity at the checkpoints.

I was told that I could carry only one change of clothing, one plain nightgown, and a comb, which were put into a worn and torn plastic bag. The rest of my belongings would come to me on a mule within the next few weeks.

Another blow came when I was told to wash my face clean of all the makeup and to pull my long hair into a bun. Zakia held my hands aloft for a few minutes, admiring my beautiful nails that were polished and painted to perfection, saying that while she had never seen such elegant fingernails in her life, they must be cut off.

"Joanna, if one soldier at the checkpoint spots these stylish nails, he will instantly know that you are *not* a mountain girl."

I could hardly bear to watch as those clipped long nails fell down to the table top, where they were gathered up and tossed into a bag of trash.

The worse was not yet over. Zakia furnished me with a plain navy blue dress, a black robe, a dark scarf, and a worn pair of plain flat slippers. I was told that it was imperative for me to look the part of a poor village girl.

Never had I dreamed that I would have to wear the veil and cloak again in my life. I was only glad that Sa'ad was not there to witness my humiliation. I struggled not to weep.

I did not want to greet my new husband in such attire, but Zakia was unmoving on those points. She was not willing to risk her own life if I was so foolish to flaunt my Baghdad sophistication. I saw her point.

I looked at Sarbast and whispered, "I'm sorry your bride had to come to you," and I looked down at my dress and slippers, "in this. I am ashamed of how I look."

Sarbast's dark eyes glittered with the purest happiness. "You are beautiful, Joanna." He tossed back his head, laughing, and I saw a flash of his perfect white teeth, thankfully all still intact. "Do I look like the groom of your dreams?" He shrugged and arched his eyebrows as he ran his hands over his threadbare shirt and trousers and fingered the thick beard on his face.

"Yes, you do, you are the groom of my dreams," I admitted. Consumed with happiness, I lightly touched his beard with one finger. "I will shave it off for you," I said, with a smile of promise.

Everyone circling us was watching and listening in complete delight. Rarely do we Kurds show any affection in public, but our traditional society excuses the affections of a young couple in love, a bride and groom just married. Our breathless reaction to each other was as entertaining as a rare visit to the cinema for Sarbast's friends.

Zakia modestly interrupted, "It is time to go now. Say good-bye to your friends, Sarbast. You will see them again in a month."

Along the trip I had been elated to learn that Sarbast and I would not go to Bergalou immediately, but that Sarbast's Peshmerga bosses had rewarded him with a month's break from the fighting. Sarbast and I were to have a month's honeymoon at the house of Zakia and her husband, Qadir Agha. I very nearly shouted out my joy, but thankfully I did not embarrass myself further in front of the others.

I was eager to leave, though. From what Zakia had described, they lived in mountain splendor, in a huge home in the village of Serwan, not far from Merge. They were so generous as to invite us to spend our honeymoon in that big house, saying that we deserved some happy, careless days before reporting for duty in Bergalou.

Never had I dreamed I would have a real honeymoon in the mountains.

I was living in a fairy tale where all dreams come true, for after years of hesitations, I could see that Sarbast finally did love me.

I did suffer one quick moment of doubt, however. For what reason had his feelings of friendship changed to love? By showing him the tenderness of my heart, had I won his?

I brushed aside all the questions troubling me. There would be plenty of time in our future for me to find out.

Sarbast and I sat as closely as possible in the jeep, our arms lightly touching. When Zakia leaned forward to speak to our driver, Sarbast glanced to make certain no one was looking, then surprised me with a quick kiss on my lips.

I felt a delicious tingling, reveling in the sensation his kiss created.

Since that first night long ago, when I had fallen in love with Sarbast, I had spent endless hours daydreaming of the moment he would be my husband. But never could I have imagined the joy I would experience by simply sitting by his side.

And that kiss! It had been tantalizing.

I was tempted to kiss him in return, in full view of Zakia and the driver, so I clasped my hands in my lap, turning to stare and think of something else, anything else. That's when I noticed the magnificent woods all around. The meandering road was shadowed by groves of chestnut and pistachio trees. Colorful wild flowers dotted the sloping mountains. Kurdistan was simply heaven on Earth.

Soon we arrived. Zakia's home seemed untouched by time, set back from the road and shaded by trees so huge that I assumed they were ancient. The house was very large and filled with children. I immediately felt at ease. Thankfully, their home was equipped with an intricate water pipe system that brought spring water from the mountains, because I needed a good bath.

Zakia took us around and out back, where there was a huge vegetable and fruit garden. I saw a barn almost as large as their home, with many cows, horses, donkeys, chickens, and ducks. The family could easily be self-sufficient.

I blushed crimson when Zakia showed me the room where Sarbast and I would spend our honeymoon. I was grateful to see that our bedroom was the most private bedroom and well away from the central area of the house where the family congregated.

Qadir Agha al-Pishderi, Zakia's husband, was a man of almost irresistible force. His title of *agha* indicated that he was the owner of vast amounts of land and the head of his tribe. Although he had jeopardized everything he owned when he joined the PUK, his eyes were calm with confidence, as though he didn't have a care in the world.

I was quickly in awe of the man, impressed by his serenity and cheerfulness. I had expected a different picture of such an important man, someone grave and pompous, perhaps. But he showed an interest in all, was solicitous and kind with his wife, laughed easily with his guests, and joked and played with his seven children. The youngest of his offspring was very mischievous and grabbed his father's precious binoculars, which were rare and difficult to obtain, for Saddam had made it an automatic death sentence for a Kurd to own a pair.

When he handled those binoculars like a toy, I became anxious and felt they should be put up high, on a safe shelf, but the *agha* laughed easily, saying, "My children are the owners of everything in this house, including their father."

I envied the relationship his children had with him, remembering how my own father's disability had kept him at such a distance from us.

Dinner was light because the mistress of the house had been away, and I was so tired that Zakia suggested that Sarbast and I retire early.

I blushed when we left our hosts, despite the fact they had done everything to make me feel at ease. But finally Sarbast and I were alone.

Becoming his wife was more wonderful than I could have ever imagined. Even after the passing of many years, when my children are grown and grandchildren are running at my feet, when I am so old that the hair on my head is glistening and white, I will remember the magic of my wedding night.

16

Under the Bergalou Sky

BERGALOU, KURDISTAN, IN NORTHERN IRAQ
June 1987

I reached the pinnacle of my dreams. Then I awoke to see a strange quivering. Nothing in life is perfect.

My mind was too hazy to know exactly what it was that I was seeing, but as I fluttered my eyes open, the roof over our little hut seemed to be trembling, a primitive roof that was in reality a mesh of small logs and twigs. Narrowing my eyes for a more careful look revealed that, indeed, the ceiling *was* moving.

Sarbast was sleeping soundly by my side.

I inched close to him, whispering, "Sarbast, wake up. Wake up!"

Sarbast opened one groggy eye. "What?"

"Look," I whispered. "Look. The roof is moving."

His voice was tired and sluggish. "No, Joanna, the roof is not moving."

"It is!" I was fully awake by then and leaned to light our small kerosene lantern. It spread only the dimmest light, although I could see well enough to know that two sides of the roof line were being stirred by something.

"Sarbast!"

Bleary eyed, he tossed back the pink coverlet and swiveled his head, then he grudgingly studied the ceiling.

"See!" I said, my excitement mounting. "There! The ceiling *is* moving!"

Without speaking, Sarbast pushed up from the floor, walked to the front door, grabbed one of his plastic slippers, stood on his tip-toes, and used the slipper to beat at the wall high up near the ceiling. Several gigantic scorpions fell to the floor.

I nearly screamed, gasping, cupping both hands over my mouth.

He slapped at them until they no longer moved.

"Scorpions?" I murmured with dread. Glancing upward, I realized the horrifying mystery behind the quivering ceiling. The entire roof over my head was swarming with scorpions!

My voice was shaky. "Oh, no, Sarbast. Oh, no. I can't sleep under nests of scorpions." I repeated, "No, no!"

Sarbast dropped heavily beside me, his arm draped loosely around my back. "Darling. Scorpions would rather retreat than fight."

I felt inflexible on the point. "No. Sarbast. No. I can't sleep with scorpions."

"They won't bother you if you don't bother them."

I then understood what the other fighters were hinting at when Sarbast bade them good night. Several men had chuckled while one muttered, "Happy hunting."

I had only been in Bergalou for a few hours, and I had already been chased out of our toilet by a snake. Now scorpions dangled over my head. I might as well sleep in the woods!

I stared upward in dread. The roof was still squirming. Those creepy creatures had amazing energy.

Sarbast kissed me lightly on the lips and fell back against the cotton mattress. He pulled the coverlet up under his armpits. "Go back to sleep. Forget about the scorpions."

I gaped. "Forget? Forget those scorpions? Never!"

I had always been a daring child. Nothing in my life truly frightened me other than snakes and scorpions. When I was six years old, a Kurdish cousin in Sulaimaniya chased me with a wiggling snake. He had dangled it by the tail, the snake's face curving close to my own, fangs threatening, causing an eternal snake phobia.

Since that incident, when in Kurdistan, I remained on special guard for serpents.

Then several years later during another summer holiday while admiring Grandmother Ameena's flower garden, I unintentionally came across the path of a large scorpion. Hearing my screams, Grandmother had run to the commotion. When I tearfully pointed out the hairy-legged creature, my enthusiastic grandmother detailed the dangers of a scorpion bite. She pointed out the six pairs of legs, describing just how handy they were. One set could grasp a toe, she said, while a second set could rip at it. Then the deadly creature could suck the juices right out of your body. My grandmother said that she loved me and wanted to keep me safe. But she gifted me with a lifelong fear of scorpions.

Before marrying Sarbast, I had contemplated the threat of shells and enemy soldiers and remained serene and undaunted. Scorpions and snakes had not been a worry. But our uninvited guests reminded me that Bergalou was surrounded by mountains and forests. I was intruding on territory inhabited by things wild and they were letting me know it.

I tossed and turned, and to get my mind on other matters, I started thinking about our beautiful honeymoon.

Sarbast and I had just spent thirty wonderful days honeymooning in Serwan, with the delightful Zakia Khan and Qadir Agha. Relatives and visitors living near the region had flocked to deliver small gifts and give us their blessings. Happily, there were plenty of opportunities for me to wear makeup and arrange my long hair in elaborate fashions as well as don my beautiful pink wedding dress that I had not worn at my wedding. I was delighted that Sarbast had the chance to admire his bride at last.

Yet there was some quiet time to share our joy in each other, plan our future, and discover all that occurred in the years after he left me in Baghdad.

There was excitement as well, as the war didn't cease just because we were newlyweds. During such moments, I learned a lot from Zakia Khan regarding the duties of a Peshmerga wife.

I learned how to pluck a chicken, milk a cow, and identify Iraqi planes as the enemy. I learned that the first thing I should do at any new mountain location was to locate the nearest bomb shelter. I learned that sharing a common enemy creates an instant camaraderie between people, even if they are different ages and from contrasting backgrounds. I learned that Peshmerga wives are never idle, that a true Peshmerga woman toils persistently to support her husband and the cause. I learned that I would be leading a primitive lifestyle. I learned that I had made the best decision of my life when I accepted Sarbast's marriage proposal and joined him in Kurdistan to share the freedom fighter life. Finally, I learned that I was in a position to fulfill my lifelong goal of supporting the Kurdish cause. As a single woman, it would have been unrealistic to live in Bergalou. It was a fighter's village, essentially for men, although there were a few courageous unmarried women as well who had a brother or a father who was a Peshmerga. I would have never been accepted before, but now that I was married to Sarbast, I would be warmly welcomed.

Sarbast accidentally pulled my pink bed cover off me when he rolled over, already in a sound sleep. How could he sleep?

Then I reminded myself that Sarbast had been living the Peshmerga life for over five years. The reality was that it was much more dangerous and demanding than I had expected. But I would learn, and I *would* make a difference. I was determined.

My eyelids felt heavy. I should sleep because tomorrow I would meet Sarbast's Peshmerga friends and acquaint myself with Bergalou. There had been no time to do so today, as we had arrived shortly after dark, trembling with fatigue after our long trek through the mountains.

I closed my eyes, then blinked them open again to keep a steady eye on the writhing scorpions, wondering what on Earth was in those twigs that kept them so busily occupied. I turned to sleep on my stomach and pulled the bedding as a shield over my head. I would prefer a scorpion on my back than on my face. I must learn to bear it. I might well live in this hut for years.

While I waited for sleep, reflections of the past month continued to flicker.

In Serwan, I had made the distressing discovery that I was woefully ill prepared for the most ordinary challenges of Peshmerga life, that while I possessed the brave heart of a freedom fighter, I didn't have the necessary skills or the adept hands. Pampered always by my mother and siblings, I was embarrassingly inept regarding the simplest matters when it came to cooking and cleaning. I had already humiliated myself on two occasions.

One morning, a few guests unexpectedly arrived in Serwan for lunch. I volunteered to help cook, insisting that Zakia assign me a duty.

Zakia made a quick gesture to the back garden. "Joanna, yes, please catch eight chickens and prepare them."

I stood helplessly, having never touched a live chicken in my life. But I was too self-conscious to admit the truth to Zakia, who had already dashed out of the room to complete other pressing tasks. Sarbast had gone on a small errand, so he was not around to help. I was on my own.

I sauntered outside. The back garden was full of plump chickens busily walking about, pecking at worms, and kicking up dust with their feet.

How hard could it be, I asked myself, as I purposefully marched toward those birds. Five minutes later I was sprawled flat on the ground without a chicken in hand, although feathers were fluttering. At least I was an amusing distraction, as the ruckus had gotten the attention of a small crowd of Zakia's guests.

I'm certain Zakia was flabbergasted at my domestic ignorance, but that kindly woman patiently instructed me on everything I needed to know about killing chickens. Soon I was standing beside her, confidently plucking a chicken and helping prepare the lunch.

Several days later, I assisted with chickens a second time by volunteering for the worst part of the job in hope of reclaiming my dignity. I was standing over a boiling pot and dipping chickens to soften the roots of the feathers, when suddenly everyone around me dashed in the direction of the barn.

Zakia seized the chicken from my hands, threw it in the pot, and grabbed me by my wrist, shouting, "Run! Run for the shelter!"

I ran.

Seconds later, Zakia pushed me into a small earthen shelter beside the barn. I heard a tremendous roar. The ground was suddenly rocked by an explosion. We were being bombed!

Although when I lived in Baghdad I had suffered Iranian bomb attacks many times since the war with Iran had begun, I had not expected our mountain paradise to be found so easily.

I looked at Zakia and remarked, "I had no idea the Iranians were bombing Kurdish villages! There was no warning roar. And how did you know that wasn't a passenger airplane, anyway?"

Everyone sharing the shelter laughed loudly. One gleeful woman even slapped her thigh as she doubled over.

I blushed crimson, the naive city girl from Baghdad.

Zakia kindly took me under her wing, gently explaining, "Joanna, that plane was not Iranian. It was Iraqi. And passenger planes don't fly low, not in these mountains. If you hear *any* airplane, it *is* an enemy plane. In these mountains, our enemy hails from Baghdad, not from Tehran."

"Oh." The moment had been bewildering, because I *knew* that the Iranians had allied with the Kurds to fight Saddam, but I had been so accustomed to being a target for the Iranians that the switch would take some getting used to. It wasn't as if I hadn't heard before leaving Baghdad that the Iraqi military had begun targeting solitary mountain villages with increased enthusiasm.

I was so embarrassed that I wanted to cry.

Zakia patted my shoulder. "Joanna, remember this: When we work, eat, or do anything, only half of our attention is given to the task at hand. The other half is listening to the sounds of the sky. You'll soon learn, for in Bergalou it will be the same. Before long, you'll identify the distant roar of a plane even before the birds hear it."

My heart skipped several beats when she whispered, "We hear that Saddam has begun testing with chemicals." She glanced around to make certain her children were out of earshot. "Who knows what that madman will do." She pulled me close to her for a brief hug, warning, "Be careful, child. Always be alert. We are entering a dangerous period."

Yes, my time in Serwan had taught me several good lessons. I had much more to learn, but I would tread carefully, watching and listening, not wishing to be a source of Bergalou jokes.

During our honeymoon, Sarbast had excited me with his stories of life in Bergalou, despite the fact that he had lost several good friends on the battlefield and that he himself had suffered many close calls.

The following day I would explore my new home and meet the brave fighters Sarbast had told me so much about. I was anxious to meet the women of Bergalou, although I had been disappointed when Sarbast reported that out of nearly two hundred fighters, there were only a few women and two children living in the village. It was too unsafe for most women, he said.

Bergalou was only one of a chain of small villages tucked away in the Jafati Valley. The villages accommodated the most important infrastructure of the PUK. While Bergalou was the home to the radio station and main field hospital, Sergalou, a twin village nearby, housed the regional command. Other adjacent villages contained equally important PUK facilities.

Over the years, I had heard Kurdish patriots ask why the PUK didn't locate its command center in Sulaimaniya, which was a one hundred percent Kurdish city. But now I understood the PUK leadership's logic. Sulaimaniya was a large city filled with civilians. Civilians could not be easily protected.

On the other hand, Jafati Valley, where all the command villages were located, was protected by tall mountains and separated from the rest of Kurdistan by extremely difficult terrain. The secure location made it nearly impossible for Saddam's soldiers to reach us.

Helping me to realize the importance of Bergalou and the other PUK fighter villages in Jafati Valley, Sarbast simplified the situation for me, saying, "Joanna. Think of it like this: Baghdad is the capital of Iraq. Baghdad is where the central command of the Iraqi military is located. Jafati Valley is the center of command for the PUK. Bergalou, Sergalou, Haladin, Yehksemar, Maluma, and Zewa are just as important to us, the PUK, as Baghdad is to Saddam. Jafati Valley is our PUK capital, the nerve center."

Happy to be a part of such an important movement, I finally drifted off to a night of peaceful sleep. Thankfully, I did not sustain a deadly scorpion bite during the night.

The following morning Sarbast woke me with a low laugh and a sweet kiss. "Wake up, wake up, Joanna. Welcome to your new home."

I stretched contentedly, pushing upright. Remembering what was hanging overhead, I glanced at the ceiling.

Reading my mind, Sarbast said, "Don't worry. The scorpions are generally quiet during the day. They like the warmth of the sun hitting the roof. They sleep." He laughed. "Just don't move around at night. That's when they get busy."

"Don't move? When I'm sleeping? I move around in my sleep, Sarbast."

"Train yourself not to move and they will ignore you."

I shivered nervously, asking, "Have you ever been bitten?"

"Never."

Taking a deep breath, I decided at that moment that there was nothing to do but to make the best of it. Never again would I concern myself with those scorpions. They could stay in their place, and I would stay in mine.

It was a good day, I reminded myself. While few sensible people would choose to leave a comfortable home in Baghdad and live in a fighter's village surrounded by a deadly enemy, for me, Bergalou was a dream come true, the fulfillment of my fondest fantasy.

A distant memory flashed as three beautiful faces came soaring into my mind from seventeen years past. The vision was of the beautiful Kurdish sisters selling jewelry at the market in Sulaimaniya. The brutal regime in Baghdad had taken their future from them, dashing their dreams of marrying men they loved and living the Peshmerga life, fighting for Kurdistan.

While those three sisters had most likely died at the hands of their jailors, they had never left my mind. As a young girl I had so envied those young women. I was now living their dream, and my own. In some way, I believed my existence kept them alive. Joy and sorrow mingled, and with tears in my eyes, I prepared myself for the first day of a new life.

I decided to inspect my new home before eating breakfast and unpacking. When I insisted that my husband show me around, I watched his face fall in worry as he warned me, "Darling, you know that revolutions are never comfortable, right?"

"You are correct, husband," I replied, as I clung to his strong arm, swinging along beside him, so happy that nothing could discourage me.

"We can take our meals here," Sarbast gestured with his hand as we stood before the small sitting room.

I looked at our meager furnishings, wondering what I might do to brighten the place. A low Japanese-style table stood in the middle of the room, with two worn cushions stashed underneath, along with Sarbast's weapons, a Kalashnikov rifle and a pistol.

Even in Serwan, Sarbast had kept his weapons within reach. He told me that the first lesson for a freedom fighter was to always keep loaded weapons on hand. Most battles struck with lightning speed.

Sarbast had refused to teach me to use weapons while on our honeymoon, saying that could wait until we were in Bergalou.

He was reading my mind again. "Tomorrow. Tomorrow I will teach you how to protect yourself."

I nodded in agreement.

But for the moment I was thinking about our home. There was nowhere to store our belongings: a few books, photographs, and clothes. We were surrounded by forest. My mind raced with the possibilities. Surely I could have a bookcase and some small tables built from one of those thousands of trees.

An unexpected sight caught my attention. A television set was pushed up against the wall.

"Oh! Does it work?"

"It's difficult to get reception here. Sometimes I can get one station. And the TV is very old, as well."

Hmmm. I would see about that. It would be lovely to watch any kind of transmission, but in any case I would keep it. Its mere presence was a reminder of normal life.

Our little dwelling had been built for survival, not for luxury. Our walls were unpainted cinder blocks, enfolding two miniature rooms for living, and a tiny area converted into a make-believe kitchen, equipped with a refrigerator that Sarbast was using as a cupboard. There was also a hot plate. Only occasionally would we have electricity when the generators were working, so neither could be used routinely. The floor was rough concrete with perceptible ridges. I would need slippers on my feet to walk comfortably over the floor.

For protection, our two windows were covered with razor wire. Few homes in Kurdish areas were equipped with glass windows. The flying glass caused by the recurring bombardments would have been a constant hazard.

"At least the water is pure and sweet," Sarbast proclaimed proudly. "It's spring water, brought directly into our homes through the water hoses."

My dear husband was worried that I found our home lacking.

"This is a dollhouse," I pronounced loyally, in that moment

adjusting fully to my environment and giving in completely to the cause. "There is no need to show me the toilet," I reminded him. I was recalling the night before, the dismal state of that bleak hole of a room and the snake coiled in a corner, its jittery eyes focused on me, the intruder.

I had fled with my clothes dragging on the floor, and Sarbast had run in to investigate, coming out with a red face and jutting chin to report that I had confused a looped twig he kept inside to kill bugs for a snake. I pretended to believe him, but thought that my husband just wanted to protect my peace of mind, suspecting that he had killed the snake and tossed it in the grass.

After my close call from the falling bombs in Serwan, I insisted on inspecting our own bomb shelter, and Sarbast obliged. He told me that there was a large concrete shelter in the village center that was more comfortable, but with bombing and shelling attacks on the rise, rarely was there enough time to dash down the hill, as our little home was at the greatest distance from the village center.

Our personal shelter edged the house, concealed under the lip of a tufted ridge of packed dirt. I knelt low to peer inside and caught a scent of dank air that smelled like the den of a fetid animal.

It was a very small space, casting doubt in my mind whether Sarbast and I could both fit. For once in my life I was glad of my slim build. Perhaps there was enough space if I would lie flat. I silently questioned how Sarbast might sidle his bulky frame into that hole, however.

I could think of nothing favorable to say about that shelter, so I said nothing at all. We walked back into the house.

"I love it here," I said to my husband, as I began unpacking my case, carefully laying my comb, brush, hand mirror, lipstick, soap, and lotion on top of my pink bedding. I had fought to be allowed to keep the bedding all the way from Baghdad, through Qalat Diza to Serwan and to Bergalou. Everyone who saw the set cautioned against it. It was too bulky. It was too luxurious. Even Sarbast questioned it, claiming that a fighter's hideout was not a place for such extravagance, but I had insisted and won, saying that surely a fighter deserved some comfort. Ironically, Sarbast slept most contentedly under that pink girlish set.

"We will make it a fine home," I said with a glad heart and a confident smile.

Relieved that his bride was truly content, Sarbast grinned, lifting me into the air and holding me there, then pulling me down beside him.

Several hours later Sarbast introduced me to Bergalou.

While our little hut was less than perfection, I could not say the same about our surroundings. We were beautifully protected.

Bergalou was one of the most secluded spots in all of Kurdistan, situated in a beautiful green valley surrounded by a natural fortress of mountains. It made a perfect setting for a guerrilla stronghold.

Sarbast informed me that there were numerous caves in those tall mountains, caves that would make ideal hideouts for the fighters, should the day ever come that our enemy succeeded in their quest to invade the valley.

I felt completely safe in that mountain refuge as I paused to look around. The high mountains ringing us were topped with peaks so tall they appeared to touch the sky. How could any army manage an invasion over those mountains? I naively believed it impossible.

The myriad chirpings of a multitude of birds entertained us as we hiked a rocky mountain path down to the village. I peered with curiosity at the chain of small huts lacing the mountainside, so similar to our own, wondering about the lives being lived in those dwellings. Modest homes had been constructed for the Peshmerga fighters, homes that stretched along the perimeter of the village with our neighborhood extending out to the base of the mountains. Most of the dwellings were constructed with their back walls braced against the hills. On one side of each home, at least, the earth provided some protection from bombs and shells.

Although I had walked through those mountains on the way to Bergalou the previous day, I was so weary after a full day of alternating between walking and riding on a donkey for the first time in my life—a particularly disagreeable donkey at that, who tried to fling me from his back on more than one occasion—that the beauty of the valley had gone unnoticed.

Before Bergalou, the PUK radio station had been located in the village of Nowzang, but with the onset of the Iran-Iraq War, the two mighty armies met there in battle in 1983, and the PUK fighters had to find a new location for their headquarters. From Nowzang, the fighters moved to a village called Sarshew, but soon that village became engulfed by the war as well. That's when the

PUK came to Bergalou, an abandoned village that had once been an important base for guerrilla fighters for the rival Kurdish leader Mulla Mustafa Barzani.

The PUK had repaired the vacated buildings and added more. There were now over sixty buildings in Bergalou that housed nearly two hundred Peshmergas. Additionally, other Peshmergas living elsewhere in the valley often used the village as a temporary stopover when going back and forth to the fighting front.

The village square had a medical clinic, a communal kitchen, and a large shelter. Those collective dwellings were roughly constructed of concrete blocks topped with thatched roofs, buildings easily erected and easily destroyed.

After settling in Bergalou, the fighters built their radio station in the mountains, anchoring their antenna in the hard rock at the mountain's highest point, a twenty-minute hike from the village. The radio station was a powerful PUK tool that recruited Peshmergas, called for Saddam's downfall, and alerted Kurdish villagers to the location of Saddam's army. Sarbast would be walking to that place every day to work.

It was then that I learned that women did not work from the station, as it was considered a particularly dangerous location given that Saddam's airmen were always trying to make direct hits on that place. I would help my husband in his work from home.

Sarbast was one of several writers and broadcasters who broadcast from the clandestine PUK radio station, "The Voice of the Freedom Fighters." I knew from his letters that he was a talented writer, although I had not yet read or heard any of his political writings. The PUK radio station had won the open hatred of Saddam Hussein, so all the broadcasters took pen names to protect their identities. Sarbast was known as Nabaz, meaning "invincible." I was immensely proud of my husband.

On my first full day in Bergalou, I saw Peshmerga soldiers everywhere, busily dashing to and fro.

Sarbast looked around uneasily. "Joanna, the village is even more active than when I left to meet you in Merge." He hesitated, adding, "Something major is happening."

"What? What do you think?"

"We'll find out soon enough. The front line is located around the Duban Mountains, not so far from here. Fighters have always passed through here to go to the front, but it's been a lot busier since the beginning of the year." Then he focused on me with his most serious expression. "They know we are here, Joanna. Saddam hates us Kurds more than all his other enemies combined. Right now, Saddam has many painful boils to lance, but the Kurdish boil is his most painful. We broadcast his misdeeds. We encourage others to rebel.

"He knows exactly where we are." He clicked his tongue. "He intends to kill us all. The instant he swirls his signature on a peace agreement with Iran, he will come to lance the Kurdish boil. That's when we start to worry."

I was quiet, thinking. I had been praying for the war with Iran to end since the first day it started. But if what Sarbast was saying was true, I was wrong to do so. At the moment, Saddam could spare only minimal troops to man the checkpoints and to drop bombs and shells on us. When the war with Iran ceased, and there was talk that the war seemed to be moving to a finale, he would have a huge land army at his disposal, armed for battle and, most frightening, not far from where we were living, for most of Kurdistan was close to the Iranian border where the war raged.

Sarbast coughed, clearing his throat, then said, "Even now the pressure is building. Every day we are under bombardment from airplanes and rockets." He glanced at his watch. "I'm surprised they have not started already. Be prepared to run with me."

Just then we stepped into the communal kitchen. Although there were assigned cooks, Sarbast whispered that none of them was an accomplished cook. He had confided while in Serwan that one of the most unpleasant aspects of a fighter's life was the lack of appetizing food. With Saddam's armies blocking most of the known roads into the mountains, it was nearly impossible to get supplies through. Smugglers mainly concentrated on transporting military equipment and ammunition, leaving fighters and their families reduced to eating very bland rations. What a pity, I thought, for Kurdish food was the best in the world.

Sarbast looked mischievous when he whispered, "The delicacies of Baghdad are not to be found here."

I chuckled, so happy to be sharing everything with him, even bad food.

And it was bad. We were served a bland meal of white rice and flat beans simmered in tomato sauce. After filling our plates, we settled at a communal table to eat the tasteless fare. Sarbast was greeted warmly by his friends and introductions went round.

Some fighters expressed stunned surprise when told that I had left Baghdad to come to Bergalou.

I truthfully replied, "I have a stake in this fight, too."

Before we could finish our lunch, someone dashed inside to shout that missiles were coming in. There was a mad scramble for the air raid shelter. Sarbast and I sprinted.

I heard a piercing crack just as Sarbast pushed me into the shelter, a rather large room that had been partially built into the earth. But compared to that cramped earthen burrow behind our hut, the concrete shelter was pure luxury. I felt a small stab of desire, wishing that our home could be closer to the village central. I'd never make it to the central shelter from that distance. More often than not, it would be the dirt lair for me.

Obviously, other villagers had no time to get to the communal shelter for I was the only woman among a large number of fighters. During the attack, everyone sat without talking. Heads were propped against the walls, hands in laps, listening to the dull thuds of the incoming shells. Most looked worried and I thought I knew why, for during our time in Serwan, Sarbast had told me that some of the conventional bombs were so large that nothing could protect against them. A direct hit on the shelter would kill everyone inside. I refused to consider the possibility. Surely I could not be so unlucky, at least not so soon.

The attack grew louder. Sarbast had mentioned that the government troops routinely dropped cluster bombs, which caused the most grievous injuries to anyone exposed outside. My thoughts focused on the human beings and animals caught in the open.

Sarbast reassured me with his arm around my shoulder, tapping me on the arm, but I was truly unafraid, thinking that being under bombardment under the Bergalou sky was not as frightening as being bombarded under the Baghdad sky. There had been many occasions that I huddled with Mother, Muna, little Nadia, Sa'ad, and his wife, all of us crammed into our tiny bathroom, which was pitifully unfit as a bomb shelter, waiting for the deadly Iranian cargo to find us there. And, here I was again, hiding from danger raining from the sky. Some things just never changed.

When the bombardment ended, everyone filed out, looking around to see the destruction. Surprisingly, there was little structural damage, although I saw two small storage buildings that had been hit. It appeared that most of the shells and bombs had missed their targets. Sarbast told me that our enemies were notoriously inconsistent when directing their firepower. Although there were casualties at Bergalou, there were fewer than one might expect.

Everyone in Bergalou then carried on as though nothing out of the ordinary had occurred. Human beings can adjust to almost anything, I decided.

Soon, Sarbast walked me home before looping back to Bergalou and then on to the radio station. He would return for dinner, and afterward, he promised, I would meet the other women.

Sarbast forgot to warn me of one very important fact, that it was a daily ritual for the Iraqi army to close each day by lobbing three shells into the village. The soldiers were so precise that the three shells had begun to feel rather ceremonial.

The Iraqi soldiers kept to their routine on my first full day in Bergalou. I was home alone when those shells burst. Wondering if the shells were the beginning of a serious offensive, I huddled in a corner, hands held over my head, locked in what I thought was a safe position.

Then Sarbast ran in through the door, looking worried. He was surprised to see that I was calm, that I was only being cautious, and he gathered me in his arms. "You are such a brave Peshmerga, darling," he whispered, then laughing, said, "Now your dreams have finally come true. Welcome to the real world of the Kurds, Joanna."

Dinner was congealed leftovers we had brought back from lunch.

Sarbast said that after dark we would join other Peshmergas gathered on the hillside. Once the Iraqi soldiers sent in their final three shells, the villagers often gathered to dance, tell stories, and visit to celebrate living through another day. The noise of many voices drew me.

The evening promised to be all that I had dreamed of.

While there were some fighters who remained on duty, guarding the village, many other Bergalou residents gathered to sit on the green grass. Although it was a night in June, there was a slight chilly breeze dipping down from the high mountains. The moon was nearly full, its light brightening the gathering.

I spotted three women among all the men, and I felt their eyes follow me. Sarbast mentioned there was a fourth wife living in the village, but she was not there that evening.

I was living in a village of nearly two hundred men and only five women. I looked closer at the three women and settled on a young woman holding a small boy on her lap. She was whistling and cooing to him. I was intrigued by that woman and her beautiful baby, wondering about her story, for every Peshmerga had a story.

I felt strangely shy in the midst of all those heroes and sat quietly beside Sarbast, a recent inexperienced bride.

But when a group of the men jumped up, forming a line to begin dancing in their guerrilla uniforms, I started to relax. Someone brought out a tamboura to tap out the beat of the dance. Several of the dancers used sticks to depict a mock battle scene. Sarbast leaped up to join them.

I clapped along with the crowd, sharing a smile with those welcoming me. Several dancers begin to sing a popular song in our Sorani Kurdish dialect.

I felt my emotions building, fighting back tears of joy. I was doing exactly what I had always dreamed of, exactly where I had always wanted to be. I was home. Home in Kurdistan. Finally.

17

Good Kurd, Bad Kurd

BERGALOU, KURDISTAN
July 1987

Wednesday, 22 July 1987
My dear Mother,

Kisses and greetings to you. I hope you and the rest of the family are all right. I must admit that I terribly miss my nephews, particularly little Ranj, for I know that I will be missing his precious babyhood. I cannot believe that he was born nearly a year ago. Please tell Alia to never let her boys forget me.

This letter of mine is a bit late, but you know the situation and why it is difficult for me to keep a regular correspondence. I have no way of knowing if you will receive this letter, as it will leave my hand to go to another hand and travel hand to hand all the way from me to you.

Dear Mother, I have been living in this village long enough to know that I have taken the correct path. I have no regrets for choosing Sarbast and this Peshmerga life. He is the man I want for my partner. He has a strong willpower and attitudes that suit me. He has chosen a life full of adventures, risks, and danger, but it is a good life that makes me proud, because he has sacrificed his life for a cause he believes in. For all of this I feel honored to be the wife

194

of this struggler and to share his hardships, because his cause is my cause.

But of course my life has changed very much. I barely remember the young woman I was in Baghdad who ate delicious food and shopped for pretty clothes and drank tea and coffee visiting with friends and family.

Who was she?

That girl is no more.

The new Joanna is experiencing each day a very hard, merciless war. From Baghdad we heard stories of the cruelties against our brothers and sisters in Kurdistan, but the reality is worse than we ever imagined. Such a savage war is being waged against our people, who are struggling to live free in this land, yet we all feel happy because of a strong determination to win.

Your little Joanna is sure of her decision, so should I make the ultimate sacrifice, let there be peace in your heart that I died doing what I wanted to do. Do not destroy your life with mourning, Mother.

I want to tell you all that has happened since we parted.

From Qalat Diza I traveled to Merge with Zakia. From Merge, Sarbast joined us on our way to Serwan, where we honeymooned for a month. There were enemy roadblocks at various locations, but after the Peshmerga April 27 Karbala-Ten offensive (which we hear caused nearly 5,000 enemy casualties in the Iraqi Fifth Army) there were some areas held by our fighters in conjunction with the Iranian troops. As you might have heard, there was another important offensive, Nasr [Victory] that targeted Sulaimaniya province. I hear that many land gains were made, and for that I am glad. Perhaps life will become easier for those we love in that area. We heard a radio broadcast straight from Tehran where Rafsanjani claimed that "Sulaimaniya is a gate of entrance to the rest of Iraq," so we assume the Iranians are going to concentrate their forces in that important area, which may or may not ease our situation here in Jafati Valley.

For now I want to tell you about my life here. Sarbast is on an important mission, which means I am alone today, a rare time of complete solitude that I will spend talking to you through the pages of this letter.

I will hide nothing from you. I will always be honest. There is nothing of normal life here. I am living in a tiny hut in a primitive village. Yet it is more precious to me than a palace in Baghdad. Our modest home is plain and simple, with the barest of furnishings. We share our home with many mice, who are quite cute when they pop out to sit on the floor on their little haunches, their little eyes watching my every move, their small paws poised as though waiting for a meal. I give them bread crumbs, and sometimes bits of cheese—over Sarbast's objections that word is getting around in the mouse community that a tender heart lives in this house. But those small mice can do us no real harm as I keep our food stored in a refrigerator. It is too bad that the refrigerator does not function, but it makes a handy storage cupboard.

Although the mice are harmless, I cannot say the same about the other creatures, especially the snakes that keep me alert with each step I take.

Yes, there are snakes. And there are scorpions.

As far as the quality of our food, it is best that I say nothing. The roadblocks are a deterrent to our smugglers, so little food gets past our enemy. Like a prisoner on a diet of dry bread and water, I often dream of your special Kurdish dishes.

But I am thankful that we do not starve.

At least ours is a home filled with love. Few married couples can match our happiness. Even my girlhood dreams fail to measure up to the joy I know living the Peshmerga life alongside my husband.

This, despite the fact we are under constant bombardment in our little village.

Let me tell you about the bombing and the shelling.

The warnings I received never prepared me for the level of the attacks on Bergalou. My ears and my eyes are now finely tuned to the danger. Finally, I understand Zakia's meaning when she warned me in Serwan that whatever one might be doing here, half the mind will not be focusing on the task at hand, but instead on the sounds and sights from the sky. When I am preparing breakfast, my hands are busy with the task, but my ears are listening for the shrill whistling resonance of shells, or for the noisy roar of an airplane or helicopter engine. It is the same when I am reading Sarbast's radio scripts, or using the toilet, or washing clothes, or visiting with other Peshmerga ladies, or walking to the village.

Never do I let my guard down.

Although we have had sad losses, there have not been as many as the frequency of the attacks might suggest. But one particular incident haunts me.

Two of the youngest Peshmergas were recently lost. The two young boys were devoted friends and very young, although I do not know their exact ages. I had seen them many times in the village. I felt badly that they were not in school, but they seemed focused and happy on their Peshmerga life. One day when they were manning the antiaircraft guns they took a direct hit. Both were killed instantly. I'm sorry that I saw their crumpled bodies because now I cannot get that image out of my mind. One day they were laughing and teasing and the next day they were dead. They were put into bags and buried in the fighters' cemetery near to the village.

The only consolation is that their lives rested on the hope of freedom. Perhaps their sacrifice will help to bring freedom to the rest of us.

It is very nerve-racking not knowing from one minute to the next if a bomb or shell might find you. Sarbast insists that I go to our earthen shelter each time I hear a plane, but I cannot make myself if he is not home. Instead, I sit it out in a corner of the house, the way we used to do in Baghdad under the Iranian attacks. But when Sarbast is home, he forces me into that dirt hole.

I would rather take my chances with the bombs. I'll describe it, and you will understand. I must be on my hands and knees to wiggle through the opening, with Sarbast pushing from behind. The shelter is very confining, so small that I cannot even sit straight. I am forced to crawl to a cramped position with the crown of my head touching the dirt ceiling.

Mother, did you know that every kind of insect species makes their home in Kurdistan? And did you know that most of them live in Bergalou?

And they all visit me when I am in the shelter. They mostly love to snuggle in my hair. One with particularly long legs tried to settle in my nose.

I fidget, unable to rest in that shelter. I marvel in admiration at Sarbast, who curls in a ball and sleeps like a contented baby.

I asked Sarbast yesterday how he could have borne this for five years, and he laughed, saying that it has never been so bad before, that while they were bombed and shelled in the past, the attacks were infrequent. But since the day I arrived in Bergalou, the bombing and shelling never ceases. Sarbast teased me, saying that I had brought this upon Bergalou.

Thankfully, we are snugly protected by tall mountains, making it impossible for our enemies to grapple with us face to face.

I have met so many *good* Kurds living in this village. Their sacrifices make the troubles we have known as Kurds living in Baghdad appear insignificant.

I am not the only female freedom fighter. There are four others, one the wife of a senior Peshmerga who sets a good example for us all. There are also two children living in this village, a toddler girl and a baby boy.

The woman I have come to know best is the mother of the baby boy. I want to tell you a little about this woman because she has been living this life of sacrifice since she was a young girl. While I was attending university in Baghdad, she was living this violent life already. When I think about this, I wonder if perhaps I should have joined this cause at an earlier age. Although my spirit was with the Kurdish cause, I was not contributing. I could have skipped university and come to the north, to take up my responsibility. When I have such thoughts, I worry that perhaps I selfishly claimed simultaneously the privileges of both my Arab heritage and my Kurdish heritage.

Regarding Ashti, the woman I so admire, you would look upon her as a daughter, as she is so dear, more brave and intelligent than most men. She is a small woman, but her courage matches that of a mountain lion. Her father was a well-known Peshmerga, murdered years ago at the hands of one of the bad Kurds, a Jahsh.

She is of a fighter family, so it was no surprise that she was born gushing with a fighter's blood. From the moment she was old enough to contribute to the cause, she did. At the young age of fifteen or sixteen years, Ashti became an undercover agent working in Hawler. As a Jahsh had killed her father, a Jahsh tried to kill the daughter. She was turned in by a bad Kurd, a Jahsh informant, and was forced to leave her home behind and flee into the mountains. Because her brother Azaad was already fighting from the PUK base in Toojhala, she went to that place, and because she was clever, she was assigned intelligence duties, analyzing political commentary broadcast from Baghdad, Tehran, and the west.

I have been told that it was most unusual for a single woman to live and work in a fighter village, but that her brother's presence made it acceptable.

Of course, some of the unattached Peshmerga men expressed interest in such a pretty, intelligent girl, but Ashti was vigilant of her reputation. She kept to herself, leading a life of social isolation.

But before long, one of the engineers, a highly respected Peshmerga named Rebwar, fell in love with her. Since Rebwar knew Ashti's brother, he was able to go through the proper channels by talking with her brother first.

There was a happy ending. Ashti and Rebwar married.

When the PUK media headquarters was moved to Bergalou, Ashti and Rebwar were among the first to arrive. I hear they lived in tents and caves in the beginning.

Even while living as a fighter, Ashti gave birth to a precious baby son, Hema. You would love this little baby. He would break your heart, as he breaks mine. He cries too much because the bombs and shells scare him, but he brings joy and hope for life to all of us living in this little village.

Hema reminds us of what we are fighting for. Even if we die, perhaps he will survive to live a free life in Kurdistan.

That poor baby endured a gas attack earlier in the year. In case you have not heard, Bergalou was hit with chemicals during the time I was in Serwan, on my honeymoon. Thankfully the chemicals were not mixed properly, or perhaps the wind was blowing in the right direction for us and the wrong direction for the murderers, so the casualties were not as high as they could have been. I heard that 200 fighters were lost, but the number could have been in the thousands had the chemicals been stronger. Sarbast and I were on our honeymoon, or my first experience as a bride would have been with those deadly gases. We were also lucky that Sarbast was allowed time away from the front during a major battle.

I don't want to worry you, but there have been other chemical attacks in the area. I believe this is because Saddam has appointed his cousin, Ali al-Majid, full authority to eliminate the Kurdish problem. Perhaps you have heard of this appointment? Ali Majid's entry creates additional worry, for he is the most fanatical servant of Saddam.

We hear that our continued rebellion has driven Saddam to a bitter fury. For this reason, the threat of chemicals has become so serious that we have all been supplied with gas masks. So try not to worry.

One of my most thrilling experiences has been to learn about weapons. As you know Peshmerga fighters are armed at all times, but I am quite upset that our leaders have ruled that women cannot join the battlefront. Is my life worth more than Sarbast's life? I believe that our lives are equally valuable. So when I stay behind and watch as he leaves on important missions, my heart skips many beats until he returns.

Although I am not allowed to go with him to battle, I must be prepared in the event of an attack. Since our home is the longest distance from the village, I suppose we would be the first to confront the enemy should they emerge over the mountains and into this valley.

I want to give you some interesting news about Kamaran Hassan. You must remember him. His mother is Nazara, sister to Sarbast's mother, Khadrja, so he is Sarbast's first cousin. He and Sarbast have lived side by side since their childhood, when they were in Qalat Diza, and for the two years after the napalm attack, when they lived in the Iranian refugee camp together with their families. So they have a bond that is difficult to break.

If you remember, Kamaran put his patriotism first, and as soon as he graduated with his economics degree, he became PUK. I am excited to know that he will be working nearby. We have not been told when he will finish his current training, but we will celebrate at the sight of him. He will contribute much to the cause.

I wanted to tell you something of our work here. Although fighters are always poised to rush to the front to share in the physical fighting, the main work coming out of Bergalou comes from the tips of pens. There are a number of writers who produce patriotic materials about the struggle for liberation. Sarbast is a part of this effort. The writings and the broadcasts keep other fighters and even civilians informed of what is happening on the battlefront, warning of areas to avoid. We transmit speeches from our leaders, such as Ma'am [Uncle] Jalal Talabani, and discussion on the demand for Kurdish freedoms. We also send out other information, recruiting young men and women to the cause, to join the Peshmerga. Although it would be lovely to produce ordinary programs for entertainment, like the ones listeners in other countries enjoy, the focus in this valley must remain on life-or-death matters.

While the government in Baghdad broadcasts its lies, we broad-cast the truth.

Often I ask myself, *where is the rest of the world?* Is there anyone out there who knows what is happening to the Kurds? Does any-one know, or care, that Baghdad has been murdering innocent Kurdish citizens for decades? Or that their sport for our blood is increasing? Does anyone know that Arabs are taught that Kurds are animals, and they are encouraged to rob and beat and murder us? Does the world know that the government in Baghdad has been emptying entire villages of Kurds, taking the men away to only God knows where, and shipping the women, children, and elderly men to live in refugee camps in the south? Does the world know that those Kurds are forbidden to return home? Does the world know that Arabs are moved into our homes, and appropriate our livelihoods?

If the world knew, would they care?

It's as though we Kurds are bleeding from thousands of wounds, yet no one knows of our sufferings.

Tears are dropping from my eyes.

The most disappointing for me, Mother, was when I was forced to acknowledge that as there are *good* Kurds, there are also many *bad* Kurds. Nothing has damaged our cause more than the *bad* Kurds, the collaborators and informers.

They join the PUK, pretending to hate Baghdad. They slip away after discovering important information and give out our positions. They cause the deaths of many fighters. It makes me believe that our loyalty as Kurds is disintegrating. I hope this is not the case, for our unity has always been one of our strong points.

Sarbast says that the war with Iran meant that rather than live in the trenches, as our Sa'ad did, many men would rather sell their honor, taking money from Baghdad to betray their fellow Kurds.

Some men will do anything to avoid those trenches of hell, I guess.

But they might as well go to hell in those trenches, for that's where they are going eventually, for spying on their Kurdish brothers.

The Jahsh are only postponing hell.

Living in Baghdad, hiding from those bombs, I hated the Iranians. But here in Kurdistan, they are our only friends.

In Baghdad the Iranians are trying to kill you, my mother, and my brother, and my sisters. In Bergalou, the Iranians are fighting to protect me, and Sarbast, and all the other Kurds.

I am torn about my feelings regarding the Iranians.

It's a dilemma.

We Kurds have been fighting against Baghdad for over sixty years. Will I stay in this fighting village for another sixty years?

My past motivated me, pushing me to come here. Now I am motivated by the future I envision, a future where my children can be free to speak the Kurdish language, to learn Kurdish history, to travel up and down these mountains without fear of ambush.

So we must win! We will never give up! Never!

Mother dear, I see that the afternoon sun is moving toward the edge of the sky. Soon the enemy will send off their finale of bombs and shells, and the frogs will start up their symphony, and my husband will come home, and we will eat our dinner together and then we shall join the other fighters on the hillside or in someone's home. There we shall laugh with giddy delight at the good luck to be alive, we shall reminisce about our days of childhood, and we shall share our dreams of a future blessed with freedoms.

May you be safe in Baghdad,

Your little Joanna

18

Chemical Attack

BERGALOU
Fall 1987

Jalal Talabani asked for a special channel of communication. I gave him one. I went to Sulaimaniya and hit them with the special ammunition. That was my answer. I continued the deportations at the same time. I told our contacts in the Kurdish villages that I could not let their villages survive, because I will attack them with chemical weapons. They said they loved their villages. I told them, "Then you and your family will die. You must leave right now because I cannot tell you the same day that I am going to attack with chemical weapons."

I will kill them all with chemical weapons. Who is going to say anything? The international community? Fuck them! The international community, and those who listen to them.

Even if the war with Iran comes to an end and the Iranians withdraw from all occupied lands, I will not negotiate with Talabani and I will not stop the deportations.

This is my intention, and I want you to take serious note of it. As soon as we complete the deportations, we will start attacking them everywhere according to a systematic military plan. Even their headquarters. During our attacks we will take back one-third or one-half of what is under their control. If we can try

to take two-thirds, then we will surround them in a small pocket
and attack them with chemical weapons. I will not attack them
with chemicals just one day, I will continue to attack them with
chemicals for fifteen days. Then I will announce that anyone who
wishes to surrender his gun will be allowed to do so. I will pub-
lish one million copies of this leaflet and distribute it to the
North in Kurdish, Badinani, Arabic and Sorani. I will not say it
is from the Iraqi government. I will not let the government get
involved. I will say it is from the Northern Bureau. Anyone willing to come back is welcome, and those who do not return will
be attacked with destructive chemicals. I will not mention the
name of the chemical because that is classified. But I will tell
them they will be attacked with new weapons that will destroy
them. So my threats will motivate them to surrender. Then you
will see that all the vehicles of God Himself will not be enough
to carry them all. I swear that we will defeat them.

I told our comrades that I need guerrilla groups in Europe to
kill whomever they see from these Kurdish saboteurs. I will do it,
with the help of God. I will defeat them and follow them to Iran.

—Ali Hassan al-Majid, secretary-general of the Northern Bureau, transcript of a tape recording at a meeting in
1987, exact date unknown

Sarbast and I were silent and thoughtful during our lunch at home
that day. Lately, we had gotten into the habit of bringing our meals
back to eat at home, enjoying our time alone together. But times
were tense, and it was difficult to relax. Much was happening in the
area between the three armies: the Iraqis, the Iranians, and the
Kurdish freedom fighters.

Sarbast and his colleagues at the radio station were transmitting
special appeals for more PUK volunteers. With the Iranians behind
us, we believed it would only take but a determined push to final
victory over Baghdad. Or so we thought. But we needed more
fighters to make this victory possible.

After Sarbast left, I rinsed our dishes clean and put them away,
then went to visit Ashti and little Hema, one of my favorite pastimes
during the few times there were no bombardments.

When I arrived, I was happy to see other Peshmerga women were there. Pakhshan, the wife of a high-ranking Peshmerga, was holding her small daughter, Lasik, in her lap. Both Bahar and Kazal were there as well. They were young wives like me, without any children, although I had been suffering with persistent nausea lately, causing me to worry that I might be pregnant. Ashti was filling a large plastic bowl with water and preparing to give Hema his bath. Although Ashti always presented a brave front, I knew that with a baby, life in Bergalou was doubly worrisome.

As I drew closer, I saw that Hema was excited, enjoying a brief time out in the sun while being surrounded by women who were giving him a lot of attention.

I picked him up and gave him a kiss. I enjoyed playing with that precious boy. But I had been uneasy regarding the well-being of Ashti's baby from the first evening I saw him in his mother's arms. Now with bombs falling and shells exploding on an almost continuous basis, the safety of both Hema and Lasik was a concern. I knew that both Ashti and Pakhshan fretted endlessly for their little children. I worried as well.

It was pitiful. When Bergalou was under attack, both children were wide-eyed with fear, listening to the bombs and the shells.

Ashti took Hema from my arms and settled him in his soapy bath. Lasik toddled over and began to splash the water with her hands. Everyone laughed.

I settled in with the women.

Kazal, whose husband was the most famous broadcaster in all of Iraq, said, "I was told that Sergalou will be receiving a shipment of meat tomorrow."

There was a buzz of excitement. Meat was a delicacy. On rare occasions when the shop in Sergalou, our sister village in the valley, received food shipments, a group of Bergalou residents would hike there and buy everything available. We would celebrate by having a small party and a barbecue.

My mouth watered. I had been eating beans and tomato sauce for the past month, without any meat, although Sarbast's brother had popped in for an unexpected and quick visit the day before and had brought us some pastries and a few other baked items from his mother. We were planning a good meal that evening.

Holding Hema by the arms as he sat in the small pool of water and splashed, Ashti looked at me and smiled, asking, "When is Sarbast going to make us a cake?"

Sarbast was a wonderful baker, and when he could get his hands on some flour and sugar, he relaxed from the rigors of war by making small cakes. Ashti looked forward to those sweets as much as I did.

"Soon, he promised," I told her.

Our lovely visit ended prematurely when Bahar's husband sent word that the food shipment had arrived in Sergalou a day early. Someone would be leaving to make the hour-long walk to Sergalou within a few minutes. Sarbast, I was told, had already given our money to buy our purchases. In a rush of excitement, everyone scattered.

In no mood to return home, I decided to take a walk. Rarely did I take walks without Sarbast, because it was one of our preferred ways of relaxing together. Generally, after the last shelling of the day, we would enjoy the pure mountain air by taking a brisk walk.

But I had a lot on my mind. We had heard from Sarbast's brother that there was chilling talk that Ali al-Majid had even more chemical attacks planned. It didn't take a genius to know that the man was planning to make Kurdistan a wasteland. Reports were rampant of the near-total destruction of Kurdish infrastructure and assets, the murder of men and boys from ages twelve through sixty, and the abandonment of Kurdish civilians in isolated areas. Something even more sinister was now brewing in our enemy's camp.

We desperately needed more PUK fighters. I had hoped that Sarbast's appeals would encourage more Kurdish men to join our fight.

As I walked, I pondered the kind of arguments that might motivate a good Kurd to make a full commitment to the cause. Although my mind was racing, I paused to take a few deep breaths of the brisk mountain air, knowing that before long the valley would be crusted with snow and ice. Once winter was upon us, I would no longer be strolling for pleasure.

Suddenly, I was startled by the roar of an unexpected artillery bombardment. While we were always subject to attacks, our enemy was off their usual schedule. Generally, we could set our watches by the afternoon and evening bombardments.

I felt a rush of confusion. I was too far from our house to make a run for safety, so I darted off the trail, crouching, waiting for an opportunity to dash home to take cover in a corner room.

Just then I noticed something strange. These artillery shells were different. Once airborne, they fell silently, puffing up dirty white clouds. I continued watching the strange spectacle, my mouth dry with anxiety, not letting my imagination go to the worst scenario. Perhaps the silent canisters were harmless?

Then another strange thing occurred: birds began falling out of the sky! I instinctively cried out, "It's raining birds!"

The combination of silent bombs and plunging birds stirred my disbelief. I whipped my head side to side, searching all around me. The edge of the afternoon sky was dotted with flashes of color, gaudy specks plummeting to earth. Those colorful specks were more birds. The poor creatures were fluttering helplessly, falling as heavily as stones, down, down, down to the ground.

I winced as I heard dreadful thumps all around me.

I had always loved birds. I couldn't bear to see the pitiful disaster unfolding before my eyes. If birds were dropping from the sky, I knew that I should move, and move fast, to run to the shelter. But I was frozen in place.

I searched the trail for sight of Sarbast. I knew my husband well. If he realized I was in danger, he would come to me. But perhaps he would think I was already in the shelter. Because of the suddenness of the danger, perhaps he would be forced to seek cover in the communal shelter in the village center.

I bit on my lower lip as I continued to search the path for Sarbast's brawny frame, feeling a rush of panic for my husband's safety. No doubt, Bergalou was in the middle of what was quickly unfolding as a dire emergency.

Just then a bird fell directly at my feet, the dull thud of its impact causing me to gasp. The creature was in great distress. Its tiny black beak scissored vigorously, then more slowly, pitifully sucking at the air.

I stayed put, for the silent canisters were still dropping from the sky. I could hear my heart thumping loudly, noticing that those strange canisters were still billowing smoky puffs that turned into a dirty brown-colored cloud that hugged the ground.

Another bird fell nearby.

I was smart enough to know that animals provide the first indication of a chemical attack. Was this the poison gas attack promised by Ali al-Majid?

With that chilling thought I threw caution to the wind, leaping to my feet and sprinting down the path home in fear of my life.

Everything was a blur, but I did catch sight of an untethered mule as it snapped and bucked into a frenzy. That mule hustled past me on the path, trotting so fast he seemed to dance. Never had I seen a mule move that rapidly.

I kept running, trying to avoid the splayed birds strewn in my path. Finally, I dashed into the house, gasping for breath. Safe!

Seconds later, Sarbast burst in through the open door. I stared at him, mouth open, panting, without speaking.

He yelled out, "Joanna, upon my honor, this is a chemical attack!"

Yes! I knew it! I now recognized the unpleasant odor I had heard about from survivors of previous chemical attacks: rotten apples, onions, and garlic. Sarbast was right. We *were* under chemical attack!

He moved quickly, reaching high to a shelf above the side door. He was getting our masks, I thought with relief, as he shouted, "Joanna! Put this on!" He handed me a gas mask as he pulled a second mask onto his own face, tightening the small bands that fastened it around his head.

I held my breath while I fumbled with the strap. In all the excitement, the simple task felt cumbersome. While Sarbast and I had discussed those masks several times, with Sarbast urging me to familiarize myself with the apparatus, I had stupidly failed to do so.

Finally, Sarbast grabbed the mask from my hands and slipped it into place over my head and face.

Hand in hand, we ran together to our earthen shelter, crawled down and as far back into the hole as possible.

Once we were settled, I realized that I had been holding my breath the whole way. I hungrily drew in a much-needed mouthful of air, but all I accomplished was to strain my throat muscles. I could not capture a single breath!

Sarbast had no idea of my problem. Desperate, I yanked at the mask until it slid from my face, shouting, "I can't breathe in this thing!" Finally I had his full attention, and he wiggled toward me. He grabbed the mask from my hands and examined it.

Feeling that I was about to explode, I was forced to breathe in the foul gases. My eyes were beginning to feel the effect of the gas, as well. I felt as if my eyes had been set on fire. The pain was so intense that hot needles probing my eyeballs could not have hurt any more. I could not stand it another moment. I started rubbing my eyes with my hands, not caring that I had been warned never to rub my eyes during a chemical attack.

"The gas is in my eyes!" I screamed, as I began to choke on the poisoned air that was fogging the shelter.

The gases were settling low over the ground, filling the shallow dugout. Sarbast moved quickly, crawling out of the shelter, then pulling me out behind him. With my mask in one hand, he grabbed my other, pulling me back into the house.

I thought we should run up the mountains, for I distinctly remembered Sarbast telling me that one should seek low shelter during a conventional bomb attack and to climb as high as possible during a chemical attack.

But first I must have a working mask.

My throat was aching, my eyes were stinging. I crumpled to the floor and Sarbast knelt beside me. A clammy fog was clotting my senses and muddling my thinking.

Well, hello, death, I thought to myself.

Forced to take another breath, I inhaled more foul-smelling air. My condition continued to worsen. I hoped that the end would come quickly. I was terrified of prolonged suffering.

Then, to my strangled amazement, I grew aware of a misty-shrouded presence in the room. A black-garbed woman appeared to float in front of me. But I was too confused to be frightened. It was Auntie Aisha!

Auntie Aisha had dropped by for a visit! That was entirely unexpected, despite the fact Halabja was not far from Bergalou. Auntie Aisha had moved to Halabja nearly ten years earlier, a few years after my father died. She was a religious woman, and as she aged she said she wanted to live near the shrine of Al-Shaikh Ali Ababaili, a revered Islamic cleric who was buried there.

Auntie Aisha had been my favorite aunt since I was a child, and I had always been in awe of her special ability to soothe all my worries away. Since I had become an adult, I realized that she received messages from God in the form of dreams.

Despite her devoutness, she was surprisingly a lighthearted woman who enjoyed having many children around her, laughing easily at our silly behavior. But she was not laughing during that gas attack. In fact, she had a grim expression on her face.

But what was she doing in Bergalou? It was an unfortunate time for a visit. Still, I felt better in her presence, with a childlike confidence that everything would sort itself out with Auntie Aisha around.

She was still floating and had me so riveted that I could think of nothing else, wondering when she learned to hover like that. She was a magical auntie in many ways, yet I had never seen her suspended off the ground before. She was an amazing woman.

Auntie Aisha bent toward me, her features only inches from my face, and sighed four shocking words, "I am dead now."

I winced, whispering, "Dead?"

Everything was too eerie. Was it Auntie Aisha's ghost?

While fighters were provided with gas masks, there were not enough gas masks for the whole Kurdish civilian population. Auntie Aisha was not a fighter. She would not have been issued a gas mask.

Had her village been hit by poison gas at the same time as Bergalou? Was she dead? Was *I* dead?

I hoped not. I was too young to die. At age twenty-five, I had too many years ahead, years and years that I wanted to share with my beloved Sarbast, years in which we would have children of our own. With signs that I was in the earliest stages of a first pregnancy, despite the fact Sarbast and I had agreed we should not yet bring children into our dangerous world, life seemed more precious than ever.

I had postponed telling Sarbast anything about the subject. He had enough worries at the moment.

Everything was confusing. I held my hands over my face to protect my eyes, but I peeked out between my fingers to see what Auntie Aisha might do next.

I was disappointed when she evaporated. I soon rationalized that Auntie Aisha had appeared to me for one reason only: she wanted to make certain I knew about the danger of the gases. She wanted me to live. She wanted me to know she was watching over me.

That idea made me feel more hopeful. For sure, Auntie Aisha was a powerful woman. How could I die with such a dynamic woman watching over me?

I looked at Sarbast, who was pulling and probing at my nonfunctional gas mask, clearly shaken that he could not discern what was wrong with it.

I began gagging. He glanced at me and then started to remove his own mask, to pass it to me, but I shook my head. "No!" *Never* would I take his mask. I wouldn't want to live without him anyhow.

I held my breath once more, squeezing my stinging eyes tight, shrouding my face in my hands, and rolling forward. I buried my face in the folds of my clothing.

Just as I felt myself losing consciousness, Sarbast finally solved the problem by removing the small cap that activated the mask's vent. He slipped the working mask over my face.

I inhaled hungrily, catching the most satisfying breath of my life. No dish had ever tasted as sweet as that welcome air, despite its rubber-scented taint.

My God! I was happy! Life!

The relief swelled throughout my body, coursing down into my legs, feet, and toes. A multitude of thoughts shot through my mind. Auntie Aisha saved me! Sarbast saved me! I would live! I pushed aside the disturbing idea that Auntie Aisha might have died in a similar attack. I told myself she was safe at her home in Halabja. She had probably come to me through one of her visionary dreams.

I chuckled. My untoward jollity seemed to frighten Sarbast. We both knew that people fatally damaged by chemicals often lost their minds right before their death.

Peshmerga commanders were so concerned that our valley might be hit by chemicals that they had filed a report on the physical effects of the previous attacks. It was said that grown men and women had giggled and danced through the chemical-soaked streets like gas-addled idiots. I hoped I would not humiliate myself in such a manner.

Deep down I knew that I was not going crazy. I was merely happy to be alive. But my joy was interrupted as two Peshmerga fighters wearing gas masks burst through our open door. Soggy towels were draped over their heads and shoulders.

One of the men cracked aside his gas mask to tell us that the bombardment was over, although the chemicals were still doing their deadly work. "Get out! Get out! Gas is heavy—it will now settle to all low areas. You are not safe here!" he shouted.

As the fighters spun around to leave to warn other neighbors, a wet towel on one man's shoulders slipped to the floor. Sarbast yanked the fallen towel from the floor and tossed it over my head. He pulled me with him out the door.

As we struggled up the mountainside, I saw everything through a murky gray color. The entire village was in chaos. Everyone was running up the valley to the mountains.

Sarbast and I pulled ourselves upward.

I moved as rapidly as possible, even though my discomfort grew worse. I could feel a sticky burning substance ooze from both eyes where it gathered on my cheeks under my mask. Even more frightening, the gas was still blunting my ability to think, to react. Each step I took suddenly required an enormous effort. Every stone on the trail loomed as a huge boulder; each small incline seemed a towering mountain face. I would never make it up that mountain.

Finally we reached a rocky outcrop high enough up the mountain to offer sanctuary from the heavy gases. My legs gave way, and I collapsed onto the damp earth.

Sarbast removed his gas mask and mine. "You are safe, darling," he reassured me. "You are safe now."

I reached out to embrace him, but he pulled away, cautioning, "Joanna, do not touch me. Do not touch yourself. We are both contaminated."

By then my eyes were nearly swollen shut. I stared at Sarbast through dim slits, curious as to how I might contaminate someone already completely contaminated.

Before I could ask that question, we heard the roar of an Iraqi airplane flying over the valley. Had we been detected?

"Down!" Sarbast shouted.

Crashing explosions erupted all around us as we hugged the rocky mountainside. Dirt and small stones were lifted into the air by explosive shells raining down on our bodies.

Sarbast lifted me in his arms, and before I realized what he was doing, he took a high dive into the void with me, as though we were two carefree lovers springing into the waves of the surf. But that particular dive was not a lighthearted caper into a pool of water. Instead, we tumbled entwined down the mountain, rolling over and over until our descent was violently halted by a large boulder that blocked our path.

Stunned by the fall, we were both silent, our bodies still loosely entangled.

My God! Sarbast could have killed us both with that jump down the mountain. I wanted to slap him, but I couldn't find the strength to move.

At least the airplane had flown away.

Sarbast was so close that I felt his deep breaths as intimately as I felt my own.

He whispered, "Sorry, darling, sorry. Are you all right?" He pulled small twigs and clumps of dirt from my hair and mouth. "Joanna?"

Winded by the fall and my slam into the boulder, I was struggling to speak, mainly because I wanted to berate him about his dangerous stunt. My efforts just produced low gurgling sounds. I wondered if I was choking on my own blood.

I slowly unwound my arms from Sarbast's neck and moved my hands over my body, from my neck to my knees, searching for an injury. It was only then that I realized my world was turning hazy with darkness.

My tongue felt too thick as well. I had to swallow three or four times in slow sequence before I could croak out, "Sarbast. Something is wrong with my eyes."

He cupped my face in his hands. "Can you see?"

I blinked. "A little. Only a little."

Sarbast must have been terrified by my news, for we both knew that blindness was one of the most common side effects of poison gas. He was breathing deeply but said nothing more; instead, he picked me up in his arms and began to rock me back and forth.

It was difficult to hold back tears. I was more frightened than I had ever been in my life. My imagination got away from me. What if the attack was not over? I could not see. If a full assault was imminent and the war front had moved to us, there would soon be fighting, hand-to-hand combat. Sarbast would be handicapped by a blind wife. Sarbast and I would be left behind to be killed, our lifeless bodies tossed into an open grave.

Such things were happening to Kurds all over Kurdistan. Perhaps it was our turn.

Sarbast was of a different opinion. "Joanna, don't worry. We'll wash them out. The bombardment has ceased. The gas will disperse, and we will return to the village."

Sarbast was right. The attack was over. My worst-case scenario did not come to pass. The gas attack was not followed by a full armed assault. I was grateful because I was in no position to defend myself.

With my useless eyes still swollen shut, I heard the Peshmerga villagers trudging past our position, returning to Bergalou. One fighter reported that the smoke was clearing. It was safe to return. Perhaps there were survivors down there, waiting to be found.

One of the fighters announced, "We must warn all of Kurdistan. They are using stronger chemicals now."

I thought of our relatives. Between Sarbast and me, we had hundreds of relatives living in Kurdistan. In truth, they were all in danger.

As voices streamed nearby, I covered my burning, swollen eyes with my hands. I felt a flash of shame that my failing sight would keep me from aiding injured villagers.

Violent nausea started to wrack my body. Reacting to the gases attacking my bloodstream and vital organs, I began to retch repeatedly. Suddenly, I realized that I still might die.

What *if* I were pregnant? Had the fetus been harmed? Even if he or she was still healthy, my own baby would open its little eyes on war. Could I really subject an infant to the dangerous life I had chosen?

I decided then and there that I could not. My life was too dangerous. If I was not pregnant, I would be more careful.

I still couldn't see, so I asked Sarbast to tell me what was going on.

He described how the Peshmerga soldiers were trekking back down the ancient pathway, returning to their homes, while bearing injured comrades on their backs or in their arms. He said many were silent and empty-eyed as they drifted haphazardly down the path that Sarbast said was now cratered by the explosions.

Still huddled on the damp earth, I listened to the murmurs as the men passed by us. Sarbast handed me the gas mask, then pulled me up from the ground. I held tight, confident that his sure hand would safely guide me down the mountain.

Instead, my beloved Sarbast lifted me up and cradled me in his arms as easily as if I were a small child. He carried me down the mountain, whispering the sweetest words of love in my ear, "My love, my queen, I will accept all the world's hardships, but I cannot endure your being hurt. Joanna, Joanna, I love this world because you are in it."

I closed my eyes and nestled my head against his shoulder, and despite my potential blindness, I was the happiest woman in the world.

19

Blinded

BERGALOU
1987

As Sarbast carried me down the mountain, he always remained alert, observing and calculating, plotting his next move. I knew that my husband was absorbed with the most lethal danger that had ever faced the Peshmergas or the radio station. Despite the fact that my eyes were swollen shut and I could see nothing, I could imagine his expression.

He made me feel safe. For once in my life I was vulnerable. I needed to depend on another person. I was glad that person was my Sarbast.

Suddenly, Sarbast's voice cracked with a decided hoarseness. "Our home is still standing."

A small cry of joy escaped my lips, my happiness as complete as if our tiny home was a costly palace decorated with ornate furnishings.

Sarbast added, "The village has not been overrun."

"Thank God for that, Sarbast."

The humble homes were dear to those who lived in them.

I was still worried. The Iraqi Fifth Army was using new tactics. Perhaps it had softened us up with the chemicals and now planned a full-scale invasion after all. For the moment, we were protected by the mountains and the dark of night. But perhaps the army was gathering. Would we be invaded at first light?

Confusion reigned throughout the village. The chemical attack had unsettled everyone.

Sarbast said, "I must get you out of here. You need to see a doctor, to check on your eyes."

I could not see, I was sick to my stomach, and I felt weak. I was struck by the thought that most likely I had spent my last night ever in our little hut, the dwelling where I had experienced the happiest yet most dangerous moments of my life.

"Is anything damaged?"

"Everything is as it was," Sarbast answered abruptly.

Relief flooded through me, and I mentally did an inventory, for I had managed to make our primitive dwelling into a real home.

Our two small mattresses were stacked in the furthermost corner from the door, where most of our worldly possessions were neatly arranged. I had piled my hoard of tattered paperback books and family photographs on that leaning bookcase. The television still had its spot in the corner of the sitting room. I had two small tables built from the trees in the forest. My pink quilt and pillow set was folded neatly on one of those tables.

Sarbast continued to stand, his breathing still labored.

The silence between us descended heavily, just like those gases. It was as though neither of us knew *what* to say to the other. What was this strange stillness growing between us, feeling impossible to breach, as if invisible particles were settling between us, hardening into an unseen wall neither could penetrate?

I had an unwelcome thought: What if the chemicals caused permanent loss of sight? Would my blindness change everything? Would I become a symbol of loss to Sarbast, rather than a source of affection, companionship, and strength?

When Sarbast had finally realized what I had always known, that we were perfect for each other, he had written me many love letters and poems. One came to my mind at that very moment, and instinctively I recited the verse I had most treasured, and now, considering my loss of sight, found the most ironic: "For me, you are the whole wide world, and my sorrows are but a sinking boat if it does not find the shore of your eyes."

I felt Sarbast drop down next to me. "Darling." He placed a steady hand on my shoulder. "Joanna, you are *still* my whole wide world."

To prove his word, and despite our contamination, Sarbast gently touched my lips with his lips. He cupped my face with his hands, asking, "Can you see anything? Can you detect light or dark, an outline at least?"

Both eyes were swollen and caked with mucus. I saw nothing but vague shadows. I avoided telling Sarbast my worst fears. I slowly touched his face. I caressed the roughness of his stubbled face. Long ago I had kept my promise and shaved off that beard, a wonderful moment of intimacy that I would never forget. I stroked his wide forehead and slipped my hand upward into his dark hair, tugging slightly on those curls that once upon a time had exercised an almost hypnotic spell over me and that were now damp with perspiration. I softly traced the outline of his full lips.

Sarbast cleared his throat and then coughed a raspy gas-induced hack that made me shudder.

"Are you all right?" I questioned anxiously.

"Fine. I am fine. So are you. Listen. Listen darling, listen to me. Your sight *will* return. This is temporary. The chemicals are known to cause short-term problems with sight for victims of gassings."

I didn't agree. I erupted, "Can a dead body rise and live again, Sarbast?" My voice spun higher in tone, "No. *No*. The chemicals have destroyed my eyesight. I feel certain of it."

Sarbast gripped my hands tightly in his own. "Come with me."

I followed his lead to the outside, where I could hear him handling the coiled water hose.

Despite the fact that Sarbast and I were living in a mountain area where cold water springs were abundant, giving us a steady supply of fresh water, water purer than any found in Iraq's major cities, transporting that water to our house had its complications. The village had multiple water hoses that the Peshmergas kept connected to the nearest mountain spring. Once a week, the chain of hoses was passed from house to house so residents could manually top the water tanks that perch on every roof. We were lucky that one of the hoses was still at our house.

"This is better than nothing," Sarbast said.

With our clothes still on us, he then hosed us both down, from our heads to our feet. We shook ourselves like wet dogs to get the excess off our face and hair. He then guided me back into the house.

"Where is the medical kit?" he asked.

"It is stored in the refrigerator."

Every Peshmerga family had been supplied with a basic medical kit. The medical clinic in the village was so low on supplies that there was no reason to go there. Recently, fighters injured during the attacks were sent to Iran for medical care.

I stood quietly while Sarbast found the kit. "Here are the eye drops," he said. He carefully lifted one eyelid and then the other, squeezing a few drops into each eye. He tried to wipe away the discharge that had coagulated in both my eyes, but my eyes still felt glued together.

"Joanna, I've read a lot about chemical blindness. Victims often regain sight, sometimes as quickly as after a day and others within a few weeks. The survivor's sight often returns to normal. There are many known cases of this."

I said nothing in reply.

Sarbast shifted his thoughts on to the urgent problems immediately ahead. "I feel certain we will get orders to take out the women and children." He paused. "I believe that they are finally coming for us."

I was of the same opinion. Something wicked was coming our way. I cocked my head, listening for the sound of enemy soldiers, but heard nothing. I made a noisy sigh.

Sarbast's voice suddenly softened. "Are you hungry, darling?"

"No. No." Truthfully, I had not thought of food once since the attack had started. I still felt nauseous.

Sarbast began to stroke my shoulders. "You will get hungry. Any food not in a can will be contaminated."

"What about those pastries your brother brought us? They were locked in the refrigerator. And our bread is there, as well."

"Yes. You are right. The refrigerator is airtight. That food is most likely safe."

"We won't starve."

"I must go to the village. I want to find out what is going on." Sarbast brushed my face lightly and reminded me again, "Then I must get you out of here."

Forcing a lightness into my voice I did not feel, I encouraged him, "You go. Help the others. I will prepare our things for departure."

"I don't like leaving you here alone," Sarbast commented.

"You must. Now go."

"Be careful. Listen out. If you hear anything unusual, take this gas mask and make your way to the shelter."

"I will," I promised, as I fingered the mask, although I knew that if our enemies were so close that I could hear them, groping my way to that shelter would be futile.

"And don't fall," he cautioned.

"In this tiny house you presented to me as a mansion?" I forced a laugh to my voice. "Three steps in any direction and I will find a wall to stop me."

There was an unanswered pause. Even though I could not see him, I could feel his strength pulsating, and I sensed his concentration.

"Good," Sarbast agreed. "Good. I will be back shortly."

"Sarbast," I implored. "Check on Ashti and Hema."

"Yes. Yes. I will."

Suddenly, Sarbast was gone and I could let my true feelings surface. Unwilling to let my husband know just how devastated I was, I had kept up an optimistic facade. In reality, I was distraught by the turn our lives had taken.

But I willed myself to survive. I had suffered too many close calls from the first moment of my conception to give up that easily. Yet that determination was capped with sadness when I was struck by the thought that an important segment of my life was ending. When we left Bergalou, I would most likely never see it again.

I steeled myself for the challenges ahead. "All right, Joanna, you cannot park yourself like a lizard in the sun. You must move now." My poor father had always inspired me, and I used his image to strengthen my fortitude. My father could not speak or hear. He had led a sad, lonely life in so many ways. Yet he soldiered on, valiantly supporting a wife and five children. I felt my father looking down on me. I could not disappoint him.

I shoved the mask aside and used my hands to push up from the hard floor, knowing that above all, I must not stumble out the door and fall down the hilly path. I had enough problems without breaking a bone.

I held my arms and hands straight out and moved one leg after the other. I was suddenly struck by the long-lost memory of a horror movie I had seen as a small girl in Baghdad: A group of zombies escaped from a graveyard to terrorize an entire town. The zombies had moved unbendingly, arms, hands, legs, and feet stiffly extended, just as my limbs must appear. I laughed faintly.

I easily found my small stock of clothing that was packed away in a plastic container. Good, I thought, these items will not be so contaminated.

When I came across a candy bar in a trouser pocket, I was struck by hunger. I had been saving that candy as a special treat to share with Sarbast. But he would be happy for me to eat it. I fingered the candy, unsure if the plastic wrapping had protected it from the chemicals. I unwrapped it and bit into it. I laughed at the sheer pleasure of the sugar on my tongue. I felt better.

When I raised my arm, I caught a whiff of pungent body odor. Oh my God, I smelled! I rubbed my hands against my clothes. My trousers and shirt were covered in dirt. I brushed my hair with my fingers and found twigs and small clods of dirt.

What would Mother say? She had raised cleanliness to a new high. Our home in Baghdad was always immaculate, and Mother had always insisted that we take a bath every day, and in the hot summer months, two baths a day. I had never *known* of anyone in our family having body odor. It would have been a scandal.

But it was not possible to maintain Mother's exacting standards in Bergalou. Learning to be modest in all needs was a requirement of being a Peshmerga. So upon my arrival, Sarbast and I had agreed to alternate bathing days.

The day of the attack had been Sarbast's day to wash, so I had not even sponged down. I had to ignore my stench. However, I did want to pack our things.

Concerned that I might fall, I crouched onto my hands and knees and began to crawl, searching systematically across the room. While probing beneath our low table, my fingers felt Sarbast's pistol. I knew he would have taken his Kalashnikov rifle with him, as it was rarely out of his sight. There was a pile of ammunition stacked under the table. I took the loaded pistol and left the ammunition.

I made several sliding trips across the uneven floor, towing our belongings behind me. The sharp ridges on the roughly made floor

Joanna and Sarbast with other Peshmergas in the Kurdistan village of Kur Kur.

Sarbast (sixth from left) in the Kurdish village of Kamchogha with Peshmergas. Sarbast is sitting between his sister Shawnim and younger brother Saman, who died soon after this photo was taken.

Joanna's friend Ashti in the Iraqi Kurdish mountains.

Joanna's friend Ashti with three Peshmergas in front of a typical PUK hut in the fighter village.

The PUK radio tower in Bergalou.

Rubble left after a Kurdish village is destroyed by Saddam's army.

scratched my hands and feet. I will not miss this floor, I thought grimly.

I soon heard Sarbast's hurried heavy steps. I smiled. Sarbast made normal walking into a form of war.

"Did you hear anything while I was away?" he asked.

"No. Nothing at all." I speculated, "They probably thought they killed us all with those chemicals. They are celebrating, waiting until it is light to come and dump bodies."

"I don't know. They probably have plans to hit us with chemicals for a few weeks, to make certain we have no uncontaminated water or food so that we will run away. Then they will come in."

Sarbast coughed loudly, a harsh gag that was beginning to concern me. I hoped his lungs had not been damaged. Choking, he said, "I brought you some food."

That candy bar had stimulated my appetite. My nausea had gone.

Sarbast was breathless. "We found several boxes of canned goods that were not contaminated. We divided them. I have some canned peas and canned chicken meat."

As he opened one of the cans with his knife, I heard the grating sounds of metal on metal. I smelled chicken.

"Ashti? Is she all right? And the baby?"

"They are well. I caught a glimpse of them both. Rebwar wants them to leave as well."

"So Rebwar is all right?"

"He was with Ashti and Hema. They all survived."

"Did little Hema suffer from the chemicals?"

"Joanna, I really don't know. I saw them briefly. I had no time to ask questions. But they looked all right. The baby was wrapped in a blanket but he was looking around. Now, I want you to eat this quickly for our entire world is now contaminated. Open your mouth."

I felt miserable instantly. Being spoon fed marked the dismal depth of my situation. But only my sight was affected. I was not helpless. I could feed myself.

"Come on, Joanna. Eat," Sarbast ordered, his words almost a shout. "Open up. Quickly, now!"

"I can feed myself, Sarbast." I extended my right arm. "Give me the can."

Sarbast talked as I ate. "Saddam has his eye on Jafati Valley. It is becoming too dangerous. It is only a matter of time before we are overrun. We have been ordered to relocate the radio station. First we'll make our way to Merge and from there to the designated station. We'll find out that location tomorrow. I believe the station will be moved closer to the border. If so, we'll get you medical attention in Iran."

I was surprised that we were running away. Yet I knew that the radio station must not be captured. The equipment would be impossible to replace. Nothing was more important to the PUK than the communication center.

"Merge is still safe?"

"Yes. I believe so. We are their first target. Once we leave the valley, our enemy will refocus to other areas."

So we would be returning to Merge, to the village where Sarbast and I had met before traveling on to our honeymoon in Serwan. Perhaps we would see Zakia and her family. Nothing would give me more pleasure.

Between bites I asked, "Have you eaten anything?"

"Later, later," he answered quickly.

"When will we leave Bergalou?"

"Tomorrow, I hope."

"Is there any uncontaminated water we might drink?"

"No. I don't think we should drink the water. Tomorrow we will find a fresh spring, high in the mountains, out of reach of these gases. You must wait until then."

I nodded as I swallowed, asking the question that was haunting me. "Sarbast. Were there any casualties?"

Sarbast hesitated, then confessed, "There are four or five fighters who are not expected to live. Others we are not certain about. Some people were caught out in the open and didn't get to their gas masks in time. We will know more in the days to come."

How I prayed everyone would survive. Death was claiming too many of our fighters.

And Sarbast was right. Baghdad's targets now obviously included the villages in Jafati Valley. While the villages had withstood daily bombardments for the past year, even the biggest and strongest fighter could not survive if chemical attacks became routine. With gas masks, one could survive the attacks themselves, but water and food and everything else necessary for life would be saturated with contaminants. Life *after* a chemical attack was the real problem.

I drank the juice from the bottom of the can, so thirsty that I drained it before licking out every drop.

"Do you want the peas now?"

Just then there was a loud thump.

He hissed, "Get behind the door. Now!" He rushed out of the room.

I decided not to hide. What good would that do? Instead, my fingers caressed the pistol. If anyone grabbed me, I would defend myself.

Tense moments passed until Sarbast reappeared. "I could find nothing."

"Perhaps it was the thrashing of an animal?" From what little I had seen with my eyes before the attack, all Bergalou animals must be dead or dying.

"Perhaps." He sounded worried, I thought.

"Get your gas mask. I will take you to the shelter. You rest there while I go back to the village. I will be back soon."

"No, no. I'll be safe here. Here in the house."

The last place I planned on going was to that earthen shelter. It would be more terrifying than a grave, and I would be alone. No. I was not going. Handicapped by the injury to my eyes, I would be unable to keep watch for squirming worms or any other many-legged creature intent on invading my clothing or crawling into my hair. And I couldn't forget about those snakes. Perhaps they had been knocked out by the poison gas. Perhaps they would wake up in a rage.

The tone of Sarbast's voice reflected his impatience. "*Joanna.*"

I circled my arms around my body. "No. I would rather *die here* than *live there*."

"I want you safe."

I spoke through clenched teeth. "I *will not* go blind into that shelter, Sarbast."

Sarbast was losing patience. "Joanna, please. I'll only be gone a short while. I could take you with me but I want you to rest, if you can. While I am away, go to the shelter. When I return, I'll get you."

I argued the main point. "Perhaps there are snakes in that shelter."

"Joanna, soldiers will *kill* you if they find you."

"Snakes, Sarbast! Snakes! Have you forgotten? My eyes are sealed shut. I couldn't see a snake if it coiled right beside me. No!"

"Ali al-Majid's soldiers are more dangerous than any snake."

"No!"

Sarbast moved quickly. His arms went round my waist and back, tight, lifting me up. My high-pitched screams blasted through the silence, prompting Sarbast to hurriedly release me.

"Well, if our enemy is near, they now know where you are."

With flattened palms I steadied myself against his chest before I pulled back and shouted, "No! Sarbast, *I said no!* I will not go blind into that shelter. I will *not*."

I clenched my fists, bracing myself for a physical fight.

Although I was born stubborn and determined, Sarbast was born even more obstinate. We were as twins in that regard.

But happy day! Sarbast relented.

In a voice tinged with admiration, he told me, "You surprise me, darling." He chuckled, "If our enemy appears, please, *do* scream. Your shouts will reach every remote corner of the village, giving everyone an opportunity to run away."

I spoke calmly and seriously, "Yes. I will do that. I will scream a warning."

Sarbast chuckled.

I changed the topic, telling him my plan for ensuring my safety. "After you leave, I will sleep with my body wedged against the door," I told him. "I will keep the pistol in my hand. When you return, call out first and I will slide away and let you in."

He gave my arm a fleeting squeeze, then he was off to the village center.

Rather pleased with the outcome of our first dispute, I squatted to the floor, carefully placing the pistol at my feet. My long hair kept falling down over my face, and I mechanically flipped it back before feeling for my pink quilt. I gave the coverlet an energetic shake, trying to remove any lingering toxins, and shook the pillows. Just as I exhausted myself with all that industrious activity, I suddenly wondered if all that shaking was a mistake. Had I just released the chemicals back into the air? Were invisible poisons propelling around me, stealing into my nostrils and settling on my exposed flesh? I stood nervously, thinking. Could those same toxins also burrow into a fetus? I patted my stomach, sending loving thoughts. *If* I was pregnant, my baby's life was more important than my own.

Then I felt them: small painful blisters were forming on the tips of my fingers. Then I noticed that small bumps had also begun to erupt from under my flesh every place my skin had been uncovered during the chemical attack: my face, neck, hands, and ankles. I had heard about blisters being a side effect of chemicals. Something else to worry about.

I decided that there was nothing I could do but give my burning eyes and stinging skin a rest. I set about getting ready for bed.

Everything was much more difficult in the murky darkness. But I managed to arrange my pink quilt on the concrete floor, and after shaping the curled edges of the coverlet down with my fingers, I fell on top of it, resting my head on the pillow and pulling half of the quilt over me as a comforter. It was contaminated, for certain, but *everything* in Bergalou was contaminated, so it didn't really matter. With my hand I patted the floor until I found the pistol, and then I placed it where I could easily reach it.

I felt I had been on the floor only a few minutes when I was awakened by a great pressure against my body.

Sarbast's voice came to me as through a hazy fog. "Joanna. Move."

It took me a few seconds to shake off my confusion.

Sarbast's foot got tangled in the quilt, accidentally spilling me onto the barren floor. I heard his heavy steps as he moved hastily from one corner of the room to the other.

"Sarbast, what are you doing? Shouldn't you rest?"

He didn't answer. Reluctantly, with an effort, I opened my sticky eyes.

Sarbast tugged the quilt off me.

"It will be clear to the east and north. That's the route we will take."

I was in a world of my own. I rapidly batted both eyelids several times and held one unsteady hand in front of my eyes. I stared in relief. My sight had already improved. There was my Sarbast! Although he was blurry, I could identify his familiar face and the outline of his muscular body.

I stood, still uncertain. My feet probed the uneven floor for a secure spot.

"Sarbast, look at me."

"Joanna, *please*."

"Sarbast, I want you to look at me. *Now*."

His breath was loud, impatiently forced through his mouth and nose. He had become a mad dragon, I thought with amusement.

"What?" Holding a pair of shoes, he turned to stare at me with visible annoyance.

"Sarbast, I can see." I paused, smiling. "I can see, a little."

His look of exasperation slowly evolved into an expression of utter delight.

"You can? Really?"

"A little."

He was suddenly close, looking intently into my eyes. He squinted and said, "Joanna, the whites of your eyes are bright pink."

"Pink?" I smiled. "My eyes are now colored my favorite color?"

I was delighted that I still had eyeballs at all. I had been obsessing over the possibility of dried-up eyeballs, like Auntie Muneera.

Sarbast added, "And a milky glaze covers both eyes. Are you sure you can see?"

"Yes!" I said, louder than I intended.

"Time will bring it *all* back. It will," he stated confidently.

"Yes?"

"Yes. Your sight will get better, day by day."

"If I can only see this well, I will not complain," I promised him, and myself.

Sarbast drew me to him, holding me tightly.

I felt happy tears running down my cheeks. I wiped them against Sarbast's shirt. Ignoring his soaked shirt, Sarbast held me at arm's length and started to laugh.

I drew away, looking at his face, smiling affectionately. "My wild stallion," I whispered. Despite the possible danger hovering over us, I felt an urge to run and shout my happiness. But that hut was too small to contain my joy, so I rushed outside.

I felt beautiful and strong. My blurred but grateful eyes rested on the contours of the rugged terrain. I wanted to run to the top of the mountain peak. My happiness had made me silly. I ran in tight circles on the small level section in front of the door, laughing, thinking, I am an untamed mare, a suitable match for my wild stallion.

Out of the corner of my eye, I saw that an amused Sarbast had followed me.

He held out his hand. "Come. Come into the house."

I went to him, and he nuzzled my neck with his sexy mustache. My knees felt weak and I only wanted one thing: to feel as close to him as a man and woman in love can feel.

I longed to tell him that I might be pregnant, but I held back. Under the current circumstances, the news would create additional worries for him.

Sarbast was looking over my shoulder. He whispered, "I feel them out there, waiting. It may be today, or tomorrow, or next week, but they are there. We are in for the fight of our lives, Joanna."

Almost as an omen, we heard the distant crack of gunfire. Where did that come from?

We scurried into the house to gather our meager belongings. There was so much to do. We must leave Bergalou. I must get medical attention. Another location for the PUK radio station must be organized.

As I looked fondly at our little home, bidding a sad farewell in my mind, I reminded myself that I should not be disheartened, that the most important thing was to survive, to live so that we could love and fight another day.

20

Escape to Merge

BERGALOU TO MERGE
Fall 1987

Quickly we arrived in Bergalou's center, where we found a small group of villagers gathered. Dirty and exhausted, they looked haunted and numb. With the chemicals, everything had changed.

I looked around, grimly nodding. I saw several people who were wearing their clothes layered. In any other setting, their balloon bodies would have been a cause for enormous merriment. I did wonder, however, if their awkward attire might make uphill climbs dangerous, although I reasoned that if they tumbled into a ravine, their puffed-up garb would protect their bones.

Only a few people had gathered. My heart thumped hard. Where was everyone else? Had Sarbast lied to keep me from worrying? Perhaps there were more dead than living?

When I asked around, I was told that most of the fighters were remaining behind to defend Bergalou, at least until a new location for the radio station was established.

Looking around, I felt incredibly sad, thinking that the once-bonded unit of Bergalou inhabitants would soon be a broken necklace, scattered like loose pearls throughout Kurdistan.

It was then that I noticed that many fighters had been afflicted with the same small blisters. They served as a scary reminder that we had all been exposed to poisonous gases. I overheard someone say that the gas blisters would heal, over time.

There was nothing to do but forget about those blisters, although I couldn't stop fretting over my injured eyes, which still hurt. My sight was diminished. Perhaps my sight would weaken even more. I was looking forward to getting out of Bergalou so that I could seek medical attention.

I had other worries. I touched my belly with my hand. I had to guard myself and make certain not to stumble and fall. I had walked over the mountains surrounding us more than once and knew that the terrain was treacherous with serrated rocks, so sharp that a touch could rip open the flesh, and unexpected drops that plunged more than 300 meters.

My stomach gave a little lurch. I didn't see Ashti with her family. Neither did I see Bahar, Kazal, or Pakhshan with little Lasik. I wondered if the other women had already left Bergalou. We had shared tragedy and sorrow, love and laughter. When would I see them again?

I turned my attention back to Sarbast and that is when I saw the outlines of a familiar face: Kamaran, Sarbast's cousin who we had heard was set to complete his PUK military training. In a worried voice, he asked, "Joanna. Are you all right?"

"Kamaran!" I laughed. His friendly face felt like a tonic.

I had forgotten how much I liked the handsome Kamaran. I had seen him a number of times in Baghdad, for he and Sarbast were not only cousins but were also close friends. Many people teased him, saying he looked just like Tom Cruise. Kamaran was not only handsome, he was genuinely nice, with a warm personality. He was also exceptionally intelligent, having graduated from college with a degree in economics. But he, like Sarbast, had forsaken a comfortable career to risk his life as a Peshmerga.

Kamaran told me, "I was on my way to Bergalou when some fighters on the trail told me that Bergalou had already been hit by chemicals. I came as quickly as possible."

Sarbast interrupted, "Kamaran will be going with us to Merge."

I was delighted to hear it.

Both men squatted on the ground, using their fingers to draw our escape route in the dirt. Although the PUK controlled a lot of

Kurdish territory, there was no way of knowing exactly the location of our enemy. The safest route for us would be to the northeast. We would walk over the rugged spine of mountainous terrain. The journey would normally take a fit man a full day of ascending and descending. But with my limited vision, I would slow our journey. I was ashamed that I had become a burden. I *hated* that feeling. I hated being vulnerable.

But truthfully, all Kurdish women were vulnerable. Papers had recently been uncovered that documented a sordid fact: Saddam's government had established the heinous position of "government rapist," attached to Iraq's prison authority, whose only duty was to rape wives in front of their husbands or daughters in front of their fathers.

Every Kurdish husband and father seethed in fury at that revelation, and every Kurdish woman recoiled at its dire possibility, as rape was considered the most dishonorable fate possible for a woman in our traditional society.

It was an unbearable thought. But if I were ever to be captured, it could be my fate. After all, it had happened to thousands of innocent Kurdish women and girls.

"Let's go, Sarbast," I said.

Sarbast agreed. "Yes. It is time."

As we stood up, he said, "We are splitting into small groups. It will be just the three of us in our group. I will be the head, you, Joanna, will be the body, and Kamaran will be our tail."

I stepped forward, my sadness at leaving suddenly forgotten. Bergalou, and indeed the entire valley, suddenly felt nothing more than a place to die.

Sarbast had thought to bring along three empty water canteens, for we would surely find plenty of uncontaminated water in the mountain springs. Both Sarbast and Kamaran were weighed down with Kalashnikovs. I had concealed the pistol in my coat pocket. But Kamaran had no baggage of his own, as he had unselfishly run to our rescue, dropping his personal items along the path the moment he was told of the chemical attack. So he accepted half of Sarbast's load and insisted on taking my satchel from my hand.

Kamaran explained with a smile, "Let's not burden our head."

The three of us left Bergalou, bidding a few solemn farewells to the fighters still making their own plans.

A steep stony pathway took us out of Bergalou. My limited vision added a new dimension of stress, so we kept close to one another. I was comforted by the fact that I could reach forward or backward at any moment for assistance. I kept my eyes cast downward, watching for the back of Sarbast's heels; but chiefly I concentrated on the path, which thankfully was worn smooth by many years of passing feet. I mechanically placed one foot before the other, counting off my miseries. My throat burned with thirst and my ears were strained by the anxious need to listen. I felt certain that at any moment I would hear the clamor of nearby enemy soldiers or the throbbing reverberations of their guns.

I looked upward at the sky. The rising sun was glossing the stony mountain with its brightness. It was a cool morning shrouded in mists. I was thankful that I had thought to add a jacket over the traditional Peshmerga man's trousers I had been wearing since the day before.

As we slogged uphill, I spotted a few tufts of wildflowers. My throat grew even more parched and painful. I glanced down at the flowers and noticed their dew-washed petals. I swiftly bent and swiped several flower stalks while maintaining my stride, lapping at the dew droplets with my tongue. Those moist drops were delicious. Keeping my eyes on Sarbast's back, I carefully tossed the stalks once the petals were cleared, my tongue and throat cooled slightly.

I heard Kamaran chuckle from behind me. I smiled, too, because I did feel better.

I was even more grateful once the trail began to wind through concealed areas, for the stony path's open exposure was disquieting. If there were marksmen watching Bergalou, our three figures would be tempting.

Suddenly, a rustle sounded from nearby bushes. I instinctively cried out.

A mountain goat leaped in front of Sarbast.

I was annoyed at myself.

Sarbast turned to look at me, expressing surprise at my lapse. I knew that Sarbast was very proud of his freedom fighter wife, as he was always proudly introducing me to newcomers to Bergalou. I hated disappointing him.

Kamaran stepped forward and reassured me with his big smile. I knew then that I was in for a very long and demanding day.

After an hour, my calves throbbed from the path's never-ending upward slant, the pads of my feet sharply ached, and my throat and mouth burned with a maddening thirst. That thirst was growing so torturous that I truly feared I might be driven mad.

I managed to walk for a brisk three hours before I began to sway dangerously.

Kamaran whispered, "Sarbast. Five minutes' rest."

Sarbast turned, surprised that the tough Kamaran needed even a single moment, but when his eyes flashed in my direction, he saw Kamaran's point.

Breathing heavily, I gladly sat down on the damp earthen trail.

In the quiet of our halt, though, there was a wonderful surprise. I heard the trickling noise of running water. The thought of clear sparkling water drew me out of my weakened trance.

"Do you hear it? There," Sarbast pointed. "There is a running stream."

"Where?" Kamaran looked.

I moved my swollen tongue around in my mouth. I was going to drink that water, whether or not Sarbast declared it safe from the chemicals. I planned my strategy. I would leap feet first into the spring before he could move to stop me. I could be quick on my feet when the occasion called for it.

"Wait." Sarbast lowered the gear he was carrying and heaved his Kalashnikov and its heavy supply of ammunition from his shoulder, carefully placing them against a bush. Then he unhooked the water canteens he had strung from a wire tied across his chest. To my relief, he said, "Up this high the waters have escaped contamination."

Through a small gap in the foliage I could see a rivulet of water as it coursed over smooth rocks and into a small pool before it flowed downhill. I licked my lips. That pool of water was a beautiful sight.

Sarbast leaned over and tasted the water. He nodded and called out, "Yes. I was right. It is clear."

The discovery of that cold stream lifted all our spirits.

Kamaran reached for a filled canteen and passed it to me. "Our pace is bound to improve now." He smiled. "We were becoming dehydrated."

I could not stop my greedy gulping. Nothing had ever tasted as delicious as that spring water. It was fresh and cold. After drinking my fill, I took a tightly balled handkerchief from my trouser pocket, soaked half, and dabbed it to my forehead and lips before tending to my swollen eyes. The water offered a surprising sting to my eyeballs, but I repeated the exercise, holding the cold cloth against my inflamed eyes.

I drank the last drop before handing over my canteen so that Sarbast could slide down the slope again to refill them.

After taking our second fill of water, Sarbast suggested that we change clothes. Before leaving our house, we had taken those clothes stored in plastic. We would change now and throw our contaminated clothing into a nearby ravine.

I was so eager to get out of my filthy clothes that I needed no urging. I leaped to my feet. The Peshmerga trousers I had purchased in Sulaimaniya were old and growing uncomfortable, binding my waist girdle-tight. I stood impatiently, waiting for Sarbast to open the container, before I plucked out another clean pair of trousers and a pink blouse made of polyester. I elbowed my way through the dense brush and hurriedly removed my tainted clothes, rolling them up and tossing them to Sarbast. "Here." I yanked the pink blouse over my head and smoothed it down with my fingers. I checked that my pistol was tucked into the pocket of my overcoat. I decided to keep on my soiled coat, for we might spend the night in the mountains, and no matter the time of the year, nights were chilly at high elevations. I kept my same shoes, for they were the most comfortable for walking. My hair had tumbled loose from its elastic band. I shook it free before gathering it once more into a long ponytail.

Too soon I was back on my blistering feet, climbing the seemingly endless serpentine trail. Were we not running for our lives, the walk could have been serene, so far away from a world troubled by wars and dictators. But there was no time to admire the tapestry of green and brown colors channeling our path, or the gentle hollows in little open spots dappled by sunlight through the trees.

As we walked over the mountains, Kurdistan's past flowed over me like the pages of history. Primitive hunters had stalked wild animals here, and campfire-lit faces had circled in local caves. Along the path where I was placing my feet, early humans had spread out from Iraq—known then as Mesopotamia—to cover the earth. My beloved land was once the center of the civilized world where writing was invented and the first laws were created. Thinking of our own desperate situation, I sadly mused where it all went wrong. At what point did the region cease its climb into civilization to revert back to such lawlessness?

Sarbast called me out of my trance. We had come to an area of the pathway snarled with stiff brushwood, and Sarbast slowed, then halted, deciding, "Let us eat and rest before we go forward."

I was saving what little energy I had left so I didn't bother to reply, although I was grateful that we would finally eat something. I reminded myself that I must nourish my own body for the sake of my baby, who was slowly evolving into a certainty in my mind.

I crumpled to the ground, tucking my legs under my body. I opened my canteen and tried to wash the toxins from my eyes once again. The pain was relentless.

Sarbast knelt down in front of me. "How are you, darling?"

I nodded, holding the kerchief to my eyes. "I am all right."

Sarbast lightly caressed my shoulder before standing up to walk over to Kamaran. I heard their low muttering voices as they conferred.

I uncurled my legs and leaned my head toward my lap. After a few moments of rest, it was with some surprise that I felt a cool, weighty object cross the lower part of my legs. I raised my head and saw a long black snake twisting slowly across my outstretched limbs.

"*Snake!*" I cried out. I moved faster than I had ever moved in my life, leaping straight into the air, my quick movement hurling the snake airborne as well. The serpent hit the ground with a heavy thud and slithered into the underbrush.

I stood panting, my hands at my throat.

Sarbast and Kamaran looked my way, puzzled by my scream.

"*A snake!*" I shouted again, pointing into the bushy area into which the snake had disappeared, a section I realized with dismay that we must soon pass through.

"Were you bitten?" Sarbast asked.

His voice was so calm that I felt a flash of anger.

I stared at him. I had *definitely* seen the flickering tongue and had even felt a delicate flick against my leg, but no, its barbed fangs had not exploded into my flesh.

"Well, he licked my leg with his tongue," I replied huffily.

I leaned down and lifted my trouser leg, searching my bare skin for any sign of a bite. There were no marks on my flesh, thank God.

Both Sarbast and Kamaran laughed merrily. "Well, then, be grateful you were only licked and not bitten," Sarbast said easily, before turning back to Kamaran to resume their conversation.

I glared at my husband's back.

I rose to my tiptoes, keeping my contact with the ground as minimal as possible, as my dim-seeing eyes scanned the ground for the snake's return.

Sarbast and Kamaran opened a can of peas, along with three cans of sardines. We would eat and resume the trail as quickly as possible. Sarbast was pleased at our progress and began to tease me, bringing me slowly round to a better humor. He said we had covered so much territory that there was a good chance we would arrive in Merge by nightfall.

I felt a rush of relief at his news, for after my brush with the snake, I shuddered to think of spending the night on the ground in the forest.

All Kurds know that snakes are drawn to the warmth of sleeping bodies. I had heard plenty of tales of Peshmerga fighters waking to discover a friendly snake coiled contentedly alongside them in their bedding.

Sarbast and Kamaran quickly ate their cans of sardines. They insisted that I eat the can of peas.

"Supermen," I chuckled, certain that without me, the two of them could sprint from Bergalou to Merge without stopping, climbing the mountains of Kurdistan as nimbly as goats.

Just as I swallowed the last of the peas, I heard a distinct rustle in the trees. I reached for my pistol while Sarbast and Kamaran seized their weapons. Sarbast motioned for me to take cover behind a large bush. Kamaran slipped behind a large tree.

Sarbast stood quietly, listening, then he left us to retrace our steps. The wait for his return felt endless.

I was uneasy when I heard the sounds of men's voices. Had Sarbast been captured? I listened for a few moments before deciding I must go see for myself what was happening. After I took a few steps, Kamaran lightly cleared his throat and shook his head from side to side, mouthing no. It took all my resolve to do as Kamaran told me.

Sarbast suddenly reappeared. "It was nothing, only another group of Peshmergas traveling through the mountains."

"What will we do if we run into enemy soldiers?" I asked, voicing for the first time my biggest fear.

Sarbast shrugged. "We fight, until . . ." and he drew his finger across his throat in a chilling motion.

Kamaran gave a choked laugh. He could always see the funny side.

I was attentive as Kamaran pushed back his heavy glasses with one hand and held four fingers of the other hand aloft.

"Joanna, do not worry, for there are four certain things I *know* will never come to pass. Number one: Saddam Hussein will *not* die peacefully in his bed." He chuckled as he raised his water canteen to his lips to drink, loudly smacking as he declared, "And number two: the fresh water springs of Kurdistan will *not* change into fine champagne, as I wish. Number three: your dear cousin Kamaran will *never* reside in a palace, as I wish. And," he paused for emphasis, "number four: neither Sarbast nor I will *ever allow* our enemies to take us alive."

Despite our dire circumstances, I smiled. Just being around him lifted my own dwindling spirits, reminding me that despite our homelessness, we still had so much to be thankful for.

Even Sarbast was amused. "Let's move on," he snorted through his laughter.

I began to feel the safety of Merge pulling on me like a powerful magnet.

Merge! The very name sounded like magic to me. It would be wonderful to be back in that village where I had met up with Sarbast before our honeymoon. It seemed another lifetime.

Mercifully, the high hills soon passed behind us and we began to cross lower, rounded mounds. That hilly terrain was easier to maneuver than the steeper rises behind us, but at the end of a long day of walking I barely noticed. Among the hills and trees, dusk came quickly, which slowed our pace.

Sarbast held up his right hand and halted.

Looking past his shoulder, I saw a graveled road threading through the valley. We could connect to that road at the base of the hill. Beyond that road was Merge.

Sarbast stood silently, surveying the area.

I gazed down from the hill, listening for the far-off sounds of life from the distant village. I heard nothing. I studied the valley below, which was still green with fields of crops and vividly colored wildflowers.

I had traveled up and down Iraq, and to my mind Kurdistan was its most beautiful asset. The lush highlands and emerald valleys were a terrestrial treasure chest overflowing with irreplaceable riches, sadly threatened by the effects of war that I feared would empty the region of all that was good.

Sarbast stepped back to speak quietly to Kamaran, but my ears were honed to his words. "Who knows what is happening all over Kurdistan, even this far north. We should split up. Meet us at Karim's house. In an hour."

Kamaran darted back into the tree line. He would wait for us to pull ahead.

My ears pricked at Sarbast's warning. Did Sarbast believe that Ali al-Majid's Fifth Army had dropped chemicals throughout Kurdistan? Would we find Merge abandoned?

An evil wind was blowing from Baghdad.

An ever-cautious Sarbast ordered me, "Joanna, walk a few paces behind me and say nothing."

"Okay." I agreed easily for I did not want my husband to observe me too closely.

I was keeping a secret from Sarbast. My sight had worsened in one way, while improving in another. I was gaining clarity, but losing expanse. My eyesight's scope was being overtaken by shadows at its periphery; only a narrow tunnel remained sharp as though I was peering into the sunlight through a thin slit. Frightened that I was going completely blind, I decided not to tell Sarbast. At least, not yet, for there was nothing he could do but worry.

Sarbast walked rapidly ahead, though not so rapidly that I could not match his pace.

When the hilly incline folded into the graveled road, we hugged to one side. Normally, the thoroughfare into Merge would be bustling with townspeople going about their routine activities, but now the road was empty. The absence of travelers convinced me that Merge had been hit by chemicals as well, but when we rounded a bend in the road, I was relieved to see a sign of normal life. Four women were walking toward us, all sauntering with an effortless willowy swing. They were wearing brightly colored cotton dresses with matching scarves on their heads. Even with my limited vision I could see that the heaviest of the women had rolled and twisted a white turban atop her head, where she balanced a large pot. Kurdish women are experts at maintaining their equilibrium and poise while they transport heavy loads on the flat of their heads, a useful skill I had never mastered, despite several hilarious attempts.

I studied the outlines of the pot. Perhaps it was filled with yogurt. I lightly touched my tongue to my lips. I would have loved some cool yogurt.

We passed the women and, not wishing to seem unfriendly, I exchanged with them a smile and a nod of greeting. But the smiles and nods did not lead to conversation, for in our uncertain times Kurds, fearful of Jahsh, did not open dialogue with strangers.

From behind, we were suddenly overtaken by two middle-aged men riding on donkeys. Their full Kurdish trousers hung wide around their waists and hips, tapering to their ankles. Both riders' legs swung out at the sides, while one of the men reached back to tap his donkey's backside with a small tapered stick.

We were soon on the stretch of the road that cut through the village, and more townspeople came into view. Strangely, none of the people passing us looked at us with the slightest curiosity, although we appeared so dirty and disheveled that I thought we should arouse suspicion.

My stomach churned with hunger when we passed a group of young men hawking Fanta orange drinks and walnuts.

An old woman was squatting on the ground, busily making homemade gas masks. She was carefully constructing the devices, using cotton wool and cloth to cover small pieces of charcoal. I knew that her next step would be to stitch the pieces together into half-moons of gauze before sewing a small string of elastic to the edges, to secure it around the head.

I had seen those homemade devices before, though I believed they were basically useless against a full-fledged chemical attack, such as the one that drove us from Bergalou. The crude screens were little more than a tool to ease the mind of victims who had no access to modern gas masks.

To my mind, it was terrible that every person in Kurdistan did not possess a gas mask. But Saddam had made it a crime for Kurds to own gas masks, and now I knew why.

But our PUK leaders had outsmarted him. Every Peshmerga gas mask had been illegally smuggled into Kurdistan on the back of a mule. Without our masks, Sarbast and I both would be dead, along with many others living in the Jafati Valley.

Sarbast made a right through a small alley and into another street. To my eyes, each house looked the same as the next. Modest and clean, most homes were decorated with pots of colorful flowers outside the door and perched on window ledges.

Finally we arrived at our destination, the home of Karim and his wife, Sozan. Sarbast knocked lightly.

I saw the glitter of Karim's intense eyes peering through the crack in the door.

"Sarbast," he said as he opened the door. "You are safe! We were worried!" He grabbed Sarbast by the shoulders. "We heard just now that chemicals are being dropped on all the villages in the valley."

My heart thumped loudly, even as we were being welcomed into their humble home. Karim and Sozan were Peshmerga sympathizers, and despite only meeting them briefly during our honeymoon, I felt their affection and returned it.

Karim and Sozan offered heartfelt, simple cordiality. They urged us to leave our shoes and belongings at the door and to, "Sit! Sit!"

Sozan said what I most wanted to hear. "You must be hungry. I will get refreshments. Later, after the children return from the neighbors, I will prepare a meal."

"Tell us what you have heard," Sarbast implored in a worried voice.

"Baghdad is bragging," Karim said in a frustrated tone, "that Sergalou and Bergalou were both hit. According to the announcement, the PUK took heavy casualties." He cast a worried look at Sarbast. "Am I hearing the truth?"

Sarbast added, "Well, it is true we were hit with chemicals. But no one died. There were serious injuries so there may be casualties to come. I have no information from Sergalou or the other villages in the valley. For sure, they meant to kill us all. We are going to set up a new radio station in a safer area, further north, away from the front and from Saddam's army." With a satisfied grin, he said, "We have our equipment."

"Many people are fleeing from Jafati Valley," I added.

I heard a sound of distress from the kitchen. I could only surmise that our hostess was expressing her fear that Merge might soon face the same dilemma. Sozan was a mother with children to protect. Her alarm was understandable.

I protectively patted my belly.

"Praise Allah no one died, at least," Karim muttered.

"We would have had many dead except for our masks."

"Ma'am Jalal?"

"He was not in Bergalou. But I assume he is safe. We would have heard, otherwise."

Karim sighed heavily. "That is good."

Jalal Talabani, called Ma'am (Uncle) Jalal by his devoted followers, had joined the Kurdish resistance when he was only fourteen years old and was elected to the party's central committee only four years later. Always serious, he studied to become a lawyer and graduated as a barrister in 1959. After clashing with the leaders of Kurdish resistance over his belief that the freedom movement should be more democratic, Talabani formed the PUK in 1975. Over the years, Talabani had earned not only the respect of Kurds, but international admiration as well. He served his fighters well and was revered by them all. To lose Jalal Talabani would be a serious blow to the movement.

Karim probed further. "Rumor is that they dropped a cocktail of toxic gases, consisting of . . ."

Sarbast finished Karim's sentence, "Most likely sarin, and other nerve agents. I saw burns and blisters."

I held up my fingers. "See," I said, "like this. Other than a cough, Sarbast was unaffected, for some reason."

Karim stared openmouthed at my fingertips. Sozan rushed in from the kitchen to have a look. "I will get some salve," she declared.

Sarbast repeated, "Without the gas masks, we would all have died during the attack."

Since the beginning of the Iran-Iraq War, the Peshmergas had more than held their own against Saddam's army, enjoying victory after victory, retaking much of Saddam-controlled Kurdistan, and chasing his army out of Kurdish lands.

With Iran's help, we had envisioned victory within the year. With a strong Kurdish hand at the bargaining table, an acceptable peace could be brokered, and we Kurds would finally achieve meaningful autonomy.

But Saddam, though weakened by the war with Iran, was now gaining in strength, for that war was winding down.

My mind raced. How could we fight back? Where could we run to for refuge? All the neighboring countries hated their own Kurdish populations.

Turkey? How could we rush into the arms of a government that distrusted its Kurdish population even more than the Iraqi government?

Syria? Syria's president, Hafez al-Assad, was as aggressively violent a man as Saddam. To hold firm to power, al-Assad had already proven he would extinguish entire communities, if necessary. The Syrian Kurdish population was as tightly controlled as were their Iraqi brothers.

Iran? Although the Iranian government was currently an ally of the Iraqi Peshmerga, that was only because they were at war with the Iraqi government, for at home they, too, repressed their own Kurdish population.

Yet, if Saddam kept ramming forward with his chemical attacks, Iraqi Kurds would be pushed over Kandil Mountain, the last geographical barrier between Kurdistan and Iran.

I buried my head in my hands. Would Kurds *ever* be free?

Karim noticed. "Joanna? Are you unwell?"

Sarbast answered quickly. "Joanna's eyes were damaged by the toxins. She was temporarily blinded, but her sight is slowly returning."

I brushed away my tears and looked up smiling. "But we are alive, Karim. We are alive to fight another day. *That* is the victory."

Sozan bustled into the room to hand me a tube of first-aid salve, which I began to smear over my blistered fingers.

She rushed back into the kitchen then quickly returned, balancing a copper tray loaded with Kurdish specialties. There was a pot of sweet cardamom-scented tea, some raisins and walnuts, and special Kurdish pastries dripping with honey. Four glasses of cold pomegranate juice were also placed on the tray.

I could barely restrain myself, but I remembered my manners

and waited for Sozan to pour the tea and to present each guest with a small cup.

Just as I tasted the delicious tea on my tongue, a soft knock sounded on the door. A questioning look flashed across Karim's face.

Sarbast explained, "That must be Kamaran, my cousin. He traveled with us. We split up outside the village. He was to meet us here."

Karim walked over to the door, carefully asking for the caller's identity first. Kamaran whispered his name and was quickly allowed entry.

The three men drank tea and munched on the nuts and raisins, discussing their plan for a new radio and communication center. I ate a pastry and listened as each fighter heatedly expressed his opinions of the next step that the PUK should take. Their voices became a buzz of background noise. Fatigue and a full stomach created an exhaustion that brought on a deep sleep even as I sat rigidly upright on the sofa.

Several hours later, I was bewildered to awake on a single cot in a small room that I did not recognize. Where was I? And where was Sarbast?

Recollections of the day before flickered in my mind. I soon remembered that I was in the home of Karim and Sozan. I was thirsty and hungry and reasoned that I had been put to bed by Sarbast, to rest while Sozan prepared the dinner meal.

I felt my swollen eyes with my fingers. I felt no more discharge flowing from my eyes, but they were still painful.

I examined my surroundings. The room was immaculate, though sparsely decorated. Aside from the cot I was on, there was nothing else to see but a small round table covered with a fancy embroidered white cloth and three pictures of Kurdish landmarks on the walls. I looked upward to see a tiny barred window high up one of the walls, covered by a lacy white curtain.

Light filtered in through the window. My vision was clearer. That cheered me up.

I stood and stretched. My entire body felt raw and aching. I hobbled out of the bedroom in my bare feet into a narrow hallway, then followed the passage into the living area where Sozan was tending one of her children.

Sozan looked up at my entrance and smiled. She had the typical Kurdish coloring, with fair skin, dark eyes, and black hair. Her features were not symmetrical, but her smile was so warm and sympathetic that I found myself wondering why I had not noticed her beauty before.

"Joanna. Did you sleep well?"

"Too well. I feel drugged," I admitted with a yawn. "Where is Sarbast?"

"Joanna," Sozan flashed a cheerful smile, "you fell into such a deep sleep that none of us could wake you." She teased me, "For certain, you were in a coma. Sarbast jokingly brandished roast chicken under your nose, but even that delicious aroma didn't cause a flicker." Sozan laughed. "Dear girl, there was nothing to do but for Sarbast to put you to bed. Then we ate dinner. Later we slept, too. You, darling Joanna, slept through the entire night. Sarbast asked that I let you sleep until you woke naturally. He said you had been so brave and strong that you had earned a long rest."

Sozan's smile faded as she studied my face with concern. I felt a little shiver of foreboding rush through me.

"Joanna, I must tell you that Sarbast and Kamaran left early this morning for Sandoulan."

"No!"

"Joanna, listen. There are so many roadblocks between here and Sandoulan that Sarbast and Kamaran must avoid the main roads and take the mountain path."

I was stunned into silence, but my mind was active. Sarbast had gone! Without me? "How long ago did he leave?"

Sozan read my mind. "You will never catch him. He left hours ago." She stroked my arm. "Listen, Joanna, we have heard that Iraqi checkpoint security soldiers are very careful now. They will allow women and children to pass, but take the men that try to cross, even boys as young as twelve. Sarbast and Kamaran are clearly Peshmerga. It would risk their very lives to chance a checkpoint." Sozan paused. "We have information that the government has a new policy to automatically execute all fighters. The soldiers murder our men in the woods, as soon as they stop them at the checkpoints."

"But I should be with Sarbast!" I shouted. "I *can* walk! See!" I marched around the room, twice.

Sozan slowly shook her head. "You, dear child, have passed your physical limit. You must rest today, and you will be taken to Sandoulan by car." She gestured at a small bundle of papers that rested on the small kitchen table. "Sarbast left your Iraqi identification papers here. As far as the government is concerned, Joanna, you are a pure Iraqi Arab, an al-Askari. There is nothing in your official papers to bind you to Kurds. You have an excellent chance of passing the checkpoints without a hassle."

Sozan's voice lowered as she glanced at her small son, who was absorbed in watching a cartoon on the black-and-white television set. "You should leave soon, though. Planes have begun to fly overhead. We don't know what is about to happen."

It was only then that I became aware of the enemy planes droning in the sky. After months of living as a target, I had come to recognize every reverberation of an airplane—I knew how a plane rumbled when it was only surveying an area, and I recognized the particular roar when a plane was approaching to drop bombs. I listened for a full minute before deciding we were in no immediate danger from those planes over Merge. Not yet, anyhow.

Sozan placed her hands on my shoulders, confirming what I thought. "We believe they are reconnaissance planes. They taunted us yesterday as well, circling over our heads for the entire morning."

I was not upset about the plane, but I was offended by Sarbast's departure. Since the first day of our marriage, I had never been a burden to my husband. Yesterday, even after being impaired by weakened eyesight, I had matched every step that Sarbast and Kamaran made.

I became so agitated that I shook with anger.

Sarbast knew how stubborn and determined I could be, so he had purposefully avoided a scene by leaving while I was asleep! I would have never let him leave without me had I been awake. I would have literally wrapped my body around his—I would have chased him through the neighborhood—*anything* to avoid a separation at this, possibly the most dangerous, time of our lives.

I circled the small room, flinging up my arms. I had *never* been so upset.

Then my stomach plunged at a new thought: perhaps I would never see Sarbast again. Sarbast might be dead, even as I stood safely in Sozan's kitchen.

I had no way of knowing where he was or what was happening to him. Unexplained disappearances were happening all over Kurdistan. How would I ever find him if he simply never turned up in Sandoulan?

That unknown made me shake in frustration and anger. I could have strangled him with my bare hands; however, I did not want anyone else to harm him.

Sozan took charge, steering my body with her hands, turning me around and pushing me into her small kitchen. "Let me prepare you a nice breakfast. A boiled egg, some bread and jam, and nice hot tea would be good, yes?"

If I planned on chasing Sarbast over the mountains, I reasoned that I had to be strong. I had to eat.

Soon, I was eating a delicious breakfast, but while eating, I caught an unpleasant whiff of my own body odor. "I must have a real bath, Sozan. Since the attack, I've only rinsed off the chemicals. I am so smelly and dirty that I cannot abide myself. What do you think? Is it safe?"

Sozan surveyed my unkempt appearance and obviously caught my scent, for she decided, "Yes. A quick one then." She added, "Very early this morning I washed all your clothes. They are hanging out in the sun drying. I will get you some fresh clothes now."

I smiled in gratitude as Sozan turned away to go outside.

As I finished the last few bites of my bread and jam, I watched Sozan through the small window. The wash was hanging almost directly over their family bomb shelter. Wonderful, I thought, it is good to know where the shelter is, in case those planes decide to attack.

Sozan maneuvered around the entrance to the shelter, first fingering my garments for dampness, then selecting several pieces of the freshly laundered clothing from the wash line.

Sozan was a genuine friend. Should she ever need a safe haven, I only hoped that I could help her in return.

She quickly returned with a dress and a small stack of clean underwear, all deliciously fragrant and imbued with the sunny breezes of Kurdistan. Then she led me into the family's bathroom, which was walled with gray concrete blocks.

The tiny room was dark and nearly featureless. I looked up to see a small window no bigger than a man's two hands flattened, located high up on the wall.

I wedged close to the metal water barrel that was placed carefully atop a liquid gas heater. An ancient faucet was installed on the bottom of the barrel and a small metal bowl was on the floor beneath. I decided I would first fill the bowl and pour water over my head and body, then soap up before rinsing.

Sozan returned to pass me a bar of soap, a small cup of shampoo, a wash cloth, and a frayed but clean terry-cloth towel.

"Be fast," Sozan cautioned me as she left the area.

"I'll create a new bathing record," I called after her.

I removed my clothing as quickly as possible. I poured the warm water over my hair and body—not once, but many times, savoring the water as it streamed over me. I poured a small amount of shampoo into my palm, then began rubbing my palm into the roots of my hair, scrubbing with my fingers as hard as possible. It felt exquisite.

But life can change in only a moment.

Standing there covered in soap suds, I suddenly heard the unmistakable roar of a plane engine so near that when I placed my hands on the wall I felt it vibrate. But I did not panic. After living in Bergalou and enduring many close calls, I simply held my breath, waiting to see what happened. The plane lifted at the last minute without dropping its load.

I exhaled. Perhaps the danger had passed.

Before I had time to rinse off, I heard the sound of the plane reapproaching. Soap suds trickled down my face and back, but there was no time for anything but to flee. I blindly clutched at the dress and heaved it over my head. If I was going to die, I would die with my clothes on.

Just as I moved one leg to run out of the room, I heard the loudest roar of my life, a blast so thunderous that my eardrums buzzed with pain.

I threw back my head and opened my mouth, shrieking.

Cracking explosions began to sound all around. I fell to the floor with my knees bent, protecting my face and head with both arms.

It was *really* the end. I was going to die. I was swept by rage at Sarbast. He did not even say good-bye. I was going to die alone.

Just as I screamed his name, *"Sarbast!"* a final blast rattled the walls and shook the floor beneath me.

In my last clear moment of thought, I remembered the baby and felt enormous sorrow.

I felt my body lift into the air. Then, like a feather in a strong wind, I was flung into the unforgiving concrete wall of the gray bathroom.

Then the darkness took me.

21

Bombed in Merge

THE FORBIDDEN ZONE, MERGE, KURDISTAN
Fall 1987

I was most fortunate to be bombed. The violence of the attack had thrust me straight into paradise. Or so I first thought.

Through the tranquil haze of what I believed to be heaven came an unfamiliar voice, drawing my attention. That's when I saw my father.

I stared in complete bewilderment, watching the silhouette of my father twist round until he became clear to me. Then I heard my formerly deaf-mute father speak.

His handsome face was strained with worry as he lightly scolded me, "Joanna. What are you doing here? You should be at home with your mother."

My father's voice sounded exactly as I had always imagined it, gentle and self-assured. I was breathless. It was a moment that I had fantasized about since I was a little girl, whispering, "Daddy. Daddy, please talk to me." He never did.

As his familiar image began to lighten, I heard an echo, a distant voice. Someone was calling my name, "Joanna! Joanna! Are you alive? Joanna?"

Groaning, I struggled to piece my thoughts together, but my memories were uneven and unable to harmonize. Moving my arms with a convulsed effort, I patted my head and face with the tips of my fingers, puzzled to find that my head was slippery wet. Had I been swimming?

"Joanna?"

I twisted to uncurl my legs.

"Joanna, yell out if you can."

My confusion mounted. Shivering, I opened my eyes and examined the dark space encircling me. Although the air was murky, I could see well enough to know that I was sprawled on a concrete floor.

Pieces of my memory slowly began to fit together. I was in Merge. I was in Sozan's house. I had been bathing when an enemy plane bombed the village.

I lightly stroked my head again, wondering how long I had been unconscious. It felt as if blood was gushing from my head onto my face and neck. I must have sustained serious head injuries. I groaned louder than before, fearing the worst, despite the fact I was free of pain.

Sarbast! Where was he?

"Joanna? Where are you?"

Desperate to make my location known, I tried to call out, but I could only manage to gurgle weakly from the back of my throat. My mouth was blocked. Was my jaw broken?

I delicately explored my mouth with my fingers. It was obstructed with a mass that felt like hardened mud! Panicking, I used my fingertips to rip that mass from my mouth. I had no idea where that hardened substance came from or what it was. I spewed out the chunks I had loosened, gagging and spitting. My gashed tongue and torn lips tasted of blood.

It brought to mind one of my mother's favorite sayings, when she warned me to hold my tongue: "Joanna, open your eyes, but not your mouth."

I supposed that, as usual, my mouth had been wide open at the wrong time. I managed a wry smile.

"Joanna! Come out! We are under attack!"

I produced a low growl. Why didn't someone come to me? Was

I buried alive? Had the roof and walls of the house collapsed on top of me?

"Joanna!"

With my mouth finally cleared of obstruction, I gave out a loud scream.

"You are alive! Praise Allah!"

I had been heard. I would meet my rescuers halfway. I imagined the entire village of Merge frantically burrowing through the wreckage, risking their lives in the open air to free me.

I was still naive, even after my time in Bergalou.

Using all the strength I could muster, I pushed upward with my hands. I could feel nothing penning me in. I began to grope, trying to find my bearings. I remembered that at my last moment of consciousness I had been in the bathroom.

I rubbed my hands over my body to make certain I was fully dressed. I could hardly pop out of the house naked.

Then I remembered my struggle to dress. I was a creation of my traditional society. I had risked my life to take additional time to cover my nudity. Better to be a fully clothed corpse than to be alive but nude and exposed to scandal. I had no regrets.

Finding my way out was a challenge. There was household debris and crumbled cement everywhere. I crawled on hands and knees to the open area between the bathroom and the bedroom. I sat back to take stock, giving myself a few moments to adjust my vision. But the house itself was still standing. The supporting concrete walls had withstood the blast.

I trembled with relief.

How many times would I beat the odds? Yet, while unlucky to undergo such close calls with death, I had been lucky that I had lived to tell the tale.

I patted my head. It was still wet with my blood. I remembered striking the concrete wall with my head. I hoped I didn't have a concussion.

"Joanna?"

I croaked out, "I am here."

"Can you come out?"

I tried to pull myself up but could not. My arms were too weak to support my body. My legs were shaking.

"I am here," I repeated weakly, tears forming in my eyes.

That's when I heard the roar of the airplane. Our enemy was still hanging about.

Hearing those thunderous roars with their promise of further disaster, I flung myself forward, crawling yet again on hands and knees. Shattered glass from broken vases and knicknacks slashed at the palms of my hands and the flesh of my knees through the fabric of my dress.

I made my way through any opening that I saw until finally I saw my rescuer standing outside. It was Karim.

I looked about. There was no one with him. I was shocked that he had come alone. Had everyone else been killed?

He extended a helping hand, "Come, Joanna. Come with me."

I checked a second time to see if there were other rescuers.

Karim answered my questioning look. "Everyone is in the shelter. This raid is too dangerous."

"Oh," I replied, understanding quickly that Karim had taken a huge risk to come out in the open during the bombing raid to search for me.

He tugged on my hand, pulling me to my feet, asking, "Can you walk?"

I nodded.

We could hear the bombs exploding nearby. Karim quickened his pace. "Come on. We must get to the shelter."

He escorted me to the main Merge shelter nearby, rather than the tiny earthen shelter next to his home. I was relieved. I had had enough of those narrow dens during my time in Bergalou.

The explosions grew louder just as we slipped into the shelter. We had barely made it.

Sozan called out, "Praise God, Joanna is alive!"

Karim released my hand and I stumbled toward Sozan. She rushed to meet me, holding my arms and leading me to a small gathering of women and children. She said, "I knew you were taking a chance to take that bath!"

The women gathered round me. Several shook out towels and began draping them over my head and shoulders, while others started examining my bleeding hands and fingers.

I choked out my fear, "Am I going to die?"

"*Na.* You will live."

"But my head?" I gingerly tapped the back of my head, which felt slippery with blood.

One woman jumped to her feet, saying, "Let me see." She stood above me, removing the towels to tenderly draw my hair left and right, examining my scalp underneath. I held my breath.

She shrugged. "You are fine. There are only a few scratches, in fact."

I perked up. "Really?"

That woman held my face between her two hands. "Your face is pitted from cement chips. Your lips are scratched raw." She smiled. "But you will live."

A third woman reported, "Your dress is ripped. Your knees are bleeding." She looked closer. "There is glass embedded in your knees."

I nodded. But my knees would heal. I was most apprehensive over my head injuries. I looked at the first woman. "But my head." I cautiously touched the top of my scalp. "What is the source of all that blood?"

"There is very little blood. You are feeling that slick shampoo in your hair."

I drew my hands to my chest, giggling. I had forgotten that I had no time to rinse off. My thick hair was still full of suds. *That* was the slick substance I had felt streaming down my back and face!

Enormous relief swept over me. But just when I was feeling respite from my worries, my lower belly gave a lurch, as if something had broke loose.

I gasped. Was my unborn child safe? I inhaled deeply, cupping my belly with my hands.

"Do you hurt there?" Sozan asked, her face twisted with worry.

I shook my head, not wanting to share my secret with anyone unless absolutely necessary. Besides, I was not certain I was pregnant at all. I decided to keep quiet.

Sozan called out for her husband to bring the pail of water that was kept in the shelter for villagers to use. There were no glasses available, so I was encouraged to drink straight from the pail, and I did. It was delicious fresh spring water.

Afterward, two of the women carefully picked the glass pieces from my knees.

Sozan rustled up a couple of blankets and a pillow, announcing, "This raid is not going to end anytime soon. You should rest."

When I curled up in a corner, she spread a blanket over my body and gave me dry towels for my head, as there was no place in the shelter to rinse off the soap.

I slept through the remainder of the raid. In fact, I never awoke of my own volition. I was finally roused by the sweet sound of Sarbast's voice.

"Joanna. Wake up."

Groggy, I turned my head to find him looking at me.

"Joanna?"

A happy moment! He was alive. "Sarbast!" I sat up, unaware of the comic figure I was cutting until Sarbast burst into laughter.

"Did you know that you have towels on your head?"

"Sarbast! See what happened! You shouldn't have left me!" I spoke in an angry tone, but in reality, I was overwhelmed with joy that he was alive and that I was alive. We had been given a second chance, once again.

Sarbast was unable to stop laughing. He pulled on the towels still draped over my head and shoulders. "What is this?"

"I was in the bath," I retorted.

He leaned down, lifting me up. "I think you need to finish that bath, darling. You have streaks of soap all over your face."

"It's not soap. That's from pieces of cement," I snapped, feeling a return of my earlier irritation that he had left me in the first place. "Trying to protect me from the trail, you left me in a worse danger! Had you not abandoned me, I would have been safe with you."

He lightly grasped my arm. "Come. Let's go back to Karim's house. We'll discuss our plans."

Tired, sore, and limping because of the sharp pain in my knees, I stepped outside, looking all around me. The sunset was especially beautiful, pink with golden streaks, but the sun was setting on a village partially destroyed by our enemy. But we were alive, and at that moment, nothing else mattered.

I felt another cramp, in the lower part of my stomach again. If I was indeed pregnant, our unborn child was in grave danger. But there was nothing I could do, for there was no medical care available in Merge. Other than the most basic first aid, the nearest medical facilities for me would be in Sulaimaniya. It was impossible for me to travel there, now. Besides, we had heard that the Iraqi government had ordered execution for anyone seeking medical treatment for chemical injuries. My eyes would quickly reveal that I was a survivor of Bergalou. They were still red, swollen, and sticky with discharge.

But I was desperate to save my unborn child. I would walk slowly and sit quietly as much as possible. Perhaps the fetus would settle down.

As far as my eyes were concerned, all I could do was administer more eye drops and hope for the best.

I glanced at Sarbast's face, wondering if I should tell him of our possible pregnancy. One quick glance at his creased face told me that he was occupied with many other troubles. I would not add to his worries.

I had not known it at the time, but when Sarbast had departed Merge without me, I could have caught up with him on the trail if I had hurried. Sarbast had warned Sozan of my determined character, so to give Sarbast and Kamaran ample time to get away, she had stretched the truth when telling me that my husband had departed hours before. In fact, I later discovered that he was only moments out of the house even as I was questioning Sozan. That explained how he was so quick returning to the shelter to find me still wet from the shower and disoriented from the bombing attack.

Sarbast and Kamaran had been only thirty minutes into the trail when they heard the bombers attacking Merge. They could even see the enemy airplanes overhead. Kamaran later told me, "Sarbast stood as stiff as a man frozen, watching those planes drop bombs on Merge. He called out your name once before turning to sprint back, hurdling over large boulders and steep gullies." Kamaran laughed. "You are very dear to your husband, Joanna. Never doubt it."

While Kamaran's words brought me a rush of happiness, I was more dogged than ever that we not be parted. But it was not to be. It was too risky for Sarbast and Kamaran to travel by the main roads. They had to cut through the forests.

But I had too many injuries to make the difficult walking journey. The situation called for transportation. With my eyes still impaired and my knees stiff and sore from cuts, it would be impossible for me to ascend hilly terrain. Because by then I felt certain I was pregnant, I thought it best to rest my body, shocking Sarbast when I meekly agreed to part at a fork in the road. He would go one way and I would go another.

Sarbast and Kamaran would meet me in the small settlement of Sandoulan, a four-hour drive by automobile, a brisk ten- or twelve-hour hike. At last we received word that Sandoulan was still held by the PUK, although the settlement was located only a few kilometers from government-occupied areas, so it could fall into enemy hands at any time. From there we would work our way to Sangaser, a dangerous location for us, for it was a town controlled by our enemies. Yet we had no choice but to go through Sangaser, for we were hooking up with a famous smuggler there who would take us over Kandil Mountain.

It would be a very hazardous journey. We would be hunted like animals for the duration of the trip.

Sarbast touched a nerve when he asked if I would consider returning to Baghdad, that perhaps I could slip back into the city and avoid what was surely coming, that he could not bear to see me die.

I stared at him in disbelief. I hissed as I shoved against his hard chest with my balled fists. He had his answer. Our fate was bonded. We were one. We would burst out alive to the safe side to rebuild our lives, or we would die together. It was that simple. Whatever our destiny might be, we would be together. While I do not doubt that other wives have loved their husbands as much as I loved my Sarbast, I am certain that none have loved their husbands more.

After Sarbast and Kamaran departed Merge for a second time, I finally completed that dangerous bath, dressed in fresh clothes, and readied my two small bags.

A few hours later, Karim, Sozan, and their children bade me farewell. Karim was not a Peshmerga, so he was hopeful that Saddam's men would not target him or his family. I joined a group that was traveling to Sandoulan. Sarbast had arranged my transportation in a car with trusted acquaintances. We did not see any signs of our enemy because the main road from Merge to Sandoulan was still controlled by the PUK. Sarbast and Kamaran could have ridden with us, but we were unwilling to take any unnecessary chances. Both men were wanted by the Baghdad government.

Along the route I gaped from the car window at groups of harried Kurdish refugees hurrying along the road, moving purposefully. All the men were armed with Kalashnikovs, the Kurdish weapon of choice, with cartridge belts draped across their chests. Many of the women walking had babies wrapped to their bodies. Toddlers trailed behind their mothers while older children, appearing bewildered by the upheaval, pulled on cords looped to the necks of cows and donkeys. Chickens and ducks were caged in wooden crates lashed to the sides of donkeys. I felt devastated for their situation. Where would the civilians find safety when the danger was erupting all around us?

The drive itself would have been magnificent had it not been for the fact that we were running for our lives. It was late fall and the frost had not yet touched the foliage. To my eyes the trees looked like mammoth bouquets of green, gold, and orange towering over the pale brown of withered grasses. The rolling hills spread out to a distant mountain range. The snow had not yet arrived, but it was cold enough to make me glad the sun was shining, bringing its daytime warmth to the brisk fall air.

I knew it would be even colder under the canopy of that thick tree cover. I stared hypnotized into those forests, knowing that my Sarbast was on foot somewhere out there.

When we arrived in Sandoulan, a tiny settlement of only a few houses, I was driven to a small dwelling where a couple by the name of Abdullah and Minich lived. They, too, were Peshmergas and were in charge of an underground human railroad of fleeing fighters from the Jafati Valley.

I was crushed to learn that Sarbast and Kamaran had not yet arrived, although common sense said it was impossible unless they had miraculously sprouted wings.

The couple offering hospitality was undeniably handsome. Abdullah was nearly as good looking as Sarbast, and Minich was a dark exotic beauty. They were fearless, too, seemingly unconcerned that they and their three small children were certain to die hard deaths should their activities be discovered by the Jahsh. No death was more brutal than that meted out to those concealing Jafati PUK fighters.

Due to my injuries, everyone insisted that I rest, but I could not until I saw that Sarbast was safe. The kindly couple settled easily around me, under a walnut tree, drinking sweet tea and eating Kurdish bread and cheese while waiting for our forest travelers. I tilted my head against the trunk of the large tree, intermittently closing and opening my eyes. With every rustle of the autumn leaves I searched the trail. After several hours, muffled voices alerted us that someone was walking up the path, and suddenly there they were, pallid from exhaustion yet smiling and waving as though walking for ten hours was a mere lark, as though we were set to embark on a family holiday rather than on another long race for survival.

I was ecstatically happy to see my husband again even as I read his intent face. Something was amiss.

After saying a quick hello to everyone, Sarbast claimed that we must leave Sandoulan as soon as possible. My husband declared that he could sense danger coming. He said that our enemy was gaining on us, that everyone in Sandoulan was in the gravest danger.

With his words, my hands felt clammy and the hair on my neck stiffened. I had been with Sarbast long enough to recognize that he had a true talent sensing real danger just before it struck. I, for one, did not want to dismiss his intuition.

I pulled myself up and was ready to leave at a moment's notice. The sooner we started, the better.

After Sarbast and Kamaran had slurped one quick cup of tea, they set off again even while eating for the first time in ten hours, quickly ingesting pieces of bread stuffed with white cheese. Their aim was to rent a vehicle to transport us over the rocky dirt road to the Jahsh town of Sangaser.

I couldn't dispel my sinking feeling at the challenges ahead, but we had no choice but to travel into the midst of enemy forces. The Jahsh had cleverly planted themselves in our mountains and hills, like poisonous serpents around the base of Kandil Mountain, the main escape route.

Luckily, Sarbast and Kamaran found an available vehicle capable of crossing the rough terrain, and the following morning we bade farewell to the hospitable and courageous Abdullah and Minich. Had I only known what lay ahead, I would have pleaded with them to accompany us, to leave Sandoulan behind and climb Kandil Mountain with us, for the handsome and affable couple's destiny was bleak. Abdullah would soon be killed in a heated battle with our enemy and Minich and their little children would be running for their lives. But we were as yet unaware of the scope of the tragedy about to overtake all of Kurdistan.

Four days after leaving Merge, we reached Sangaser.

Entering Sangaser was relatively simple, for the Jahsh living there would have never believed any Peshmerga so foolishly reckless or even courageous enough to voluntarily enter their armed camp. Indeed, most Peshmergas avoided the town by traveling through the woods, but we could not climb Kandil Mountain without a guide, so we drove directly to the door of the famous Kurdish smuggler known as "Crazy Hassan." It was claimed he was crazy for the chances he took, a man celebrated for his daring as well as for his knowledge of every footpath crisscrossing Kurdistan. The man looked the part, a true mountain man: he was only a few years older than Sarbast, tall, and wiry, and he had bushy hair and a large mustache.

Hassan told us to sit and have tea. He solemnly announced, "You have come at the worst time." He made a clicking noise with his tongue, adding, "My brother is a Jahsh, and he tells me that over a thousand Jahsh have congregated here, and more are coming."

With a quick jerk of my head, I looked at Sarbast. Our smuggler was the brother of a Jahsh? Sarbast's face was a mask, revealing nothing, listening. I exchanged a grim glance with Kamaran.

Hassan reported, "They have their orders. The PUK camps in the Jafati Valley are the first priority. Baghdad means to shut down the radio station forever. The Jahsh role is to harass and kill retreating fighters. This means you. They will inflict punishment on any civilians who lend assistance to the Peshmergas. That means me. From now on, they will be flushing villagers out of their homes, killing the men and boys, and relocating the women and children to the south, to refugee camps. They mean to empty Kurdistan."

My heart raced.

Sarbast's response was cold and calculating. "If this is true, we must leave now."

"It is too dangerous," Hassan replied with a wobble of his head.

Sarbast sneered, "I thought you were a real smuggler."

Crazy Hassan did look crazy then, crazy with rage at Sarbast's insult.

Sarbast leaned back lazily, as though he didn't have a care in the world, yet as I watched I saw his muscular arms tensing.

Oh my, any moment now I knew there would be in an altercation. Sarbast had always been more daring than most, but I feared he was pushing his luck now. Both Sarbast and Crazy Hassan were powerful men, but we were in Crazy Hassan's territory. What would keep this man from calling out for the Jahsh to come and capture us all?

Crazy Hassan's eyes narrowed. "I will see."

"Yes or no," Sarbast said quietly. "If you don't have the skills to get us up Kandil Mountain, then I will find someone else."

Crazy Hassan took the challenge. "I will do it. But you will do what I say."

Sarbast's eyes were glittering. "When do we leave?"

"Not today. I will talk with my brother. He will give me the information I need."

Sarbast got up. "We will go with you."

Kamaran stood beside Sarbast. Both men adjusted their weapons.

Crazy Hassan looked over at me. "She will stay here. With the women."

"Yes," Sarbast agreed. He nodded at me, his eyes conveying a hidden message that I should remain calm.

I was paralyzed with fear, watching as the three men marched out of the house. Why on Earth was Sarbast willingly entering the house of a Jahsh? Had he gone crazy as well? *If* he made it back safely, I decided from that time on I would nickname him "Crazy Sarbast."

I couldn't believe the dangerous turn our journey had taken. Would Sarbast be killed? If so, would I be turned over to our enemy?

Just then, Crazy Hassan's wife and several other women collected me from the sitting room, chatting easily as though all our lives were not in the balance. Finally, I found the courage to question his wife, asking, "And your brother-in-law is a Jahsh? How does that work?"

She appeared to be a coarse-mannered woman with a pitted and prematurely wrinkled face that hinted of many years of hard work, but she soon proved herself to be kind natured. She laughed at my question. "Oh, he is not *really* a Jahsh. He takes the government's money but he is harmless. He protects his brother, my husband."

I hoped what she was saying was true because my husband's fate depended on her husband and his brother.

Her tale was believable, for the history of the Jahsh was complicated. In the past, most Kurds would honorably die rather than accept one dinar from the Iraqi government to spy on their friends and neighbors. Jahsh were so despised that they were known by the derogatory term *donkey foal*. But some Kurds changed their attitude during the long war with Iran. That war changed every Iraqi's life, including the Kurds in the north.

Every Iraqi man was expected to go to the trenches and defend the Baghdad government. If a Kurd refused to fight in the trenches, his family members were imprisoned, homes were leveled, and young men were killed. And then there was the embargo. The government in Baghdad tried to starve the Kurds by launching an austere food embargo. With families starving, a few Kurds began accepting the government stipend, pretending to be informers to avoid having to fight.

Greed became a factor, for the Jahsh were well paid. There were even bounties placed on the heads of certain Peshmergas such as Sarbast, who became famous by writing and broadcasting over the radio station. With so much money at stake, Jahsh numbers swelled to several hundred thousand.

We now found ourselves in the thick of Jahsh territory, uncertain whom we might trust. Nobody, was my guess.

My worst fears were kindled when Crazy Hassan returned without Sarbast and Kamaran. Perhaps he had traded my husband's life for a new car!

I became wild with rage, set to claw his eyes from his skull.

Sarbast had obviously predicted my reaction. He soon sprinted in, reassuring me that all was well, saying that it was too dangerous for the three of us to be together at Crazy Hassan's home. I would be safe there with the women and unnoticed when the Jahsh start searching homes, for they were doing just that in Sangaser, making nightly raids. But Hassan's brother's house was less likely to be searched, because he was a known Jahsh.

Sarbast and Kamaran were going to spend the night there in the home of Hassan's brother. Sarbast trusted both men, the smuggler and the Jahsh. I trusted neither.

That night was the longest night of my life.

The following morning Sarbast and Kamaran returned. While Kamaran looked rested, Sarbast appeared gaunt, with hollow eyes ringed by wide black circles. During a moment of privacy, he confessed to me that he had not slept for a moment. While Kamaran slept, Sarbast had sat in the hallway guarding the house.

Nothing had happened, thankfully, but Sarbast was an exhausted man on the edge.

Sarbast argued against Crazy Hassan's protests that it was still too dangerous to depart Sangaser. He carried on until finally Crazy Hassan agreed to make an attempt. He led the way on his mule, while we followed on foot. But shortly after leaving the town we spotted a Jahsh roadblock ahead. They were swarming like angry bees all over the area. We quickly turned around for a second sleepless night.

The following evening we made our second attempt to flee the town. We ran into another roadblock and returned once again to Sangaser.

By this time Sarbast was a man crazed. For the first time in my life, I began biting my fingernails. Only Kamaran kept his cool.

On the third evening, Sarbast confronted Crazy Hassan again, telling him, "We are leaving tonight, Hassan."

When Hassan demurred, saying he would wait and see, Sarbast shouted, "Even if Saddam Hussein himself is standing guard at the roadblock, we are going through!"

We finally found some luck. At the third attempt to leave Sangaser, we managed to creep past the roadblock without being noticed while the Jahsh guards were busy interrogating other unfortunate travelers.

Success was sweet, but I could not forget that the journey ahead would be even more treacherous. We knew that the Jahsh would menace us until we reached the top of Kandil Mountain.

As we followed Crazy Hassan and his large gray-colored mule, I gazed into the distance. I could already see the white veil of snow covering the peaks of Kandil Mountain, which would be a beautiful sight in any other circumstance, yet I declined to enjoy the view, for I knew that I was expected to climb that mountain.

My heart gave a lurch. Perhaps we would perish along the way, but should we live to find ourselves at the base, how would I ever manage to ascend to the top of that towering peak? God would have to intervene on this one, I decided.

Once again, I soldiered on.

22

Climbing Kandil Mountain

During my twenty-five years of living, I had given little thought to mules. But after only a few moments of desperate clinging to Crazy Hassan's pack mule, that mule became my entire world. I was acutely aware of its every move, from the positioning of its enormous ears to the placing of its hooves. My only goal in life was to hang on tightly and to avoid tumbling out of the saddle and spilling onto the hard ground. My arms were clinging to the animal's neck and my backside stuck up in the air. Mine was obviously an incorrect position for a rider, and the mule appeared as uncomfortable with me as I was with him. I was as terrified as I had ever been.

As soon as we were safely out of town, Sarbast and Crazy Hassan had joined forces to insist that I ride the mule. I was walking too slowly, they claimed, although I felt confident I was keeping up. Sarbast counted off other reasons for their decision. The journey to the Kandil Mountain range would take two or three days of hard walking. My injuries were not yet healed. I would slow the journey.

I reacted indignantly. While I had ridden a small donkey on occasion, donkeys are quite low to the ground, and my long legs would very nearly brush the hilly grasses. If I tired of the ride, I would simply stand tall, allowing the donkey to trot off under me.

But Crazy Hassan's mule was a different story.

I have always had a fear of heights, and Crazy Hassan's mule was massive. Undoubtedly, it was considered a magnificent specimen, with his beautiful light gray coloring and broad chest, and the movement of his large ears was very expressive. Crazy Hassan was very proud of it. I had reason to believe that our guide loved his mule nearly as much as he loved his little children. But for me, the mule was terrifyingly tall, much taller than many horses.

I resisted riding the creature until Sarbast made a desperate plea. "Please get on the mule, Joanna. There is no time to waste! You are going to get us killed."

I stared up at the animal. It was already loaded with my two sacks of belongings, hanging like saddlebags on either side. My pink bedding, which had caused disagreements with Sarbast all along the way, was thrown across its back, giving the mule additional height that it did not need.

The three men were watching me. I took several deep breaths, deciding that since my knees were throbbing perhaps I should give mule riding a chance.

"Okay. I will try," I told Sarbast meekly.

I had no idea how to mount the mule. I circled it warily, looking for a good spot to make my climb. That mule's eyes opened wide, alert to every move I made. The mule obviously believed me unworthy of a ride because when I stepped toward him, he stepped back.

With a harsh sigh, Sarbast finally handed his Kalashnikov to Kamaran and in one quick move lifted me in his arms and settled me on the mule's back. I remembered Sarbast's sister teasing me about my Peshmerga trousers and finally realized that she had been correct. I *could* accomplish daring feats in the adaptable pants.

Kamaran, who was full of quips, said a joke I did not hear, bringing chuckles from Sarbast.

I would have shot both men a filthy look but I was too unnerved to make any sudden moves. Nothing was amusing about sitting on that mule. I was so high off the ground that I felt dizzy.

Crazy Hassan gestured with his hands as he instructed, "Rock your weight from side to side. Let the mule get a feel for you."

I gaped at Crazy Hassan. He *was* certifiably crazy if he thought I was going to do anything to upset his mule. *Rock?* I bent low as I hugged the mule's neck instead.

Crazy Hassan wiggled his head in disgust, and with his thick mustache twitching, he lifted one of the reins and gave me the other. Then he led the mule down the trail.

While I hung on awkwardly, the mule plodded on mechanically, surefooted even in the dark, its large graceful ears moving in perfect rhythm to his rolling gait. I decided to privately name the mule Beauty, for his owner was justifiably proud of his appearance. Still, I knew it best not to touch Beauty unnecessarily, because when I accidentally brushed the back of his head with my face, he suddenly stretched his neck out so far that my upper body was stretched along with him, and I nearly fell off.

No, Beauty was not happy with his reluctant passenger.

I was barely breathing I was so anxious. But the mule finally relaxed and his pace lengthened.

Sarbast asked, "How are you, darling?" and I grunted without further explanation. I didn't want to upset Beauty with aimless chatter.

I found the strangeness of mule riding the greatest misery, with every moment exhausting me. Every nerve felt alive, throbbing and tingling, and I expected every moment that I would be tossed to the ground.

Crazy Hassan was a longtime smuggler for the Peshmergas. For years, he had been in the risky business of supplying the Peshmergas in the area of Kurdistan that Saddam labeled the "Forbidden Zone." Crazy Hassan and his mule were experts at supplying the Peshmergas with medicine, food, weapons, and ammunition. Saddam intended to starve out the Peshmergas, but smugglers such as Crazy Hassan thwarted that strategy. To decrease personal danger, other smugglers even trained teams of mules who learned to cross the mountains unaccompanied by their human owners from the Iranian villages that were the main supply depots for Iraqi Kurdish Peshmergas to the smugglers who were waiting on the Iraqi side of the border to unload the goods. After a rest and a feeding, the mules would be sent back to Iran and the process would repeat itself. The situation often turned tragic for the poor mules. Should a mule be packed carelessly and the load shifted while on the trail, the mule would lose its footing and tumble to the ground, unable to rise. Unless the mule was discovered by a sympathetic traveler, the fallen animal would lie there until it was attacked and eaten by wild animals or until it died from starvation. Kurdistan could be a cruel place, for man or beast.

Crazy Hassan was appalled that any smuggler would risk sending his mules on those solitary runs. "I would never risk my beauty," he professed as he looked at his mule with such affection that I thought for a moment that he might kiss it on those large loose lips.

I had to admire Hassan's courage. The smuggler's life was a perilous occupation. None of us could ever forget that the Peshmergas would not have lasted a month without the help of the smugglers.

Within a few hours, a terrifying incident occurred.

Crazy Hassan abruptly halted, and began shouting loudly, directing his voice in the direction we were heading, "This is Crazy Hassan! This is Crazy Hassan! Who is there? I'm crazy! Get away or show yourself! This is Crazy Hassan!"

Sarbast and Kamaran both raced to stand beside me. I watched with a sort of horrified fascination as they raised their weapons.

Who was in front of us? The Jahsh? Saddam's foot soldiers?

When Beauty's entire body quivered, I decided it wise to leap off his back before he bolted. But then I looked at the ground that seemed so far away and changed my mind. If I was pregnant, such a dive to hard ground would surely cause a miscarriage. Deciding not to risk it, I tucked my head as low as possible, for I knew that Beauty and I were a tempting target.

Hassan continued screeching his wild threats that he was a crazy man and that the intruders would be even crazier to give us a problem. Crazy Hassan was clearly proud of his nickname, and I knew then where he got it.

Just then we heard a voice from the night respond to Crazy Hassan. Crazy Hassan obviously recognized the voice and calmed down. He walked toward the voice to sort out any misunderstanding.

When he returned, we were told that it was a gang of four smugglers who often preyed on travelers in the area. They were opportunists, not murderers. Without Crazy Hassan we would have been robbed.

I snorted, thinking of their disappointment had they indeed robbed the three of us. We were the poorest of the poor.

The night seemed to have no end. Perched miserably on the back of my mule, I only half-listened to the men's muted conversations. I fretted over the child I believed I was carrying. A physical mishap might cause new problems.

I became so weary that I began to see visions of Baghdad. I longed for my old bed and was desperate for a real meal. And then I began wondering for the first time since I had married Sarbast what I was doing in Kurdistan in the middle of the night, sitting on a mule that did not even like me.

Finally, just when I thought I was going to drop off the mule like a stone, Crazy Hassan called a halt beside a small stream. He said, "We have passed a danger point. We can rest here for a while and then leave before dawn."

His words were the sweetest I had ever heard.

While Crazy Hassan petted Beauty, whispering sweet nothings no doubt, Sarbast struggled to help me to the ground.

It was not a night that encouraged aimless chatter. We gathered in a silent circle to share our simple fare. Crazy Hassan had packed fruit and nuts and Sarbast had bagged some Kurdish bread, bread that after being baked hardens like a cracker, but when sprinkled with water becomes soft and edible. Kamaran took our bread to the stream and prepared it for us.

I ate very little, then walked over to the stream to slurp cold water from a small puddle that had formed beside it. While I was drinking, Crazy Hassan and Beauty came up beside me to share the same puddle.

I stared for a startled moment at Beauty's open mouth and large teeth. Then I sighed noisily. I was beyond caring, so I scooped up another handful and drank greedily.

Sarbast guarded me while I squatted behind a small bush because Crazy Hassan had cautioned that we were in area frequented by wild animals, mainly wolves and bears. After I told him that I was more worried about snakes and scorpions than bears, Sarbast watched for ground movement. Then Sarbast tenderly bundled me in my pink bedding, whispering that his Baghdad bride had made him proud, that I was so brave.

I was too tired to respond, but before I closed my eyes to sleep, I saw that he was sitting guard over me, watching for bears, I assumed.

Only in Kurdistan could we have found such a lonely place. I fell asleep with flickering visions of Sarbast wrestling a wild bear in our little camp.

Hours later, a loud noise woke me. Birds were singing and muffled human voices hummed all around. *What?* I sat up in a hurry and warily looked around. I was stunned to see that our campsite was crowded with a mass of humans and a large group of pack mules.

My mouth went dry. I looked at Sarbast in alarm but he was smiling. "It is all right," he assured me. "This is a smugglers' haunt. They all know about this place. It is a popular stopping point for them."

Although none of the smugglers did anything to cause the slightest concern, I was the only woman in the camp, so I was in an understandable rush to leave. We ate our breakfast of bread and fruit, and after witnessing several mules slurping from the stream, I postponed quenching my thirst. Water springs were abundant in Kurdistan. Shortly after departing we would stumble across another stream. I would relieve myself later, as well, I decided, as the bushes in the area were too small for complete privacy.

Sarbast reluctantly agreed that I could walk for a short distance before returning to Beauty's back. Crazy Hassan agreed, stating that we would soon be at the base of Kandil and once we started that climb, his mule would need all his strength. My dread of climbing that mountain slowly shaped into a terrifying goal.

Delay marred the day's journey as Crazy Hassan constantly gestured for us to stop. We were still in the area controlled by the Jahsh and government troops, and only he knew exactly where the government checkpoints were located. There were moments we were not even allowed to whisper, and if Hassan had his way, we would have ceased breathing altogether.

It was truly a miracle that we were not discovered. Crazy Hassan didn't make us feel any better when he shared a few hair-raising tales about previous travelers who had been caught by the Jahsh. Those poor families had been separated, the men taken off to be executed and the women sent to jail to endure horrors that

Crazy Hassan refused to describe. However, we were reassured when he bragged that he had never been caught by his enemies. His missions were always successful.

I felt somewhat better knowing of his perfect record. But we were soon crouched in the grass again after hearing enemy voices through the thicket.

Even Beauty sensed the danger. He seemed in perfect harmony with his owner, stepping softly at the same moments Crazy Hassan was most fixated on the noises around us. Beauty gave every indication of being a very intelligent mule.

Soon there was reason to feel sorry for Beauty. Sarbast was conferring with Crazy Hassan when it became obvious Beauty had eaten a certain food that created terrific intestinal problems. Kamaran and I were speaking quietly when we were startled by the explosive passing of mule gas. I blinked, silenced by the sound and the smell, too embarrassed to acknowledge what I had heard. But Kamaran, who was born a prankster, could not resist making a few jokes. We fell further behind Beauty, keeping a safe distance, for he continued to expel gas loudly. The situation worsened. With each step Beauty made, more gas blasted, the explosive sounds becoming louder and longer. Unable to restrain himself, Kamaran began imitating the mule by making revolting noises with his mouth.

Although at first I did not find Beauty's misery funny, Kamaran was making the most of the predicament, finding something to laugh about in our joyless situation. He carried on until I was infected by his laughter.

Hearing our peals of laughter, Crazy Hassan took offense. He walked back to us, scowling. "You mock my mule?"

Crazy Hassan's reaction fired Kamaran's enthusiasm. Kamaran's forehead wrinkled and his bright eyes glittered as he laughed boisterously. Unable to restrain my merriment, I cupped my hands over my mouth.

Sarbast was displeased as well. His face was grim when he sternly ordered us, "Stop it. This is not a game."

With the greatest effort, Kamaran and I restrained our hilarity.

But that poor mule found no relief. Because of his predicament, I convinced Sarbast that I should walk for a few hours more, until finally he and Crazy Hassan ruled that my walking pace was holding us up and that I must ride again.

And so I did. In fact, I was beginning to feel some affection for Beauty, admiring his tirelessness in twisting in and out along the trail. I soon felt relaxed enough to look around me at the landscape. I became hypnotized by the sight of the magnificent Kandil Mountain range slowly coming into full view.

While the daytime journey was not as frightening as the nighttime experience, there were still many reasons for discomfort. The sun was shining with fiery strength, surprisingly strong for that time of the year. Then I reminded myself of our high elevation. The sun would remain intense from that point on. The rays were so dazzling that I bent my head to my chest to guard my eyes from the glow. I was thankful that the snows had not yet come, however. Snowstorms would have added extra peril to an already difficult journey.

Our travel routine was simple: We moved forward. We stopped and listened. We moved forward again. We halted to listen. Only rarely did we stop for a rest. Our biggest concern was that checkpoint locations had changed since Crazy Hassan's last trip through the area. A number of times we could actually hear the voices of our enemies through the thick foliage. Those moments were the worst of all. If we were discovered, we would be executed. Unfortunately, we would almost certainly be tortured before being executed.

Sarbast pledged that he would not allow us to be taken. "Better to die in a gun battle than in the armpit of your enemy," he swore. He looked into my face. "Do not worry. I will kill you myself, rather than see enemy hands on you."

I was unsure whether to be relieved or terrified. Certainly, I knew that my husband possessed an iron core. If it became necessary to save me from torture and death at the hands of our cruel enemy, he would find the strength to fulfill his challenging pledge, even if it meant looking into my eyes for a final farewell while firing a bullet into my brain. I shivered at the morbid prospect, for I knew that if such a tragic moment was our destiny Sarbast's sorrow would be more agonizing than my own.

Crazy Hassan was energetically working a large tooth stick in his mouth, even as his eyes swept the landscape, searching for danger.

Only Kamaran seemed relaxed in the face of threats, amazing me with his ready smile and quick wit. Of our group, I decided that it would be the greatest loss for Kamaran to die. He was young and unmarried and had not yet experienced the love of a woman.

Perched high, and on a journey that did not encourage point-less prattle, I decided I would take responsibility for watching the horizon for any sign of our enemy. Thankfully, I saw none.

The countryside was increasingly interesting. Scrub grass was everywhere and the land was getting ever more hilly, a promise of what was coming. My stomach lurched. The hills we were crossing were growing into a mountain. I became somber, aware that I was nearing the biggest challenge of my life. Even Beauty sensed the gravity of the situation, becoming even more strained and tense. The famous Kandil Mountain range loomed higher and larger until finally we arrived at its base.

I was awed into silence, staring upward until my neck muscles began to throb. I could not even see the top! Sunbeams were danc-ing on the polished rock. I had anticipated climbing a mountain covered with trees and dirt paths winding like ribbons to the top. But Kandil Mountain was not the mountain of my dreams. A spe-cial kind of dread settled in my stomach as I realized I was expected to scale bare granite so ruggedly high that I could not believe that Sarbast truly believed me capable of climbing it.

And how would a mule find its footing on that glossy rock? Were we going to leave Beauty behind? Surely not, for Crazy Hassan openly loved his mule. And Beauty was carrying our goods, as well.

For the first time since we had started the trip, even Kamaran was silent.

That's when Sarbast gave me the worst news: "You will not be walking, darling. You will be on the mule for the entire ascent."

Mouth open, I stared at Sarbast. He was asking the impossible of me.

The news became even more grim when Crazy Hassan instructed, "It is too dangerous. If we start the climb now, we will be spotted from below, tempting enemy fire. We will wait over there"—he pointed at a bushy area—"until dusk."

I looked once more at Sarbast. So, he planned for me to sit on a mule and trust that mule to climb the steepest mountain in all of Kurdistan and to accomplish that amazing feat in the dark of night. Sarbast had lost all good sense.

While waiting for the sun to go down, I sat rigid, openly staring at the mountain. From what I could see from my ground position, Kandil Mountain had steep cliffs and drops thousands of feet deep.

I would be sitting high on a mule while flanked on one side by serrated rock and on the other side by ravines so deep that if Beauty
suffered one tiny misstep, we would both plunge off the mountain
to certain death.

I had never been more miserable. For the first time in my life, I
had been presented with a test I couldn't pass.

Sarbast attempted to cheer me. He sat by my side, encouraging
me to eat the last of our fruit, patting my hands, and even stroking
my shoulder, a sign of intimacy rarely seen in public in our Kurdish
world. He was leading up to something ominous, I felt certain.

Finally, he said in an offhand way, "The mule can climb that
mountain blindfolded."

I gasped loudly. So! *Now* I knew! So! That was how they coaxed
mules over such a high mountain! That was how they kept fidgety
mules from leaping off mountains! I jerked my hands back from
Sarbast, my words coming in a rush. "No! It is settled then. I will
go back to Baghdad."

"What are you talking about, Joanna? There is no going back to
Baghdad from here. Tehran, perhaps, but not Baghdad," he added
with a chuckle.

I glared at my husband. "Listen to me, Sarbast. I am *not* going
to sit on a blindfolded mule who is being coaxed over a mountain
over three thousand meters high!"

Sarbast was baffled for a moment. Then a tentative smile
twitched, slowly shaping into full laughter. Once started, he could
not stop, laughing with such intensity that tears began to roll down
his face.

I thought, well, Sarbast has finally gone mad. I had been expecting it. No man could live under the extreme stress Kurdish fighters endured, day after day, year after year, without paying a mental
price.

Kamaran popped out of the bushes to see the source of the
merriment. Even Crazy Hassan and Beauty looked our way with
interest.

Sarbast wiggled his head back and forth, still laughing. "Oh,
Joanna. That is funny. That is *really* funny."

I was shaking with anger, suddenly realizing that I had mis-
understood, that he had not been literal. The mule would not be
blindfolded. But it was no wonder I had suspicions. The entire trip

had been a mist of deceits. I was never given the full truth, but instead was fed the truth bit by bit.

Of course, Sarbast made merry over my confusion. Crazy Hassan thought it a good joke that I had even considered the possibility he would blindfold Beauty during a dangerous mountain climb. On the contrary, he said, "My mule is so intelligent, sometimes I let him select the best route."

Confirmation that our path might be selected by the mule failed to reassure me. Yet my concern at crossing the mountain on Beauty's back was suddenly less frightening. I had discovered that any situation could be even worse.

Our little caravan was soon on the move again. The sun had dipped below the earth's horizon, but a glow of pink light remained. My nervousness returned when Crazy Hassan walked ahead to coax Beauty to start the climb. My weight shifted as the mule's head, neck, shoulders, and barrel rose higher than his rump.

Crazy Hassan detected my gathering alarm and warned me, "Sit lightly. If a mule feels the weight is shifting incorrectly or if the load is too heavy, it will leap off the mountain."

I'm certain I looked a wild woman. "Sarbast! Overloaded mules will fling themselves off mountains! Here"—and I nudged one of the two bags with my knee—"Take this bag." I pleaded, "Kamaran, take the second bag."

I overheard my husband and his cousin chuckling. At that moment I wanted to slap both their faces.

It was then that I knew my fate depended on the good graces of Beauty. Flashes of regret haunted me. How I wished I had fed Beauty my fruit, petted his nose, and kissed him. I should have cupped water in my palms for him to drink. But I had missed my opportunity to bond with Beauty.

That was the beginning of a nightmarish night. As Beauty's hooves clattered on the granite, his neck and shoulders strained and his veins popped. Perspiration broke out all over his body. I trembled in fear when I heard pieces of rock break off under Beauty's hooves, gathering with small stones to crash down the mountain. For the first time I understood the true wisdom of the PUK choosing the Kandil Mountain range for their new rebel hideaway. No regular army could fight their way up to the top of such a mountain. The new radio station would certainly be safe.

Within an hour of starting the climb, ever-alert Hassan sensed we were being watched. He quickly guided us to a section of wide crevices between the rocks, an area offering protection, and gestured that we must hide. He returned with the news that there were enemy soldiers lingering at a new checkpoint almost directly below us and that they had a clear vision of our position. He had to find another route. He left to explore.

We waited for an interminable time. I was too edgy to rest, but Sarbast and Kamaran were true warriors, using the time to grab a few moments of sleep. My vision was not yet perfect, but it was improving, and was helped by a slight light from the moon.

My eyes were drawn to the outline of my husband. I speculated on the times Sarbast had probably spent in similar situations, fighting and hiding from his enemy. All the while I had been back in Baghdad, unaware of the reality of the Peshmerga life. I had always thought of the fighter's life as one of constant action and adventure, unaware that the truth was much less exciting. For every moment of action, there were many more moments of endless delays, trapped out in the open and tormented by hunger.

Determined not to be the weak link that I knew the men considered me to be, I vowed that I would be as strong and brave as the other Peshmerga women I had met, that I would not cause further problems for Sarbast.

Finally, Crazy Hassan returned, passionately gesturing for us to follow him.

Adrenaline was high as we inched to yet another mountain passage. After an hour of climbing, Crazy Hassan seemed satisfied that we had escaped the eyes of our enemy, eyes that were focused on the mountain face.

I believed us unlucky to be making our journey at the cusp of high tension between Baghdad and Kurdistan. But I was wrong. We were lucky to be among the first Kurds climbing Kandil. The *real* rush was yet to come. The situation would deteriorate until a huge crisis erupted, leading to a virtual Kurdish holocaust. Many Kurds would soon be forced from their homeland, fleeing Kurdistan on foot. Thousands of men, women, and children would ultimately perish on Kandil Mountain. But on our night of escape that part of our Kurdish future was as yet unknown.

The evening was a series of close calls. When we were not seeking shelter to hide from prying eyes, we were climbing on rock crags so narrow that I could not bring myself to look down. For some bizarre reason, Beauty was more comfortable walking on the very edge of the precipice. Even if there was ample space for him to hug the mountain wall, he seemed to take perverse pleasure in living life on the edge, literally.

Once or twice the mule really overstepped, teetering inches away from plunging over the cliff. Each time Crazy Hassan managed at the last minute to pull Beauty back.

The continuous plunging and straining while maneuvering narrow paths made me rigid, locked up my muscles, and caused my entire body to throb.

After four hours of complete terror, Crazy Hassan said we would stop for six hours. Beauty, he said, had reached his limit.

Sarbast lifted my trembling body off the mule, and I stood flexing my legs and arms, every muscle coiled with tension. I couldn't believe that I had survived.

My heart sank when Sarbast mentioned that we had not yet reached the most difficult part of the climb. I stared at my husband in disbelief, so mentally numb that I couldn't think of a retort.

We ate a snack while Crazy Hassan fed, watered, and wiped down the sweaty Beauty. After eating, we silently arranged our sleeping quarters.

It was cold on the mountain, but we spread all our clothes over us. I was lucky to have my pink bedding, as well. But I could not relax on that stony ground. And despite my exhaustion, I was unable to sleep. When I looked around, I saw that both Kamaran and Sarbast were draped easily on the hard rock surface. Even in the cold mountain air they were sleeping with complete abandon, as contented as lizards in the sun.

Crazy Hassan took the first watch, then Sarbast, then Kamaran. I had offered to take a turn as well, but Sarbast refused, saying that I was using all my energy just getting up the mountain and that was the most important thing of all.

Despite the dangers, it was beautiful at the high elevation. The dark of night was slightly lit by a crescent moon and twinkling with stars that appeared so close I felt I might pick one out of the sky.

Staring reflectively up at the heavens, I placed my hands on my belly, feeling confident that my child was finally anchored securely inside me and was resting safely. I enjoyed fully for the first time the idea that I might really be pregnant and that as soon as we were out of danger, I would tell Sarbast. I imagined the unrestrained joy he would feel and how he would twirl me round with happiness. Later, we would cuddle and plan our child's future together.

"Child of my heart," I whispered. I hoped our baby would look just like Sarbast, even if it was a girl.

Thinking about how I so desperately wanted my child, for the first time in my life I allowed myself to wonder how my mother could have ever considered harming me when I was in her womb. Although she had been a perfect mother to me, she had conscientiously attempted to abort me because she had no help, she already had four children, the youngest being twins, and her husband had lost everything during the 1958 revolution. Although her situation had been undeniably bleak, it was not as bleak as my own at that moment.

Never could I consider intentionally harming my baby, despite the fact I was basically homeless, on the run for my life, perhaps soon to be a refugee, and without a single dinar to call my own. I would have sacrificed my own life to protect my unborn child.

I fell asleep staring at the stars, sleeping splendidly, enjoying a full five hours of unbroken sleep.

When Sarbast woke me the following morning, the sky was pale with the fleeting dawn.

I was filled with anticipation to finish the dangerous climb. In only a few hours we would reach our destination of Dohlakoga, the site of the new radio station. We were all eager to get the final leg of the journey behind us.

Our day was filled with many challenges. I experienced moments of sheer terror combined with grim satisfaction. The path deteriorated, with the trail becoming so narrow that there was barely space for Beauty to walk. He appeared to be struggling, wincing with hooves tender from the sharp ridges rising from the mountain floor.

I was faring little better, and once when I accidentally glanced down I saw trees and bushes so far below that they appeared no larger than matchsticks. I swayed dangerously. It didn't help the situation when the morning sun became a torment, hammering against my head and face. The journey *must* end, I thought. Another hour will break me.

Enduring the glare of blazing rays, I stared upward to see that we could not climb much farther. The massive rock was running out. My excitement escalated. For the first time, victory over the mountain seemed possible. I then glanced to the distance below, the view compensating me. Our enemy was *down there*, owning only the ground where they stood. They would never conquer Kurdistan. Never! We Kurds were too focused on victory, willing to sacrifice everything for freedom.

We arrived at a wide plateau a short distance from the very top of the mountain. We were at Dohlakoga. We had not failed. With Beauty's last step I felt I had been presented with a priceless gift.

Sarbast lifted me from Beauty's back for one final time. I stroked Beauty's forehead, knowing that I owed the mule my life. When I leaped into the air for the first time on the trip, Beauty opened his lips, showed his teeth, and brayed, "Whinee . . . aw . . . ah . . . aw." I laughed with complete pleasure, petting Beauty a second time.

I looked around the plateau. We were not alone. Forty or fifty fighters were there to greet us, including two women, one of them Ashti from Bergalou. Mostly I was happy to see little Hema, with his little full cheeks and his cute budding mouth. Hema appeared to be thriving, despite the harsh environment. Thankfully, that precious baby had not suffered any long-term ill effects from the poison gases. Ashti's husband, Rebwar, was the radio station engineer, so he was most important for the success of the new radio station.

There were few buildings at Dohlakoga, and they were not built in any particular order. Most of the fighters were living in tents, although more permanent construction was ongoing. Simple dwellings were rising up, including a bomb shelter, simple one-room homes, and even a communal bath and toilet, which sounded good to me. I was in a desperate need of a bath but would have to wash from a basin for the time being.

Taking off my soiled clothes, I gratefully washed, my skin refreshed by the feel of the cool water. Just at the moment when I believed that our worst troubles were behind us, pain flared like a burning fire in my belly.

That's the moment I lost my already much-loved baby.

I cried bitterly.

23

Searching for Auntie Aisha

Saddam's army was on the move, bringing death from the south to the north, his soldiers firing bullets, his airmen dropping gas canisters. The only question remaining for most Kurds was: When will we be struck by our bullet or inhale our gas pellet? Certainly, I no longer expected to survive. How could I be hopeful of life when so many others were dead or dying? And just when we thought the situation was as bad as it could get, it grew worse.

Since we had fled Bergalou, all of Kurdistan had erupted in chaos as Saddam's troops swept in. The mountains and valleys were swarming with Kurds literally running for their lives. The threat had escalated when Ali al-Majid unleashed his chemical weapons not only against the Peshmergas, but also against all of Kurdistan, including the civilian population. Thousands of terrified Kurds perished during the gas onslaught. Mothers and fathers were driven to such panic that they lost babies and left toddlers behind to die alone on mountain passes.

We Kurds believed that once the rest of the world learned of the chemical gas attacks, civilized people would demand that the Baathists cease their barbaric actions. To our surprise, no one seemed to notice. The world's disinterest made the Baathists even bolder, so they began using chemical weapons in an even more brutal manner. And so the Kurdish genocide gained momentum.

Sarbast and I had not had a home since we had fled Bergalou. When we reached Dohlakoga, it became obvious that it would be impractical for us to spend the coming winter months there. The radio station was not yet operational, thus Sarbast's skills as a writer and radio broadcaster were not yet needed. Housing was scarce, consisting of nothing more than a cluster of small buildings. Even with winter approaching, many fighters were still living in tents. There were three Peshmerga wives in Dohlakoga, but no special exceptions would be made for women. Sarbast and I lived in a small shed used to store tools. But winter would bring heavy snows. Flimsy buildings would not offer protection from those high-elevation winter storms.

As we had witnessed firsthand, Dohlakoga was challenging to reach even when the weather was perfect. During the harshest winter months, travel would become impossible. Snowdrifts were often twenty or thirty feet deep, making delivery of supplies extremely difficult. The circumstances meant that the number of fighters must be trimmed to the minimum, at least during the winter months. All unnecessary fighters were asked to leave.

Our journey to Dohlakoga had been such a dangerous trek that we were keenly disappointed. But once our frustration ebbed, relief flickered. Dohlakoga was a harsh environment for someone with ailing health. My eyes, although much improved, remained troublesome. There were many days when my vision unexplainably blurred. Although the cuts and bruises I received during the Merge bombing had completely healed, I was experiencing various female problems from losing my unborn child. I needed medical attention.

Sarbast and I had to leave and travel on to Iran, at least temporarily. Kamaran was told to remain in Dohlakoga. The three of us had become a team, so the split was painful. But Sarbast and I stoically said our good-byes as we prepared for the difficult journey down the mountain. Crazy Hassan and Beauty had departed Dohlakoga shortly after we arrived, so we had to hire another mule for the trip. The trip down the mountain proved easier than the trip up. It helped that there were no enemy soldiers looking to shoot at us from the Iranian side of the mountain. Despite the more favorable conditions, however, I was within mere inches of literally falling from a cliff several times. Thankfully, we survived our downward trek.

Our destination, the Iranian border town of Al-Wattan, was only seven or eight hours' travel from Dohlakoga. There we hoped to find temporary housing until we received orders for Sarbast's next assignment. I was looking forward to the rest, but my heart skipped a few beats when Al-Wattan popped into view. "It's very remote," I said. "And it looks as primitive as Dohlakoga." I was speaking truthfully. Everywhere I looked I saw crude dwellings and poorly dressed residents. "It's cold here, too." I took a deep breath. "I hate the cold."

Sarbast grew impatient with my complaints. "Of course it is cold, Joanna. We are still very high up." He looked at me reproachfully. "Be thankful you won't be living in a tent."

He had a point. We were fortunate on that one issue. As Peshmergas, Sarbast and I would be allowed the privilege of settling in an ordinary Iranian village, unlike the Kurdish civilians fleeing the chemical attacks, who were kept confined in refugee camps. We had heard that the camps were bleak and that the refugees living in them were unbearably miserable.

With the proper documents, which Sarbast had obtained, we were free to come and go across the border as we pleased.

That was the theory. But when we arrived in Al-Wattan, I was struck by the number of Iraqi Kurdish Peshmergas already in the village. It was an ill omen. We soon learned that all rooms were taken. We were told, "The town is full of Iraqis."

After following rental leads for the remainder of the day, we still had nowhere to stay. I grew tense, knowing that even though it was still summer, the nights at high elevations were very cold. When the light began to fade, a desperate Sarbast began to approach strangers on the street. A tent was beginning to sound desirable.

Every villager turned us away. We had very little money, for Peshmergas were poorly paid. The only gold we owned were the wedding bands on our fingers. We were determined not to barter those.

Soon I began to feel weak. I became quite ill, limply hanging onto the mule.

Finally, an Iranian man took pity on me. He told Sarbast, "My rooms are all rented." But with a quick glance at me, he offered, "I do have a stable. You are welcome to sleep with my animals."

Sarbast shocked him by accepting. "Yes. That will do. Temporarily."

In fact, the man's words were like music to our ears. We were so exhausted that sleeping in his stable with the animals sounded like a grand idea. We meekly followed him home.

I was so hungry that I enjoyed visions of a hot meal. I was naive. Despite the fact that we were Peshmergas and had been fighting with the Iranians against Saddam, the eight-year war had festered in the hearts of the Iranians, for the war had proved a bloodbath for their men. The reception from that man's family was as frigid as the mountain snow.

Thankfully, I had thought to stuff a few pieces of bread and a chunk of cheese in the wide pockets of my Peshmerga trousers before leaving Dohlakoga. At least we had something to eat before sleeping.

The stable was a small room attached to the house. The moment we stepped into that makeshift barn, the door to the cozy house was firmly closed. Sarbast and I stared at each other and then at our sleeping quarters. We saw a very tight space located between the stable entrance and the house. The floor was dirt. Mercifully, there was a knee-high barrier erected to contain the farm animals in their designated area.

There were mules, cows, chickens, ducks, and rabbits. We were serenaded throughout the night with a chorus of animal noises. The sounds and odors of large animals passing urine were nauseating. The room was infested with fleas, and during the night I felt them scampering about in my hair. The misery of it all!

Sarbast and I cohabited with the farm animals for a week. Throughout it all, Sarbast was an angel, maintaining a positive attitude and constantly repeating that our situation could be worse. "Joanna, we could be in the refugee camps."

I grunted in reply, but did understand that our living conditions could indeed be even more ghastly. Other Peshmergas verified our earlier information: the refugee camps were horror camps.

I understood the Iranian government's position. It was still embroiled in a lengthy and bitter war with Iraq. It was understandably wary of the flood of Kurdish refugees from Iraq, suspicious that spies were mixed with the people seeking refuge. Iraqi Kurdish refugees had been rebellious in their own country. Once settled in

Iran, would they link up with Iran's own defiant Kurdish minority? Quite simply, the Iranian government did not know what to do with the Iraqi Kurds, so it shut them away in refugee camps, hoping for a military victory over Saddam so that they could be sent back to Iraq.

Our wishes were the same on that one point.

Yet I would never forget that although the refugee life was deplorable, at least the Iranians were not intent on eliminating the Iraqi Kurds. Truthfully, the Iranian government was more humane to Iraqi Kurds than was our own government in Baghdad.

Sarbast and I continued our search for a room. With the rising of the morning sun, we would hose off with cold water, trying to discourage the fleas, and then flee our dreadful quarters to walk about in the village, hooking up with various Peshmerga acquaintances. After seven days, we met a Peshmerga friend who invited us to move into a house he had rented for his wife and two small children.

I was in heaven, despite the fact that there was no electricity, no running water, and no toilets. Residents walked up the mountainside to use the springs as a toilet, which was inconvenient and unsanitary. Sarbast solved our personal situation when he and his Peshmerga friend bought water hoses and connected them to a nearby spring, rigging up a welcome water supply for the household.

Six months later, when Sarbast received orders from PUK officials to travel farther into the interior of Iran, to a larger village named Saqqez, we were delighted, wishing to avoid a second winter in Al-Wattan. The PUK had gained permission to erect a new radio station in Saqqez.

Upon arriving in Saqqez, however, our Al-Wattan difficulties were repeated, as we found it nearly impossible to locate suitable living quarters. Our luck changed when another Peshmerga alerted us to a vacancy in a home owned by an Iranian woman named Shamsa. She was reserved when agreeing to the deal, coldly examining the two of us with her wide-set brown eyes. Her attitude expressed distrust of Iraqis, even Kurdish Iraqis. But Sarbast and I were very grateful for our little room in a decent home, and we took every opportunity to show our appreciation and to be good tenants.

After a few weeks, Shamsa became less formal, appearing sincere when she advised me, "You should return home to your mother, child. You are too young and innocent to live the life of a Peshmerga."

My heart fluttered with a vague hope. Perhaps over time Shamsa and I could become friends, in spite of the suspiciousness that Iranians and Iraqis felt toward one another. But it seemed that my destiny was not to anchor in any one place. Sarbast received orders to leave Saqqez to travel to a mountainous area near Halabja, southeast of Bergalou and Sulaimaniya. Once more the Iranian government and the PUK Peshmergas had liberated the area from Saddam's army, and the PUK had plans to set up another radio station there.

"I am going with you," I promised, although Sarbast was fiercely opposed to my plan.

For our last three months in Al-Wattan, Sarbast had been forced to leave me behind while he traveled back and forth across the border to join raids attacking Saddam's forces. During his absences I was frantic with worry for his safety, certain that each farewell was our last, for Peshmergas were dying in large numbers. For me, the only advantage of the obligatory physical rest was the restoration of my health. Even my damaged eyes had finally healed.

For long months I had believed that my eyes were permanently injured, that perhaps I would even lose my vision altogether. To my relief, over time my eyes returned to normal. After learning that permanent blindness was one of the most common side effects of the poison gases, I felt incredibly lucky.

But before we left Iran to return to Iraq, we had an important task to accomplish. While we were in Al-Wattan I had managed to contact my family, telling them that we were alive in Iran. During that call I learned that Auntie Aisha was missing, that she had been out of touch since the March 16, 1988, chemical attack on Halabja. Her son, Sabah, and three daughters were alarmed, fearing that their mother had died during the attack. I convinced myself that she had taken refuge in Iran, in one of the many refugee camps. Sarbast and I decided to search for her before we left the area.

There was one particular refugee camp on the border area that seemed most likely because it specifically housed refugees from Halabja. I hoped that Auntie Aisha was one of those displaced. If so, we would take her back to Sulaimaniya to be with her children.

Soon we were on our way there. I could smell the refugee camp long before I could see it. I sniffed the air, led by the stench, looking until I saw a soft cloud of dust tinting the skyline. As we drew closer, a gigantic city of white tents slowly emerged on the horizon. Mesmerized by the repetitive tent tops, I paid little heed to where I placed my feet, stumbling over rocks hidden by tufts of grass. After stumbling two or three times, a concerned Sarbast asked, "Are your eyes bothering you?"

"No. No."

All I could think about was our mission to find Auntie Aisha. Sarbast gently held my elbow, guiding me through the field.

As we drew near, I spotted a meandering line of color in the midst of white, a bewildering sight until I identified the spiraling line as colorfully dressed Kurdish women. I assumed that the women were queuing for bread or water.

I shivered, even in the heat of a summer day, remembering what Halabja had once been. Now its citizens were living in tents.

Before the attack, Halabja had been a busy town of approximately fifty thousand Kurds located only a few miles from the Iranian border. The bustling town was a magnet for trade and the location of a shrine honoring Al-Shaikh Ali Ababaili, a revered Islamic cleric who was buried there.

That shrine was the reason Auntie Aisha had moved from Sulaimaniya to Halabja in the first place. Always a pious Muslim, after raising her children she drew even nearer to her faith, expressing a desire to live close to the shrine of Ali Ababaili. She bought a small house in Halabja and spent many pleasurable days during her aging years joyfully worshipping at the shrine.

The chemical strike on Halabja had become well known because the Iranian government had the foresight to transport photographers to the scene to authenticate the death and destruction. Foreign journalists and photographers documented the deaths of five thousand innocent men, women, and children. Numerous other victims died over the coming days.

I only hoped Auntie Aisha was not suffering from painful injuries. She was of an age that it would be more difficult to overcome poor health. A strong sense of resolve flashed through me: I *must* find her. She was nearly as dear to me as my own mother. She had never failed us when we were in need, whether it was at the unexpected death of my father or during one of our many financial crises.

I felt another very important reason to find her. I had never shared with anyone her mysterious spiritual appearance to me during the Bergalou poison gas attack, not even with Sarbast. I had been mere moments from death when her shadowy appearance inspired me to live. I had a strong desire to describe that puzzling scene to Auntie Aisha, to ask her if she had been at prayer during that time, or even if I had been on her mind. There had to be a rational explanation, for she had been physically real to me, although I had learned since then that she had been alive and well in Halabja during the time I believed her to be in Bergalou.

I briefly closed my eyes and muttered a prayer, asking that when I opened them Auntie Aisha would appear from inside that refugee camp to grasp me in a heartfelt hug. I opened my eyes expectantly. My prayer had not been answered.

"We will find her," I said to Sarbast with an emotional catch evident in my voice.

The camp confining the Halabja refugees was the most populous refugee camp on the border, since Halabja had been the largest of the Kurdish cities emptied by the gas attacks.

There was a reason the Iraqi government had specifically targeted Halabja. Before the chemical attacks, the PUK and Iranian forces had liberated Halabja from Saddam's forces. The liberation of Halabja had reportedly caused Saddam to fly into a rage. He ordered the Iraqi army to use all measures to retake the town, regardless of the loss of life.

When the Iraqi army attacked Halabja, the town's population of fifty thousand people had swelled to seventy thousand from the overflow of refugees from neighboring villages who were also under attack. Our enemies first pounded Halabja with mortars and rockets. Then on March 16 the intensity and severity of the attacks increased when Halabja was bombarded with a cocktail of mustard gas, sarin, and tabun. Many residents remained in their shelters, wrongly believing that they were in the safest place. Because toxic chemicals concentrate in the lowest levels, entire families were trapped to die in low-lying shelters. Those who caught a whiff of the chemicals and realized the horrifying truth of the weapons being used against them ran outside to escape. But without gas masks, there was no time for many to reach high ground before succumbing to the poison gas. Many of those exposed suffered a host of painful symptoms before dying on the streets. Witnesses reported seeing stricken victims dying of laughter or vomiting green bile until they died. During and after the gas attack, Halabja emptied.

Was the bustling city of Halabja I remembered from my youth now a ghost town? We would soon know because Sarbast and I had plans to travel to the area. A lump of dread gathered in my throat. What might we discover in Halabja?

But for that day, I put my mind on the problem at hand: finding Auntie Aisha.

After Sarbast presented our identity papers to an unsmiling Iranian revolutionary guard, we were allowed entry into the heavily guarded and fenced camp.

Silently, we walked side by side into the enormous refugee camp. I saw members of the Iranian Red Crescent in charge of distributing food rations.

The camp was dismal, with its flapping flimsy tents and garbage strewn everywhere. Displaced Kurds were standing or sitting all around us, staring at us with curiosity. After taking a few steps, we hesitated, pondering where we should begin our search. Forked pathways were packed with clusters of people. We had heard that during the past six months over one hundred thousand Kurds had sought refuge in Iran. From the looks of that crowded camp, I believed that most of the one hundred thousand were staring directly at me. How would we ever find Auntie Aisha in that mass of humanity?

"Which way?" I asked my husband, flinging both hands palms up at the enormity of it all.

Sarbast lifted his shoulders in a shrug. "What difference will it make which path we take?"

I sighed deeply. The large number of refugees was disorienting. "Maybe you will see someone you know and they will help us," I said hopefully. Other than the few years Sarbast had spent at the university in Baghdad, he had lived his entire life in Kurdistan. During his years of being a PUK Peshmerga, he had traveled the entire region, often staying over in Kurdish villages for a meal or for a night's rest. Perhaps he would recognize one of the refugees.

"I will search the faces on the left and you search the faces on the right," I finally proposed.

When Sarbast did not respond, I glanced at him. His face had grown pale. To hear descriptions of the refugee camps was depressing. To see the catastrophe with his own eyes was the most painful revelation possible.

I understood the damage to my husband's pride and honor. The tent city represented total failure regarding everything the Peshmergas and the PUK stood for. My husband had sacrificed his entire adult life for freedom for the Kurds, forgoing a career and postponing marriage and children. At age thirty, when most men have settled in a career, he was a poor man without a home and a job, with each meal possibly being his last.

Our despair deepened when we heard the saddest sound of all: the haunting cries of ill babies. Remembering my own recent loss, and convinced that the chemical attack and the bombing and the mountain climb to Kandil had cost me my precious child, my sorrow gathered. It was at that moment that I realized we Kurds had lost everything. All our hopes and dreams were finally smashed. Nothing would ever be the same.

A terrible new world had been born to replace our familiar world. Kurds accustomed to living in the scenic beauty of bountiful valleys and mountains, tilling their fields, tending their thriving livestock, and raising their sons to inherit the land had lost it all. Their dreams dissipated in the brown puffs of smoke unleashed by the poison gases. Kurds were now scattering all over the earth, forced to adjust to new lives inferior to what they had known before. It was the bitterest loss.

Sarbast and I walked on, cautiously, in silence. As we moved through the camp, the ring of my sorrow widened along with the refugees pressing in all around me. Each refugee was trapped in a crowd, yet seemed very much alone. The forlorn faces of the camp children drew me like a magnet, their sad eyes reminding me of flickering candles, half-burned out, their little shoulders hunched down into their chests.

One small boy of only four or five years of age wandered aimlessly past me, unaware of the world around him, his dreadfully blistered face tucked low. What horror had that child lived through? What tragedy had befallen his community, his family? I trembled for his lost life, imagining that one moment he had been a child at play and the next he was running behind his parents, screaming in agony at the invisible fire falling on his face. Where were his parents? Had he been left a lonely orphan?

My hands bunched into fists. I want answers, God! What will happen to the children?

Everywhere I looked I saw children of sorrow. I closed my eyes, wanting to escape those haunted stares, longing for the power to lift those children up and whisk them out of the camp. But I could do nothing. I didn't even have the money to buy them a piece of candy. I was completely broke.

My thoughts were interrupted by exclamations of "welcome" from a group of refugees sprawled around one of the many tents.

"Come, come!"

"Sit! Sit!"

Sarbast gave me a perceptive look. We must accept their hospitality.

We entered the refugee circle, sitting cross-legged on the ground to talk. A crowd began to form and raised voices were eager to know what we were doing there, impatient to learn the latest news of the outside. They wanted the violence to end so that they could go home.

Sarbast and I exchanged yet another meaningful look. I read my husband's mind. We could not tell those poor people the bitter truth: that their homes no longer existed. Sarbast and I had recently learned that as the Iraqi army emptied the towns and villages of Kurds, it had become common procedure for crews of army engineers to follow and blow up all buildings. Bulldozers followed to level the rubble. Flourishing communities of Kurdish homes, businesses, schools, and mosques had been turned into piles of rubble. Wells were poisoned. Livestock was exterminated. Wicked Saddam sowed that willful destruction with the intention that Kurds would have nothing to return to.

But the refugees did not know what had happened after they ran from their homeland. News of the outside world was kept from them. Perhaps there are times when ignorance can be for the best.

To put their minds on other matters, Sarbast and I both began asking about Auntie Aisha. "My auntie is Aisha Hassoon Aziz. She moved from Sulaimaniya a few years ago, to be close to the shrine.

Her granddaughter Rezan was living with her shortly before the attack. Rezan was away on the day chemicals were dropped. She was spared the assault."

I was not surprised to learn that Auntie Aisha was a popular and well-known Halabja resident. Nearly everyone claimed to have heard of her. She was quite famous, in fact, a virtuous Halabja resident, making such an exceptional impression that word had spread through the community of her goodness.

When Sarbast gravitated toward the men, I turned away from him to talk with the women, telling them about Auntie Aisha, hoping that there was some firm news on her whereabouts.

One woman named Jamila who was so elderly and so skinny that her face was virtually concave, said loudly, "Aisha Hassoon Aziz's reputation was as pure as the saints she revered. Her acts of goodness were numberless." Her brow wrinkled. "I believe that she was chosen to read the Koran at the gathering of the women during the Eid Al Mawlid Al Nabawi."

I nodded eagerly, familiar with the annual celebration of the Prophet's birth.

I even remembered a time when Auntie Aisha had led the females in our family during that particular ceremony. I was only a young girl, but I had been mesmerized by the magic of that evening. Auntie Aisha had sat with her back to the wall, chanting songs praising the Prophet. As she chanted, she lightly shook a leather tambourine, adding magic to the entire ceremony. Afterward, a feast was served, the dishes spread on a colorful carpet laid out on the floor. I distinctly recalled a whole lamb stuffed with rice, with lots of vegetables, delicious minced meats, and every kind of fruit.

Jamila continued, "She took care of the poor, your auntie." She glanced around, a glint of excitement in her dark expressive eyes. "You say that Aisha Hassoon Aziz is in this camp?"

"I hope so," I replied. "She did not go to Sulaimaniya, where we would have expected her to flee. Now her son and daughters cannot find her."

By this time more refugees had gathered around us, for news of PUK Peshmergas being in the camp had spread rapidly. The PUK was much admired in Halabja. The conversation rapidly swung from Auntie Aisha to the mass murder of Kurds, to the flight of the refugees, then back to Auntie Aisha, and again to the dark tragedy they were living.

"How can Saddam kill women and children?" one young woman muttered, who was cuddling a tiny baby. Someone whispered to me that the baby had been born early during the shock of the exodus, but without medical care, it was not expected to live.

The aged Jamila snorted, slapping her hands together. "When a cat wants to eat her kittens, she says they look like mice!"

Three or four cute teenage girls jostled each other, smiling at the old woman's witty remark.

My eyes could not avoid the suffering of the children. Almost every woman was holding a child. They all bore visible wounds.

A fussy toddler continually rubbed her eyes that were oozing thick mucus.

A waiflike little boy complained, "My feet, Mommy." His mother held them high so that I could see his wounds. The soles of his little feet bore inflamed cuts. She explained, "There was broken glass on the roads. There were so many little feet freely bleeding that when we got to the mountain snow, that snow turned pink."

Another small face was furrowed with infected blisters. The smallest of the children wheezed and struggled for breath. Her lungs had been affected by the poison gas.

A mother with thin black hair robotically reported, "My husband died last month during a raid. When the chemicals came, I had to leave three of my five children. I only had two arms. I could only carry one child in each arm. The other three could not keep up. I will never forget their screams, pleading with me not to leave them behind."

One particularly sad-faced woman said dreamily, "I left my baby on the mountain. He was dying from the gases. I had to save my other children. When I laid the baby on a flat stone, he opened his little eyes and stared at me as though he knew his fate." Her brown eyes dulled black and her long fingers fluttered around her head. When she began sobbing loudly, two of the teenage girls led her away.

Every refugee had a tragic story to tell. Faces and stories began to merge. I was robbed of all sense of a response. What could I say? There were no words. What could I do? I had no resources, no way of helping those helpless women. When I brushed away my tears, the old woman Jamila patted my stomach and announced, "Kurdish wombs will have to make up the loss."

I was jolted by her insight, her remark prompting memories of Auntie Aisha, who always knew what was in my mind and in my heart.

Sarbast, unaware of the solemn turn our women's conversation had taken, tapped me on my arm. "Joanna. You need to hear this. Come."

I nodded at the women and edged away to listen to a man with thick features and a mustache framing thin lips. He was describing a sight he had seen. "After the gases in Halabja cleared, and before the army bulldozers came, I slipped back to my neighborhood to find my wife and three daughters. I found them. They were all dead in the house. Praise Allah I had taken my two sons with me for the day, so they were spared. After burying my wife and daughters I took the time to check houses in our neighborhood. Aisha Hassoon Aziz lived nearby. I called out her name. Like this," and he cupped his hands around his mouth and opened his mouth so wide that he fully exposed his stained and broken teeth. 'Lady Aisha Hassoon Aziz!' I then called out her granddaughter's name. No one answered. The house was unlocked, so I walked through the rooms. When I stepped out the back door I saw her. Aisha had been praying in the back garden and she had collapsed on her prayer rug."

"No!" I cried out. "No!"

Startled by my outburst, the man looked at Sarbast for guidance on whether he should continue.

"Go ahead," Sarbast affirmed as he patted me on the back.

I hunched forward. "Tell me only this: *was she alive?*"

The man answered quickly and decisively. "No. She had been dead for a day or more by then."

I could not absorb the words I was hearing. Perhaps the man was mistaken. Why would she go in the garden to pray *during* a gas attack? But with a sudden and certain flash of insight, I knew that the man was describing Auntie Aisha's reaction to the chaos. She would have turned to prayer at the moment of greatest danger. While everyone else was rushing to survive, she instinctively turned to God.

Joanna's beloved Auntie Aisha, who was murdered in the chemical gas attacks.

Joanna and Sarbast in 1988 in the Iranian village of Al-Wattan after their harrowing escape from Iraqi Kurdistan.

A pregnant Joanna in 1988 with Sarbast in Iran after their escape.

A pregnant Joanna in 1989 with the kindly Shamsa (standing, far left), the
Iranian woman who became a second mother to Joanna.

The passport photo of Joanna, Sarbast, and their son Kosha, readying to flee the area to go to England.

A happy Joanna, safe and free in England, with her son Kosha.

I was struck with a sorrowful certainty that he was telling the truth, that the woman he was describing was indeed Auntie Aisha. I had a flash of joy that Rezan had not been at home. She was alive and well, thank God.

"I wanted to bury her but I was afraid to wait much longer. I covered her up with two or three prayer rugs I found inside her house. When I returned several days later, I saw that someone else had buried your aunt in her garden. At the time, there were groups going around the city, burying the dead before the enemy soldiers had a chance to desecrate the bodies." He repeated, "She was buried in her garden. I am certain of it. There was a new grave next to where I left her."

There was nothing else left for the man to say.

I sat. Numbness crept through my body. Auntie Aisha was dead.

And I knew who had murdered her. Ali al-Majid, fulfilling the wishes of his cousin Saddam Hussein, was the man responsible for the deaths of many thousands of innocent people, one of whom was my saintly Auntie Aisha.

Soon, Sarbast and I made our way from the camp back to Saqqez. I fretted endlessly as to how I would notify Auntie Aisha's four children of her demise. Making telephone calls was expensive and difficult. A letter was too cold and impersonal in matters of death. What about Mother? She would be stricken by the news. Finally, I got a call through to my brother Ra'ad. He was the one who shared the bitter news.

My only comfort was knowing that Auntie Aisha went to God doing what she loved best: praising and honoring Him. As far as her unexplainable appearance in Bergalou, it was a mystery that I would never solve.

The weeks following I could not get out of bed. At first my lethargic state was blamed on depression about Auntie Aisha, but I felt so ill that Sarbast and I finally concluded that I had food poisoning. Nothing I ate would stay down. Knowing that we were set to leave Saqqez soon and understanding that Sarbast was looking for any excuse to leave me behind, I struggled to find a doctor to request medicine to ease my violent nausea.

That's when I discovered the news that threw our life plans into a tangle: I was pregnant. The lady doctor said that there was no doubt. I was going to have a child. In less than eight months Sarbast and I would be parents.

Suddenly, I remembered the old woman in the camp, and her penetrating look into our futures, understanding that "Kurdish wombs will have to make up the loss."

I wept with complete joy.

24

Kosha, Child of My Heart

SAQQEZ, IRAN
May 8, 1989

I was sleeping soundly when I was stirred by abdominal pains so sharp that I found myself hunched over in the middle of our small bedroom, incapable of recalling how I got there. My breath was shallow and fitful as I waited to see what would happen next. To my misery, the pain soon struck a second time. I gasped loudly as I cupped my hands over my protruding belly.

I looked at Sarbast. He was snoring.

I had spent most of my pregnancy alone in Saqqez: Sarbast was off fighting our enemy in Kurdistan, but thankfully he had made arrangements to be with me as my pregnancy progressed. We were uncertain of my exact due date. I had seen a doctor only once, the lady doctor who had enlightened me of my pregnancy. Since that first visit, I had not undergone any additional examinations, so I had studied the calendar on my own, guessing when our child might be born. Pregnant Kurdish refugees, even pregnant Peshmerga refugees, were not provided with Iranian medical care. Without money to spend on medical services, I could only hope and pray that my child would be born without complications.

For the third time pain radiated from my back and lower abdomen throughout my body. Something was dreadfully wrong. I stumbled to Sarbast, pulling on his shoulder. "Sarbast, wake up."

Sarbast's warrior reflexes were sudden and sure. His eyes shot open as he automatically reached for his weapon on the floor, his full attention directed to the only entrance to the room. When he saw there were no intruders to battle, he looked at me. "What? What?"

"Sarbast, I am very sick. I am having terrible pains."

"It was the milk," Sarbast replied with quick certainty. "You didn't boil it long enough. You have milk poisoning again."

I considered what he was saying. Believing that my pregnancy required a lot of milk, I had been drinking large quantities of Iranian milk lately. It had to be boiled before drinking. On several occasions I had miscalculated the length of time necessary to make the milk safe, and I had become violently ill.

Actually, I had been sick for most of my pregnancy, unable to retain most foods or liquids. Even the smell of food made me gag. Often the smell of foods prepared on the hot plate in our one room would drive me outside. To help keep food down, I was forced to eat my meal on the outside stoop. I could eat only small amounts, and although I was nearly nine months pregnant, I was very skinny. A small pregnant bump was the only proof that our family was about to increase. Few people believed that I was nearly nine months into my pregnancy.

My landlady, the wonderful Shamsa, had become a friend by being a marvelous support. After discovering my pregnancy and remembering the serious consequences of the journey from Merge to Dohlakoga, I had agreed with Sarbast that it was too risky for me to accompany him on further Peshmerga incursions into Kurdistan. I had to keep our unborn child safe. Because Sarbast was away much of the time, Shamsa became my main support. In the beginning she was aloof, but ultimately she had grown to love me. During my difficult pregnancy, she had expressed her affection by preparing special soups and Iranian rice and vegetable dishes, encouraging me to eat. Although no one could ever replace my mother, Shamsa had become a wonderful substitute.

Sarbast was staring at me.

"Sarbast? I am having severe stomach pains. What should I do?"

"Come back to bed. It is only the milk. You will feel better in the morning."

I turned on the light and looked at my watch. It was four in the morning. Everyone would be asleep. He was right. I would be better in the morning. I dragged myself to the bed.

Sarbast pulled the cover up to my chin. "You will be okay, darling. Go back to sleep."

He turned away, his voice muffled. "Wake me again if you need me."

Sarbast, who, after ten years of the fighter's life was accustomed to sleeping on the hard ground, quickly fell into a deep sleep on our cotton mattress.

The pains failed to cease. In fact, they increased in intensity and frequency. I knew nothing of what to expect in a pregnancy, but something was starting to tell me that my pains had nothing to do with milk poisoning.

The pains increased in severity until I could no longer remain in bed. I got up to pace. Sarbast never heard me. Two hours later I became frightened and decided to go to Shamsa. She would know what to do.

There were two floors to Shamsa's small home. She rented out the downstairs and lived on the upper floor. Her husband had died years before, leaving her with five children. Two of her daughters were married and her two sons lived at home while attending university. Her youngest child, a daughter who was seventeen years old, was still in high school. Despite her responsibilities, Shamsa had found room in her heart for me.

I knocked on her door and stumbled into the room at her command.

Before I could speak, Shamsa gave me a single glance and declared, "You are having the baby."

"No. No. I have milk poisoning."

"No, my daughter, you are having the baby."

I stood frozen to the spot, suddenly terrified.

I knew nothing of babies. What had I done? I should have guarded more carefully against pregnancy, at least until I could be with my mother.

Shamsa was all business, giving instructions to her children before grasping my arm and leading me downstairs. "Where is Sarbast?"

"He is asleep."

"Wake him. Tell him that we need to go to the hospital. While I get ready, you take a quick bath."

I nodded numbly. I had never been more frightened in my life. I was ill prepared in every way. I had nothing ready for the baby. Although Shamsa and I had been knitting some tiny clothes, nothing was finished. It had all seemed a game, a preparation for a doll, but suddenly the truth blared: soon, a helpless baby would be living with us! I rushed about, confusion mounting. I called out, "Sarbast! Get up! Get up! I'm having the baby."

The cover was over his head. A muffled voice came from underneath. "It's the milk."

"No. No, Sarbast! Shamsa says the baby is coming!"

Sarbast sprang to his feet. He scrambled to find a clean shirt and trousers while I took a cold bath. There was no hot water in Shamsa's home.

In fact, few Iranians took baths at home. Their homes were not equipped for bathing, but there was a huge marble Turkish bath in the city center of Saqqez. There were rooms for families, women, and men. Sarbast and I had often utilized the family bath, enjoying the luxury of the plentiful hot water and the luxurious accommodations. The one thing I had enjoyed about living in Iran was that Turkish bathhouse.

But there was no time for a hot-water bath that morning.

We left in a rush, taking nothing with us. The hospital was an agonizing thirty-minute walk from Shamsa's home, and despite being in the middle of labor I was going to have to walk every step. The unrelenting birth pains were so agonizing that I felt a primitive urge to lie down on the sidewalk and let nature have its way with me. But I knew I could not. I must get to the hospital to make certain my baby was safely delivered.

And so, once again in my life, I found that there was nothing to do but to soldier on. But I knew nothing of the torment awaiting me.

The pains were so intense that I had to stop walking during every contraction. I stopped, held my breath, and braced myself against the buildings on the street. Trying to stifle full-fledged screams that might bring the police, I groaned instead. Sarbast and Shamsa were helpless bystanders. Our odd trio received many peculiar stares.

We finally arrived at the local hospital. It was no surprise to discover that I was not welcome there. Although Shamsa told the admitting clerk, "My daughter is having a baby," they soon discovered that I was a refugee, and by that time the Iranians had wearied of Iraqi refugees. We refugees were enemies in their minds, people who were using up medical services needed for their own people.

A nurse was called to guide us to the delivery wards. I received a shock when she told Sarbast that he could not accompany me. "No," she said, "men are not allowed in the maternity ward."

I looked anxiously at Sarbast. It was the most pivotal event of our lives and I wanted us to share it. Besides, I was frightened. I did not want to be alone.

When Sarbast saw my look of despair, he became forceful. "I must be with her. This is our first child. My wife needs me."

That nurse's face became a mask of fury. She had a thick neck and a powerful frame. She was a frightening opponent, ready to battle any Iraqi Peshmerga. She glared at me and then at Sarbast. "No! It is the rules. You go and stand behind that mesh." She gestured in a direction straight behind us.

Sarbast and I both turned to look. Heavy wire mesh from ceiling to floor divided a large room behind us into a waiting area. Were husbands in waiting considered wild animals in that hospital?

I told Sarbast, "Wait there, it's all right. Shamsa will be with me."

The nurse then turned to Shamsa, gruffly demanding, "Where are her things?"

"I have nothing," I stammered.

The nurse ordered Shamsa, "Go and get her a gown and clothing for the baby. We do not supply those items."

With tears in my eyes, I watched as Sarbast dutifully went away to stand behind the mesh. Shamsa followed him.

Terrified, I trailed behind that inhospitable nurse, making the loneliest walk of my life. It's doubtful I could have been more miserable if I had been told I was being led to my grave.

I was admitted to a ward where other women were waiting to

have their babies. I was informed that there was no physician available to deliver my baby, but that I would be provided with a midwife or a nurse, according to the difficulty of the labor. Without a comforting word, I was put to bed and told that I would be taken into the delivery room when the time came.

Everything was wrong. Never had I felt so vulnerable. The unrelenting pain was destroying my body. I was frightened. I was the youngest child in our family and had foolishly paid no attention to the business of childbirth. I was the most uninformed woman in the world about what was coming. My ignorance created enormous fear.

I was on my own at a time when I needed my mother or my sisters. Tears of fear and loneliness rolled down my face. I wanted my mother!

I turned my head and faced the wall, sobbing, "Mother."

A nearby voice responded, "Child. What are you doing here alone?"

I opened my eyes to see a friendly face, an Iranian Kurdish woman of middle age. "You are such a sad little thing! This is a happy occasion." She glanced around the room. "Where are your sisters? Where is your mother?"

I felt the greatest misery for my circumstances. "I am a refugee," I confessed tearfully. "I am alone."

That kindly woman was overweight in a cuddly sort of way. I smiled through my tears as she leaned to me. "Hug me, child. Pretend I am your mother."

And I did.

That lovely lady spent the next few hours darting between my bed and her daughter's.

Around 10:00 in the morning, a grim-faced midwife came to take me away, saying, "It is time."

Along with my fear of what was about to happen, I felt a rush of doubt. How could she know it was time? No one had come to examine me.

My sweet companion hugged me good-bye, whispering, "It will be over soon. And when they place your little son or daughter in your arms, that baby will become your whole heart."

The next stop was a chamber of horrors.

I was told to climb onto a wooden birthing table. It was so

narrow that I was in danger of falling off onto the hard concrete floor. I could not lose myself in contractions for fear I would lose my balance.

Every moment of that birth was a nightmare. I was in a delirium of pain, but I was given nothing to relieve that pain. There was no attempt to calm me. There was no sympathy, no care. With brusque incompetence, someone roughly pulled my baby from my body before he was ready to appear. I was screaming and so was my child.

I heard my child!

Just when I was sinking to a murky place I feared I might never leave, I heard the sound of Shamsa's voice. Oh, the joy! She had been allowed into the delivery room. She clasped my hands and spoke soothingly, "It is over. You have a son, Joanna. You have a son."

I was too exhausted to understand the significance of what had just happened.

While a nurse cleaned my son and wrapped him in a blanket, the midwife stitched my torn body. Claiming, "There is no topical anesthesia available for Iraqis," she stitched mercilessly, with a sort of angry joy as she inflicted stabbing sutures.

When I cried out, she jabbed harder. I whimpered, pleading for her to be gentle. She ignored my pleas. That torture seemed endless, but finally it was over.

And then I saw my son.

He was so beautiful. I could not stop staring at his tiny oval face. His adorable eyes were large and dark. His slender nose and full lips reminded me of Sarbast. His dark hair lay smooth as if it had been combed.

Shamsa held him close to my face and I breathed in his baby scent. My eyes clouded. I looked at Shamsa and said with delight, "I am a mother."

Several hours later I insisted on showing Sarbast our son. I could not wait until the following day for my husband to see the little miracle that had come into our lives.

Gloomy Sarbast was still behind the wire mesh, Shamsa told me with a little chuckle.

There were no wheelchairs for Iraqi refugees, so I limped stiffly down the long corridor. Shamsa had my son cradled in her capable arms.

Sarbast slowly came into view, his fingers clutching through the wire. His eyes were on me.

I stepped as close as the wire would allow. My voice was breathless, "Look, Sarbast. Look at your son."

Sarbast's glittering eyes fixed on his son.

His face broke into a smile. "Kosha," he said.

Over the past few months, Sarbast and I searched for the perfect name. We had decided that if our child was a son, we would name him Kosha, which means "struggler" in our Kurdish language.

"Kosha," Sarbast repeated.

I stared at our little struggler, our little Kosha, who already had my whole heart.

But Kosha seemed to resent our absolute adoration. He opened his mouth and produced a cry of protest.

We laughed with complete happiness. Our son was perfect.

Sarbast turned back to me, smiling with pride and joy. "You've done it. You've done it, Joanna."

"Yes," I replied. "We have done it in the end. We triumphed."

And we had. We had been hunted like animals, but we had fought to survive. Although Kurdistan was in disarray, and Kurds by the thousands had died while we lived, we would regroup, and we would return. The Kurdish dream would live on.

Kurdish wombs had already started making up the loss of life.

Epilogue: Freedom!

LONDON, ENGLAND
July 20, 1989

At Immigration Control at Heathrow Airport, Sarbast turned to face me, a small smile of triumph on his face. His eyes met mine as he gave a quick nod. Without saying anything, he began to gather our few belongings.

My knees were as weak as my nerves. I felt my legs trembling beneath the folds of my skirt. I could barely stand.

Sarbast was the most persuasive man in the world. To my amazement, his words prevailed with the somber-faced immigration officer. We would not be turned away and placed on the next flight returning to Damascus, where we had arrived from. We would not be arrested and put in prison. We were accepted as refugees seeking asylum in the United Kingdom. Sarbast and I, with our baby son, Kosha, could enter England freely and would be given help and support while we applied for legal residency.

We really were safe, removed forever from the chemical weapons of Saddam Hussein, free from the gloomy refugee life in Iran, and far away from bullying Syrian officials. We were in England. In England we could create a new beginning. In England we could live safely. In England we could raise Kosha, our precious son.

I looked into Kosha's little face and tightened my hold. The enormity of the moment caused me to weep, sobbing in happiness.

We were the lucky ones.

My darling Sarbast looked so worn and weary. During nearly three years of married life, we had lived through more troubles than most couples married for fifty or sixty years. Yet those trials and tribulations had made us so close that I knew even if I lived for another hundred years, Sarbast was the only person in the world who would perfectly understand my every thought and emotion. My husband had shared my every grief, and even at that moment I knew that he was missing the same people I missed, and, like me, was still dreaming of our beautiful Kurdistan.

I was amazed by the kindness shown by the immigration officials at Heathrow. They rallied round, arranging accommodation and food, providing us with money and even offering assistance to help us attain legal status. After years of dealing with Iraqi government officials who routinely harassed us, I simply couldn't believe the compassion of strangers.

My thoughts drifted back to one of the happiest days of my life, the day when I had traveled from Qalat Diza to Merge to greet my new husband. How could I have known then the tears in the making inside me, the countless tears that were still to be wept. I was so young and in love that I had truly believed that dreams do come true, that our battles would be won, that our sacrifices would produce the greatest victory: freedom for Kurds.

But Kurdistan was not free, and so many who had loved Kurdistan's mountain ranges were now dead or were living as unwelcome refugees.

I had finally come to realize that even if Saddam succeeded in massacring every living Kurd, the world was never going to take notice. Saddam was the darling of the Reagan administration, and his genocide of nearly one hundred thousand Kurds had been virtually ignored.

Like Sarbast, I could have endured the refugee life forever, but motherhood changes everything for a woman. After bringing Kosha into our world, my husband and I finally agreed that we should leave the area, that we must seek a new life in a different country where we could raise our children safely.

My brother Ra'ad was there for us. He sent money for us to pay for our passports and to bribe officials in Iran and later in Syria. Without my brother, Sarbast, Kosha, and I would have ended up refugees in a tent city, like those we had visited in the camp for Halabja survivors, for with the nearly total defeat of the PUK, there was nowhere in the area left to run. After the war between Iran and Iraq ended, Iraqi Kurdish refugees became a festering sore for Iran, and we were no longer welcome there. Nor was it possible to return to Iraq to live: most likely Sarbast would have been executed and I would have been imprisoned. Our newborn son would not have survived.

In a world so corrupt, money can solve most official problems. With Ra'ad's generous help, Sarbast had managed to arrange some papers, and we left Saqqez and traveled to Tehran, taking the first flight we could get out of Iran. From there, the plan was to work our way to a country, any country, that was accepting Kurdish refugees. I had to fight hysteria when I discovered that we were heading for Syria, yet another Baathist country. Although Sarbast stoically assured me that we could handle the situation, I could think of nothing but the dour Baathist faces I knew we would face upon arrival.

To my despair, I was right to worry. The Syrian officials who met us at the airport were furious to see Iraqi Kurds had flown into their country. Suspicious eyes lingered over our documents and passports, and we were abruptly pulled from the immigration line and refused entry into Syria. We were put into isolation in a primitive shelter located under the airport terminal. If we didn't like it, we could go to jail. There were other Kurdish travelers locked away with us, but I was in such a fog of worry that to this day every traveler's face sharing our bleak plight remains blank, every conversation heard forgotten.

I was worried also over the lack of water and food. Our bags were confiscated, and I had only two spare diapers for my son. Too soon those diapers were dirty. I was unable to nurse, and my two-bottle supply of milk for Kosha was soon gone, too. He screamed with hunger. After twenty-four hours we were taken away in a police car, to a police station in Damascus. There we were to be interrogated. There was an underlying threat that we would be turned over to the Iraqi government, back to a certain death.

When I requested milk for my hungry son and was given water instead, it seemed so callous that it triggered a wild rage that burst from me in a mighty roar. Everyone around was startled by my outburst, with Sarbast urging me to get control, but I could not, feeling wild and strong and capable of slaying them all. Screaming insults, I suddenly realized that my outrage had changed the officials' attitude. Suddenly we were welcome guests, taken from the police station to an apartment in Damascus and given assistance.

I refused to leave that apartment for two weeks. I saw nothing of the ancient city of Damascus, wanting only to flee from a world where Baathists ruled. While I guarded my son, Sarbast set about obtaining forged papers and tickets and arranged a direct flight to England. My new passport claimed that I was a citizen of the United Arab Emirates. Unable to organize British visas, we decided to leave Syria anyhow and throw ourselves on the mercy of the British immigration.

Feeling like criminals, we were so nervous boarding the flight from Damascus to London that we could barely speak. I was certain that at any moment we would be pulled from the plane and forced onto the next flight to Baghdad.

When the airplane made an unscheduled stop in Cyprus, I was so paranoid that I convinced myself that our illegal status was the cause. After disembarking, all passengers were told that we would be there for ten hours, so we were encouraged to leave the airport, to go out and visit the pretty little island. But I refused to budge from the terminal. I would do nothing that required exit and entry through yet another immigration office.

Once again, my worry was unjustified. We boarded without mishap, and the plane took off. When we finally entered the customs area at Heathrow Airport, my heart was in my throat. I watched Sarbast step forward to the desk. He explained our predicament, confessed that we had fake documents, and asked for political asylum on the grounds that we would certainly be murdered if we were forced return to face Saddam and his Baathists in Iraq.

I remember little of that first night in England, for Sarbast and I were both so exhausted from our long journey to freedom that we barely spoke. Our only concern was for the comfort of Kosha, who was understandably crying and fussy.

The following morning I woke early. I stared up at the dingy ceiling of the hotel room, a room that had been generously provided by the immigration officials until we could find an apartment. I was looking forward to having a place of my own, something better than a single room without a ceiling stained brown by years of drifting smoke and grime. The ceiling was symbolic of my own life, I decided. I, too, was once young, fresh, and beautiful, but the past few years had aged me, toughened me.

But we were reprieved! We found ourselves suddenly free, living in a hotel room in a country where we weren't in danger of being taken away to be shot for the crime of being born Kurd.

I quietly turned my head and stared at the face of the man I loved more than my own life. My heart tightened with sadness. Sarbast's face was so weary looking, even in the midst of a deep slumber, but at least he seemed not to be enduring nightmares, the first time since we started our journey. I hoped that there would be many restful nights to come. A warrior since he was a young man, perhaps Sarbast could finally heal in England.

Through the thin door I heard the muted sounds of laughing children running through the hotel corridor, fortunate children who had never known the fright produced by crashing bombs or booming artillery or the horror of having to run away from one's home in the dark of night.

I turned to stare at the crib beside our bed, to watch the sweet face of little Kosha, out of physical danger for the first time in his young life.

I quietly eased from the bed, lightly touching Sarbast's cheek, walking over to kiss then cover little Kosha's tiny pink feet, before slipping behind the heavy-weighted curtain to stand and peer out the window. I took a few quiet moments to gaze into the distance, seeing the diminutive backyard gardens of several English homes.

Would Sarbast and I one day grow such a garden? How difficult would it be to leave behind the chaos of our life as freedom fighters, to live a normal settled life? For years we had lived as beautiful winged butterflies, our wings pulsing with Kurdish passion. Could we really become a settled, refined English couple?

After breathing a heartfelt sigh, I walked to the small desk wedged against the wall and settled into the wooden chair. I took a cheap piece of hotel stationery, staring at the blank page for many long moments.

Then I wrote down words that were really too good to be true: Sarbast and Joanna and Kosha Hussain are free!

We are free!

Where Are They Now?

World-altering events have occurred since Joanna fled her beloved Kurdistan, greatly affecting the lives of her family and friends, who are now spread around the globe.

Joanna is still living in England, the country that offered her freedom. She and Sarbast are the proud parents of two sons. Kosha, who inherited his father's artistic talents, will be eighteen years old in 2007. Younger son Dylan is a lively six-year-old. Joanna has an enjoyable career with British Airways, which allows her extensive travel.

Sarbast divides his time between Northern Iraq, still called Kurdistan by devoted Kurds, and England. He is currently working on projects to help rebuild Kurdistan.

Joanna's aging mother, Kafia, is still quite the lively personality, living now in England, where she enjoys the company of some of her children and grandchildren. Older sister Alia and her husband, Hady, along with three of their four sons, live in England as well and see Joanna and her family frequently. A fourth son lives in Dubai with his wife. Oldest brother Ra'ad, along with his wife, Christina, and teenage son, Omar, divide their time between

Switzerland and Dubai. Brother Sa'ad and his family still live in Iraq and are facing many hardships due to the precarious situation there. Recently Sa'ad and his family were forced to flee Baghdad in the middle of the night to seek safety in Kurdistan.

The moment it was safe for them to do so, Auntie Aisha's children returned to Halabja and exhumed their mother's body to bury her in beautiful Sulaimaniya, the Kurdish city where she knew much happiness. Sadly, Uncle Aziz passed away after Joanna fled Iraq.

To Joanna's best knowledge, Ashti, her husband, Rebwar, and their children live in Australia. Sarbast's amiable cousin, Kamaran, is now married and living in Austria with his wife and young daughter. Many other Peshmerga fighter friends are scattered throughout Europe, while others have returned to Kurdistan, now free for the first time in modern history.

Tragically, Crazy Hassan is dead. The events surrounding his untimely death are not known by Joanna. The whereabouts of Beauty, the intelligent mule so loved by Crazy Hassan and who saved Joanna by taking her over Kandil Mountain, are unknown.

Iraqi Kurds and Iraqi Shiite are finally receiving some small measure of justice as they follow the war crimes trials of former president Saddam Hussein. Found guilty in his first trial for crimes against the Shiites, he was sentenced to die on the gallows and was executed on December 30, 2006. Joanna, along with many other Kurds who suffered under Saddam's regime, felt his execution was just, although she was keenly disappointed that the former dictator was executed before the conclusion of the ongoing Kurdish al-Anfal trial, when it is estimated that two hundred thousand Kurdish men, women, and children were murdered.

Hussein's removal has placed Kurdish heroes at the forefront of Iraqi leadership. KDP hero Massoud Barzani, son of the father of Kurdish nationalism Mullah Mustafa Barzani, was elected president of Iraqi Kurdistan. PUK leader and politician Jalal Talabani was elected the first Kurdish president of Iraq, an event few Kurds could have imagined during the dark years when Kurds were hunted to be tortured and massacred.

With Saddam gone, Joanna, along with other Kurds, hope that the door finally closes on an era of oppression and genocide, opening on democracy and personal freedoms.

Hope is alive in Kurdish hearts!

CHRONOLOGY
of Key Events Affecting
Modern–Day Iraqi Kurds

1918 The Ottoman Empire is defeated. British forces occupy Iraq, bringing Kurdish-populated areas under British control.

1918 Winston Churchill orders the Royal Air Force to drop chemicals on the rebellious Kurds.

1919 Kurdish areas are added to the new Iraqi state, which comes under a British mandate.

1920 The Treaty of Sevres provides for a Kurdish state, subject to the agreement of the League of Nations.

1921 Faisal I is crowned king of Iraq, including Kurdish areas.

1923 Sheik Mahmud Barzinji rebels against the new Iraqi government. Sheik Mahmud declares a Kurdish Kingdom.

1923 The Treaty of Sevres fails to be ratified by the Turkish Parliament.

1924 In a rebellion against the new British-backed Iraqi government, Sulaimaniya falls.

1932 Barzani leads a rebellion, demanding autonomy for the Kurds. Autonomy is refused.

1943 Barzani rebels yet again but is more successful, with his Kurdish fighters gaining large areas of territory.

1946 The Kurdistan Democratic Party (KDP) is formed by Massoud Barzani. It is a tribally based Kurdish political party.

1946 The British Royal Air Force bombs Kurdish forces. Kurdish fighters flee into Iran seeking exile.

1946   Barzani has to flee Iran over a dispute with Iranian forces. He seeks exile in the Soviet Union.

1951   Barzani is elected president of the KDP even though he is still in exile in the Soviet Union.

1958   Barzani returns from exile after the Iraqi monarchy is overthrown. The new Iraqi government recognizes Kurdish national rights.

1959   The first Baathist coup fails. Saddam Hussein flees to Egypt.

1961   The Iraqi government dissolves the KDP after another Kurdish rebellion.

1963   The Baathist coup succeeds. Nine months later, a countercoup overthrows the Baath government.

1968   Baathists return to power. Saddam Hussein is second in command.

1970   The Iraqi government and the Kurdish political parties agree to a peace accord that grants the Kurds autonomy.

1971   Peace between the Iraqi government and the KDP is strained.

1974   Barzani calls for a new rebellion after rejecting the autonomy agreement.

1975   The Algiers Accord between Iran and Iraq ends Iranian support for the Iraqi Kurds.

1975   Jalal Talabani, a former member of the KDP, organizes a new Kurdish political party, the Patriotic Union of Kurdistan (PUK).

1978   Talabani's PUK and Barzani's KDP clash, leaving many Kurdish fighters dead.

1979   Saddam Hussein replaces Ahmed Hassan al-Bakri as president of Iraq. Barzani, the head of the KDP, dies. His son, Massod Barzani, assumes leadership.

1980   Iraq attacks Iran, and war breaks out.

1983   The PUK agrees to a cease-fire with the Iraqi government. Talks on Kurdish autonomy begin.

1985   The Iraqi government becomes increasingly repressive to Kurds. Talks break down. Iraqi government militia murder the brother and two nieces of Jalal Talabani.

1986   Kurdish fighters from the KDP and the PUK join forces with the Iranian government against the Iraqi government.

1987   The Iraqi military uses chemical weapons against Kurdish fighters.

1988   The Iraqi military launches the Anfal Campaign against the Kurds. Tens of thousands of Kurdish civilians and fighters are killed, and hundreds of thousands are forced into exile in Iran, Turkey, and Syria. The town of Halabja becomes the most recognized symbol for the heinous chemical attacks.

1991   After Iraq is expelled from Kuwait, there is a Kurdish uprising. The Iraqi military wages war against the Kurds. Many thousands are killed and over a million are forced into exile. Many are forced to seek refuge in the mountains.

1991   A no-fly zone is established in northern Iraq to protect the Kurds from Saddam Hussein.

1994   Clashes between the PUK and the KDP turn into civil war.

1996   The KDP leader Barzani appeals to Saddam Hussein for help in defeating the PUK.

1996   PUK forces retake Sulaimaniya.

1998   A peace agreement is reached between the PUK and the KDP.

2003   Saddam Hussein's government is overthrown by Coalition forces. Kurdish people are safe for the first time since Iraq was first formed after World War I.

2005   Iraqi and Kurdish history is made with the appointment of the first Kurdish president, Jalal Talabani, on April 6, 2005. Talabani was the original founder of the PUK.

GLOSSARY

Abu Ghraib Prison   Notorious prison complex in Iraq that was built by the British in the early 1960s and became known as the place where Saddam Hussein's government tortured and executed dissidents. Joanna's brother was imprisoned there. The prison gained worldwide notoriety when it became the site known to be used by U.S. forces to torture Iraqis.

Ahwaz   Iranian city located on the banks of the Karun River. It was a place of some of the most vicious battles during the Iran-Iraq War. Joanna's brother Sa'ad fought in the Iraqi trenches outside of Ahwaz for many months and was nearly killed there.

Al-Dawa Party   Formed in Iraq in the late 1950s by a group of Shiite leaders to combat Baathist socialism, secularism, and communism. It became more prominent in the 1970s and waged armed combat against the Baath government.

Al-Askari, Jafar Pasha (1895–1936)   Paternal great-uncle of Joanna al-Askari. Jafar al-Askari was from a prominent Baghdad family. During World War I, he served with Prince Faisal and Lawrence of Arabia in command of the Hijaz regular troops. After World War I ended, he served King Faisal I and King Ghazi I, both of Iraq, in many government posts, including minister to Great Britain, minister of defense, and prime minister of Iraq. Jafar was the uncle who arranged for Joanna's father to be educated in France. Jafar was assassinated in 1936.

Al-Majid, Ali Hassan   (1941–)   Iraqi Arab, a first cousin of former Iraqi president Saddam Hussein. He led the violent repression to quash the Shiite and Kurdish rebellions against Saddam Hussein's Baath government. He was given the name Chemical Ali for his role in the Anfal Campaign against Iraqi Kurds, including Joanna. At the time this book was written, he was being tried for that war crime and for others he is accused of committing.

Arab Linguistic group of approximately 270 million people that originated in Saudi Arabia.

Arabic language A written language since the early fourth century, Arabic belongs to the Semitic language family with its sisters Hebrew and Aramaic. Arabic is written from right to left.

Ayatollah Ruhollah Khomeini (1900–1989) Religious leader of the Shiite Muslim sect who was instrumental in overthrowing the shah of Iran in 1979. He led Iran during the eight-year Iran-Iraq War.

Baath The Arab Baath Socialist Resurrection Party was formed on April 7, 1947, by Michel Aflaq and Salah ad-Din al-Bitar, two Syrian university students. The tenets of the Baath Party include adherence to socialism, political freedom, and pan-Arab unity. The Baath Party still rules in Syria. The Baath Party in Iraq was toppled in 2003 when Coalition forces overthrew Saddam Hussein's government.

Baath Socialist Party, Iraq Formed secretly in 1950. The party increased in size and overthrew the Iraqi government in 1963. Out of power only nine months later, the Baathists came back in 1968 and remained in power until 2003.

Baghdad Capital city of Iraq, with a population of approximately 5.8 million. The city is situated by the Tigris River. Baghdad was once considered the heart of the Arab empire and was second only to Constantinople in terms of size and splendor during the city's golden age from 638 to 1100, when Baghdad flourished as a center of learning, philosophy, and commerce.

Bakir, Hassan (1914–1982) Baathist president of Iraq from 1968 to 1979 and a cousin to his second-in-command, Saddam Hussein, who succeeded him in 1979.

Barzani, Mullah Mustafa (1903–1979) Kurdish nationalist leader and president of the Kurdistan Democratic Party. He was a legendary ruler and was committed to the struggle for Kurdish causes. He was a hero in the minds of Joanna and her brother Ra'ad.

Barzinji, Sheik Mahmud (?–1956) Revered Kurdish leader who opposed the British by declaring himself king of Kurdistan and taking over Sulaimaniya and the surrounding area.

Halabja A Kurdish town in the northern province of Sulaimaniya located approximately 260 kilometers northeast of Baghdad and approximately 11 kilometers from the Iranian border. Halabja became famous after the March 16, 1988, chemical attack, the largest-scale chemical weapons attack against a civilian population in modern times, that left five thousand men, women, and children dead of poison gas. The town was later destroyed by Saddam's forces but has since been rebuilt.

Hussein, Saddam (1937–2006) The son of a landless peasant who died before his birth, Saddam was raised by his uncle, rose to power through the Baath Party, and became the president of Iraq in 1979. Saddam led a reign of terror over all Iraqis and attacked his neighbors Iran and Kuwait, creating war in the region. During the Iran-Iraq War (1980–1988), Saddam waged extensive military campaigns against the Kurds in northern Iraq, ordering the use of chemical weapons in 1987 and 1988, which forced Joanna to flee her country. At the time this book was written, Saddam was on trial in Baghdad for atrocities committed in Iraq, including the Kurdish massacres of 1987 and 1988. During the Kurdish trial proceedings, an Iraqi special tribunal convicted Saddam of crimes against humanity for the execution of 148 men and boys from the Shiite town of Dujail, 35 miles north of Baghdad. Saddam was put to death by hanging in December 2006.

Iran Islamic Republic of Iran, also known as Persia. Iran is located in southwest Asia and has always been an enemy of Iraq.

Iraq, Republic of Middle Eastern country encompassing most of Mesopotamia, the northwestern end of the Zagros mountain range, and the eastern part of the Syrian desert. The country was made up by combining the Ottoman provinces of Baghdad, Basra, and Mosul. Iraq shares borders with Iran to the east, Turkey to the north, Syria to the northwest, Jordan to the west, and Kuwait and Saudi Arabia to the south. Modern-day Iraq was created in 1923 at a European convention led by the British and French governments.

Islam Religion founded by the prophet Muhammad. The emphasis in Islam is on submission to the will of a single god.

Jafati Valley Mountainous region in northeast Iraq where the Patriotic Union of Kurdistan (PUK) located its command center. It was one of the first places where Saddam Hussein's army unleashed chemical gases. The Jafati Valley was the location of Bergalou, the place where the PUK radio station was located and the little village Joanna called home.

Jahsh   Kurdish informers who worked for the Iraqi government to spy on their Kurdish neighbors.

Kandil Mountain   Highest mountain in Iraq.

King Faisal I (1885–1933)   The third son of the first king of Hijaz (modern-day Saudi Arabia), King Hussein bin Ali. Faisal was born in Taif, educated in Constantinople, and aligned with Great Britain's T. E. Lawrence, popularly known as Lawrence of Arabia, to fight against the Ottoman Empire. Faisal became the king of both Syria and Iraq after the defeat of the Ottomans in World War I. He was very close to the al-Askari family.

King Faisal II (1935–1958)   The only son of King Ghazi I. He was only four years old when his father died in an automobile accident. Faisal II was murdered in the revolution that occurred on the morning of July 14, 1958, the revolution that caused the destruction of the furniture factory owned by Joanna's father.

King Ghazi I (1912–1939)   The only son of King Faisal I. He ruled Iraq for only six years and was killed in an automobile accident on the palace grounds.

Koran   Islamic holy book. The paramount authority of the Muslim community, the Koran is the ultimate source of Islam. It is composed of the divine revelations received by the prophet Muhammad over the last twenty years of his life.

Kurds   A group distinct from the Arabs, Turks, and Persians. They are estimated to number thirty million and inhabit areas in Syria, Iran, Turkey, and Iraq.

Kurdistan   Literally meaning "the land of the Kurds." It is an area of northern Iraq, southern Turkey, western Iran, and northeast Syria. After World War I, Western powers promised Kurds they would have an independent state, but it did not happen. Since that time, Kurdish nationals have continued to seek independence, but their cries for freedom have been repeatedly rejected. Today, the Kurds of Iraq enjoy almost complete autonomy, and the Kurdish region of Iraq is prospering.

Kurdistan Democratic Party (KDP)   Kurdish political party and military tribal group formed in 1946 and led by Massoud Barzani. It was the first Kurdish political party formed for and by a Kurd. Later in the 1970s, a member of the KDP, Jalal Talabani, would break off and form a rival party, the Patriotic Union of Kurdistan.

Mesopotamia   Greek term meaning "the land between the rivers," including the area between the Euphrates and Tigris rivers. Early civilization emerged in this area, which is known today as Iraq.

Mosque   Islamic place of worship.

Muslim   Adherent of the religion known as Islam.

Patriotic Union of Kurdistan (PUK)   Founded in 1975 by Jalal Talabani, who became the president of Iraq in 2005. The PUK is a principal Kurdish and Iraqi political movement with a large following among the Kurdish people. It is a rival group to the KDP.

Peshmerga   Literally meaning "those who face death." The Peshmerga were armed Kurdish fighters who were affiliated to political parties such as the PUK in Iraq. Joanna's husband, Sarbast, was a PUK member. As of January 2005, it is estimated that there are still eighty thousand Iraqi Peshmerga fighters in northern Iraq. They are the only militia not prohibited by the Iraqi government.

Shatt al Arab   Waterway created by the joining of the Euphrates and Tigris rivers. The Shatt al Arab flows into the Persian Gulf.

Shiite   Islamic sect at odds with the Sunni sect over the successor to the Prophet Muhammad. In Iraq, the Shiite are in the majority.

Sulaimaniya   Kurdish city in northern Iraq. Joanna's mother was born there.

Sunni   Leading Islamic sect in terms of numbers. In Iraq, the Sunnis are in the minority. Joanna's family was Sunni Muslim.

Tigris   One of two main rivers in Iraq. The Tigris flows through Baghdad.

INDEX

Page references in *italics* refer to illustrations.